Global Perspectives in Urban Law

The growing field of urban law demands a collaborative scholarly focus on comparative and global perspectives. This volume offers diverse insights into urban law, with emerging theories and analyses of topics ranging from criminal reform and urban housing, to social and economic inequality and financial crises, and democratization and freedom for individual identity and space. Particularly now, social, economic, and cultural issues must be closely examined in conjunction with the rule of law not only to address inadequate access to basic services, but also to construct long-term plans for our cities and our world—a bright, safe future.

Nestor M. Davidson is the Albert A. Walsh Chair Professor of Real Estate, Land Use and Property Law at Fordham Law School and the Faculty Director of the Urban Law Center. Professor Davidson has published widely in the fields of property theory, urban law, and affordable housing law and policy. He earned his AB from Harvard College and his JD from Columbia Law School. Professor Davidson previously practiced with the firm of Latham & Watkins and served as Special Counsel and Principal Deputy General Counsel at the U.S. Department of Housing and Urban Development.

Geeta Tewari serves as Associate Director of the Urban Law Center at Fordham Law School. She earned her BA in Government from Cornell University and her JD from Fordham Law School. She has practiced public interest law for the New York City Law Department and the Washington D.C. Office of the Attorney General. Tewari also holds a Master of Fine Arts in Fiction Writing from Columbia University, where she taught creative and expository writing to New York City high school students and the Columbia undergraduate and alumni community. Information about her writing is available at www.geetatewari.com.

Juris Diversitas

Rooted in comparative law, the *Juris Diversitas* series focuses on the interdisciplinary study of legal and normative mixtures and movements. Our interest is in comparison broadly conceived, extending beyond law narrowly understood to related fields. Titles might be geographical or temporal comparisons. They could focus on theory and methodology, substantive law, or legal cultures. They could investigate official or unofficial 'legalities', past and present and around the world. And, to effectively cross spatial, temporal, and normative boundaries, inter- and multi-disciplinary research is particularly welcome.

For more information about this series, please visit:
www.routledge.com/Juris-Diversitas/book-series/JURISDIV

"This volume persuasively demonstrates that the global and the local increasingly overlap. In case studies ranging from the United States to Hong Kong, the Netherlands to India, and Ireland to South Africa and Australia, an internationally diverse collection of legal scholars and social scientists show that such problems as housing, crime control, water supply, management of public space, social conflict, and popular engagement in governance characterize cities around the world, even as differences in local economics, culture, politics, history and law lead to varying solutions. The reader comes away impressed with both the wide range and complexity of urban responsibilities, and the many creative ways in which they can be addressed."

Richard Briffault, Joseph P. Chamberlain Professor of Legislation, Columbia Law School, USA

"This book is further evidence that urban law, as a discipline, has arrived. The book's diverse contributions reflect the various ways that law shapes how we live in cities, how we interact with each other in city spaces, what kind of resources are made available to different kinds of urban residents, and who gets to participate in the variety of decisions that make a city what it is. The contributions powerfully demonstrate that while urban law is intensely local a comparative analysis between cities and regions can yield trenchant insights into the power of law in addressing many of the challenges ushered in by this era of global urbanization."

Sheila Foster, Professor of Law and Public Policy, Georgetown University Law Center, USA

Global Perspectives in Urban Law

The Legal Power of Cities

Edited by Nestor M. Davidson and Geeta Tewari

Routledge
Taylor & Francis Group
LONDON AND NEW YORK

First published 2019
by Routledge
2 Park Square, Milton Park, Abingdon, Oxon OX14 4RN

and by Routledge
52 Vanderbilt Avenue, New York, NY 10017

First issued in paperback 2020

Routledge is an imprint of the Taylor & Francis Group, an informa business

British Library Cataloguing-in-Publication Data
A catalogue record for this book is available from the British Library

Library of Congress Cataloging-in-Publication Data
Names: Davidson, Nestor M., editor. | Tewari, Geeta, editor.
Title: Global perspectives in urban law : the legal power of cities / edited by Nestor M. Davidson, Geeta Tewari.
Description: New York, NY : Routledge, 2018. |
Series: Juris diversitas | Includes index.
Identifiers: LCCN 2018027457 | ISBN 9780815372271 (hardback)
Subjects: LCSH: Municipal corporations. | Local government–Law and legislation.
Classification: LCC K3431 .G56 2018 | DDC 342/.09–dc23
LC record available at https://lccn.loc.gov/2018027457

ISBN 13: 978-0-367-66403-9 (pbk)
ISBN 13: 978-0-8153-7227-1 (hbk)

Typeset in Galliard
by Swales & Willis Ltd, Exeter, Devon, UK

For Clare Huntington
ND

For Avanti, Uma, and Livia
GT

Contents

Contributors

L. Michelle Bruijn, Ph.D. Candidate, Faculty of Law, University of Groningen, the Netherlands.

Laura Delgado, Doctoral Candidate, Massachusetts Institute of Technology, U.S.A.

Ernesto Hernández-López, Professor of Law, Fowler School of Law, Chapman University, U.S.A.

Abigail Jackson, Solicitor and Lecturer in Law, Royal Docks School of Business and Law, University of East London, U.K.

Ronit Donyets Kedar, Associate Professor of Law and Co-Founder of Corporate Social Responsibility Institute, College of Law and Business, Israel.

Alice Lee, Associate Professor of Law and Associate Dean for Academic Affairs, University of Hong Kong, Hong Kong.

Rebecca Leshinsky, Barrister-at-Law, Senior Lecturer, School of Property, Construction & Project Management, Royal Melbourne Institute of Technology University, Australia.

Malcolm MacLaren, Privatdozent, Faculty of Law, University of Zurich, Switzerland.

Scott McKenzie, Doctoral Candidate, Institute for Resources, Environment and Sustainability, University of British Columbia, Canada.

Daniel B. Rodriguez, Harold Washington Professor, Northwestern University Pritzker School of Law, U.S.A.

Nadav Shoked, Professor of Law, Northwestern University Pritzker School of Law, U.S.A.

Julian Sidoli, Barrister, Pendragon Chambers, Swansea; Member of the Wales and Chester Circuit and Member of the Chancery Bar Association, U.K.

Justin Steil, Assistant Professor of Law and Urban Planning, Massachusetts Institute of Technology, U.S.A.

Padmapriya Vidhya-Govindarajan, Yenching Scholar, Yenching Academy of Peking University, China; Development Studies, Indian Institute of Technology, Madras, India.

Michel Vols, Professor of Law with a Chair in Public Order Law, Faculty of Law, University of Groningen, the Netherlands.

Phoebe Woo, B.A. and L.L.B. (Literary Studies), University of Hong Kong, Hong Kong.

Acknowledgments

Our thanks and sincere appreciation go to Emily Mastoloni and Isedua Oribhahor for their assistance in the preparation of this volume.

We also wish to thank all of the participants in the second and third annual International and Comparative Urban Law Conferences, which took place in June 2015 and June 2016, for launching the dialogue that inspired this book.

Lastly, Alexandra Buckley and the editorial and publishing staff at Routledge, all of whom shepherded this book to press—thank you for bringing urban research and ideas to the world.

Introduction

The chapters in this second volume of the Global Perspectives on Urban Law collection within the Juris Diversitas series reflect the eclecticism and serendipity of the urban experience itself. From Hong Kong affordable home ownership schemes, to drug eviction tactics in the Netherlands, spatial reorganization of Chennai street vendors, even conflicts over sriracha hot sauce manufacturing in Los Angeles, and more—each diverse issue addressed in this book incorporates urban communities' desire for new legal frameworks to resolve conflicts while trying to foster a sense of secure and functional belonging.

The chapters in this volume grew out of a series of annual International and Comparative Urban Law Conferences that, since 2014, the Urban Law Center at Fordham Law School has hosted to gather urban scholars from around the globe. These Conferences have provided forums to reflect together on comparative urban legal experiences and insights. What has emerged from these gatherings—held so far in London, Paris, Hong Kong, Cape Town, and São Paolo—is that the challenges that drive the intersection of law and cities has a surprising number of commonalities in comparative perspective, despite the significant differences in disparate legal and urban systems. Perhaps this tells us something about underlying deeper structures that unite cities in the ways in which law mediates urban governance and daily life.

This volume is a culmination of scholarship presented at the Urban Law Center's Second and Third Annual International and Comparative Urban Law Conferences, held in Paris and Hong Kong, respectively. The diversity of selection in the chapters that follow reflects two overarching themes. First, the challenge of law and belonging in the urban context, with scholars examining resistance to de jure segregation, subsidized housing, eviction, privacy, even mediating conflicts on the sidewalk. Second, the promise of innovation and urban governance through a legal lens, as cities react to financial crisis, foster democratic decision making, and advance corporate responsibility. Across all of these contributions, it is clear that urban law is inherently multifaceted because cities are inherently multifaceted.

Part I of this volume, Law and Belonging in the Urban Context, begins with a historically based chapter by Laura Delgado and Justin Steil exploring U.S. segregation ordinances from the early 1900s. Baltimore, Maryland, to begin, used property market value as a scapegoat for prohibiting black families from relocating to primarily white neighborhoods. Delgado and Steil explain how at the time, the ordinances were considered a "novel extension of the police power, and state courts grappled uncomfortably with how to evaluate them." After *Buchanan v. Warley*, 245 U.S. 60 (1917), declared that segregation ordinances violated the Fourteenth Amendment, racially restrictive covenants rose as the next effort by white homeowners, property developers, and city public officials to maintain segregation, again invoking the negative effects of gentrified neighborhoods on property value. The authors explain how this utilitarian approach advanced segregation of cities, and should be remembered by law and policy makers to avoid similarly rationalized consequences in the future.

Next, Abigail Jackson and Julian Sidoli examine urban inhabitants' dichotomy between privacy and participation, as city dwellers carefully balance public personas and their private nature. Citing criticism of a marketing company in a central London neighborhood for embedding sensors in recycling bins so as to monitor movement of individuals in the vicinity, these scholars confront the difficulty for individuals to enjoy privacy in urban settings. Invoking Aristotle for the premise of humans as "social animals"; Sennett to explain "while man *made* himself in public, he *realized* his nature in the private realm"; and Lefebvre for the individual's fundamental "right to the city," Jackson and Sidoli argue that for a city to succeed, its residents require a certain degree of private space.

The volume continues with a chapter by Alice Lee and Phoebe Woo addressing the world's increasing housing dilemma through the lens of one global city, Hong Kong. In navigating the conflict between rising property markets and the public's increasing need for affordable housing, Lee and Woo analyze how the government's "Home Ownership Scheme" (HOS), implemented as part of a greater mission to create equality for different income groups, has in fact resulted in conflict among families seemingly tied to ownership of the HOS flats. In discussing Hong Kong's highest court's appeals of several cases, Professor Lee and Woo point out that while the goal of the HOS is to aide lower middle income class and public rental housing tenants in home ownership, the program's loopholes, lawfully allowing ineligible persons to become owners, yields the opposite. These scholars accordingly call upon the Hong Kong Housing Authority to review its policies and goals.

Related to housing, L. Michelle Bruijn and Michel Vols examine eviction as a legal tool for crime control in the U.S. and the Netherlands. Bruijn and Vols cite the growing trend of law and policy makers to decentralize crime control so as to create a "new crime control establishment" including terms such as third-party policing and community-based law enforcement. The authors explore how eviction has been used to control drug crime from exploratory, legal, and theoretical perspectives. In the United States, their research focuses on New York City in particular because of its Narcotics Eviction Program, which led to "one strike" evictions in public and private housing. Using NYC data, they provide a comparative legal analysis with Dutch law and data from the Netherlands, noting that there is a lack of recent comparative research on this issue. The authors also argue that a consequence of third-party policing in the War on Drugs is that citizens, landlords, and tenants that reside with the person responsible for drug activities are accountable. This drug eviction practice has received criticism over the years, and Bruijn and Vols's intention here is to show the power of eviction in the Netherlands and the U.S.

Next, Scott McKenzie applies a legal pluralism framework to analyze aspects of water governance, particularly, the "international human right to water, state protections, and local implementation." The United Nations, McKenzie notes, has been at the fore in securing the right to water as a substantive human right. Pointing to two cities, Johannesburg and Dublin, McKenzie demonstrates "how the human right to water is implemented and experienced" in different urban centers, ranging from a problematic lack of regulation to secure the right, to a financial model of charging for water after a certain point. McKenzie notes that effective enforcement mechanisms of the right to water are essential to prevent "racial, ethnic, or gendered differences in water access."

The chapter that follows is Padmapriya Vidhya-Govindarajan's collection of field work and research on the spatial reorganization of the Pondy Bazaar street market in Chennai, India. Vidhya-Govindarajan begins with an offering of the cultural history of the bazaar, how over 600 vendors sold their wares along the sidewalk pavements of Pondy Bazaar and Usman Road until 2013, when the Chennai Municipal Corporation shifted these businesses into a single complex. Vidhya-Govindarajan notes that the government's regulation is "a form of informality from above—the convenient alternation of regulation and deregulation" with no way for the vendors of Pondy Bazaar to consider legalizing ownership of the former "sprawling horizontal market." However, the sidewalk structure created peripheries, too, Vidhya-Govindarajan points out, such as a form of spatial violence, where vendors were forced to barter with each other for space. Vidhya-Govindarajan goes on to map the conflicts that emerged from the altered arrangements for these vendors, with an understanding of their perception of "authority, legality, threat, and change," especially legality, which vendors viewed as "simply something they did not have."

The final chapter of Part I, by Malcolm MacLaren, crystalizes his research on conflict, peace, and state-building in the urban context, assessing strategies and challenges of urban transformation. MacLaren examines subsidiarity and democracy, and how democratization can effectively be applied to local governments. He points to immigration, and how movement of people results in tensions of "ideational strife" despite that urban areas are "traditionally more tolerant and cosmopolitan than rural areas." Especially in the Global South, MacLaren notes, urbanism has "been characterized more by conflict than by consensus" and governments in these areas should be evaluated, "alternative approaches should be considered," and the author continues on to suggest that subsidiarity and democracy, broadly speaking, may not be suitable for urban areas with histories of internal conflict. MacLaren proposes to assess cities' best approaches to government, which he suggests consists of augmenting democratic self-government.

Part II: Innovation and Urban Governance in Legal Perspective begins with a chapter by Daniel B. Rodriguez and Nadav Shoked, shifting the volume back to America, specifically its 2008 economic collapse, a breakdown that generated "reverberations throughout the globe." While the interdisciplinary focus in the aftermath of the Great Recession has been largely at the national level, Rodriguez and Shoked suggest that, local institutions may equally contribute to the social and economic environment of financial bodies. Rodriguez and Shoked focus on the severe downturn of U.S. cities such as Detroit and Chicago during the Great Recession, and argue that in their plight cities devised new tools to generate revenue—tools that happen to be "more private market oriented than ever before." In moving forward, Rodriguez and Shoked argue that financial market stakeholders should draw on the experiences of urban governments locally and globally.

Next, Rebecca Leshinsky focuses on the importance of community involvement in local government decision making. Leshinsky notes that citizen involvement assists in "municipal transparency" and "avoiding conflicts of interest." Leshinsky showcases stakeholder views on local law-making in Melbourne, the capital city of the state of Victoria. While not disagreeing with the theses of Jackson and Sidoli, encouraging space for privacy in the urban realm, Leshinsky draws from the Melbourne study the message that there must also be citizen involvement in local law-making, and that municipalities must share their results nationally and internationally, to make the law-making process more transparent and inclusive.

Heating up the discourse, Ernesto Hernández-López brings us to Huy Fong's sriracha sauce company in the city of Irwindale, California. From 2012 through 2014, the company faced pressure to shut down from the city, arguing that the company's "chile pepper grinding created a public nuisance with smells." Due to the popularity of the sauce, the dispute received global attention. Hernández-López points to frameworks from the Los Angeles School of Urbanism, the history of Irwindale, and the initiation of the public nuisance proceedings, as he analyzes the legal power and doctrines behind the city's litigation. Hernández-López utilizes this conflict for a theoretical discussion of spatial urban justice disputes, noting that law plays a substantial role in discourses such as regional urbanization and economic restructuring.

Finally, Ronit Kedar closes the second section pointing to the growing need for scholarship focusing on cities vis-à-vis corporations, examining cities' roles as regulators and corporations' necessary expectation of social responsibility towards the cities they are based in. Perhaps, Kedar proposes, a "dual concept of responsibility will mitigate negative influences corporate conduct may have on cities as such, and secure a better protection for the city as a unique, meaningful human arena."

In preparing this volume, we are reminded how fast the urban context around the world is changing, increasingly in need of collaborative engagement from the full range of urban stakeholders. Across all aspects of urban life, law is central to problem solving as well as urban identity, and the urban legal scholars collected in this volume bring careful thought and deep insights into those fundamental dynamics.

Part I

Law and belonging in the urban context

1 Contested values

How Jim Crow segregation ordinances redefined property rights

Laura Delgado and Justin Steil

Introduction

In the spring of 1910, George McMechen, an attorney, and his wife Ann, a schoolteacher, moved from their home at 1704 Presstman Street in Baltimore to a new home, less than a mile away, at 1834 McCulloh Street. Geographically, the move was short. Socially, however, it was significant. The McMechens were black, and their new neighborhood was almost exclusively white.

Several of the McMechens' new neighbors were not pleased. Some white residents quickly organized the "McCulloh Street and Madison Avenue Property Protective Association" explicitly "for the purpose of preventing negroes moving into the neighborhood" and petitioned the Mayor and City Council to "prescribe a limit beyond which it shall be unlawful for them to go."[1] Milton Dashiell, a fellow attorney who lived at 1110 McCulloh Street, then drafted a municipal ordinance making the McMechens' move, and any other move like it, a crime punishable by a fine and imprisonment of up to a year. The City Councilman for the area, Samuel L. West, sponsored the ordinance, and, after heated public debate, the council approved it on December 10, 1910, and Mayor J. Barry Mahool signed it into law nine days later.

Section 2 of the ordinance provided as follows:

> [I]t shall be unlawful for any colored person to move into or use as a residence or place of abode any house, building or structure situated or located on any block . . . so far as the same are occupied or used as residences or places of abode . . . in whole or in part . . . by white persons.[2]

In an effort to avoid falling afoul of the Equal Protection Clause, the ordinance contained parallel language prohibiting white persons from occupying houses on

1 *Baltimore Tries Drastic Plan of Race Segregation*, N.Y. Times, December 25, 1910, at SM2; *Negro Invasion Opposed: Residents Protect Against Sale of House to Colored Lawyer*, Baltimore Sun, July 6, 1910, at 7.

2 Balt. Md., Ordinances and Resolutions of the Mayor and City Council of Baltimore Passed at the Annual Session, 1910–11, 379, Ord. 692, § 2 (1911).

"colored blocks" as well. And Section 3 of the ordinance excepted domestic servants who lived with their employers from the prohibitions in the preceding sections. Baltimore's segregation ordinance quickly spread to other cities, such as Richmond, Virginia; Winston-Salem, North Carolina; Atlanta, Georgia; and Louisville, Kentucky. In the following seven years, more than thirty cities enacted municipal segregation laws modeled after Baltimore's.

The proponents of these segregation ordinances were generally white property owners who expressed concern about the effects of black families moving to their neighborhood, particularly the effects on the value of their homes. In Baltimore, Dashiell elevated his opposition to the McMechens' move and his support for the ordinance to a public duty in defense of white property values:

> When one considers how whole blocks by the half dozen have had their values cut in two by the advent of a half a dozen negro families, it seems conclusive that the city, under its police power, has a right—indeed, not only has the right, but should hold it as its bounden duty—to step in and, by the prohibition of further influx of negro population into the white districts, prevent further destruction in value.[3]

At the initial meeting of the Property Protective Association in Baltimore, a local pastor, Reverend Philip A. Heilman, similarly argued that "the settlement of negroes" in formerly all-white neighborhoods "greatly reduced the taxable property and sacrificed the homes which white people had worked long and earnestly to purchase."[4] Parallel themes drove campaigns in favor of the adoption of segregation ordinances in other cities. A postcard from the United Welfare Association in St. Louis read: "LOOK At These Homes NOW! An entire block ruined by negro invasion ... SAVE YOUR HOME! VOTE FOR SEGREGATION!"[5] The ordinances were seen by white homeowners as an effort to protect their home values by exerting collective control over the occupancy of the rest of the homes in the neighborhood.

These efforts by white property owners to control the sale and the use of others' property challenged accepted conceptions of property rights at the time. To protect their property values, the proponents of these ordinances wanted to limit the property rights of all other owners and tenants in the city—to limit others' rights to acquire and to dispose of property, as well as their right to lease or even occupy their own home. These restrictions on the acquisition, use, and alienation of property were a novel extension of the police power, and state courts grappled uncomfortably with how to evaluate them.

3 *Baltimore Tries Drastic Plan of Race Segregation*, *supra* note 1.

4 *Negro Invasion Opposed: Residents Protect Against Sale of House to Colored Lawyer*, *supra* note 1.

5 Postcard from United Welfare Ass'n (1915) *in* Missouri Historical Society, http://collections.mohistory.org/resource/166747 (last visited Jan. 25, 2018).

Today, we take local ordinances regulating land use and occupancy for granted as perhaps the most paradigmatic and banal example of urban law. Local laws excluding toxic industries from dense residential neighborhoods and codes designating minimum bedroom sizes or requirements for light and air are central to the quality of urban life and the protection of environmental health. But some of the early laws testing the power of local governments to regulate property and shape land use were highly contested and for good reason, as discussed below. And even today, local ordinances regulating land use are often still used for invidious, exclusionary purposes. The struggle over the early twentieth century municipal segregation ordinances can illuminate some ways in which the social conflicts over group hierarchies and spatial conflict over urban geography are fought in local laws and state and federal courts.

I. An initial survey of litigation upholding and against segregation ordinances

McMechen's partner in law practice, W. Ashbie Hawkins, litigated the first challenge to one of these segregation ordinances to reach a state high court. Hawkins was the most well-known African American lawyer in Baltimore at the time. He had attended the University of Maryland law school, but was expelled in 1891 because of his race when the school resegregated. Hawkins then completed his law degree at Howard University and returned to Baltimore to work as a schoolteacher and, ultimately, to start his own law practice. Hawkins had been active in the Niagara Movement from 1905 to 1909 and then in the National Association for the Advancement of Colored People (NAACP), founded in 1909 as the Niagara Movement waned. Hawkins was married to George McMechen's sister, Ada, and was also the owner of the McCulloh Street property into which the McMechens had moved.

Shortly after the ordinance went into effect, Hawkins together with C. Ames Brooks, a black lawyer from New York also working with the NAACP, represented John Gurry, who had been convicted for violating the ordinance after buying a property on a "white" block. Hawkins and Brooks were successful in *State v. Gurry*, at having the ordinance struck down as "a practical confiscation of … property."[6] Subsequent challenges on property rights grounds to segregation ordinances in North Carolina and Georgia were also successful. In *State v. Darnell*, the Supreme Court of North Carolina noted that the ordinance "forbids the owner of property to sell or to lease it to whomsoever he sees fit"[7] and held that "this right of disposing of property, the *jus disponendi*, has always been held one of the inalienable rights incident to the ownership of property which no statute will be construed as having power to take away."[8] The Georgia Supreme

6 88 A. 546, 552 (Md. 1913).
7 81 S.E. 338, 339 (N.C. 1914).
8 *Id.*

Court similarly held that "[t]he effect of the ordinance ... was to destroy the right of the individual to acquire, enjoy, and dispose of his property. Being of this character, it was void ..."[9] It seemed as though courts' attention to property rights would spell the end of the municipal segregation effort.

But in *Harris v. Louisville*, the Court of Appeals of Kentucky upheld Louisville's segregation ordinance, noting that "[t]he advance of civilization" had "resulted in a gradual lessening of the dominion of the individual over private property and a corresponding strengthening of the regulative power of the state" to impose regulations such as the segregation ordinance.[10] The decision stated that the "*jus disponendi* has but little place in modern jurisprudence"[11] and found the ordinance valid and consistent with the state's commitment "to the principle of the separation of the races whenever and wherever practicable."[12] The Virginia Supreme Court of Appeals followed the Kentucky decision. In *Hopkins v. Richmond*, the court held that because "close association of the races tends to breach of the peace, unsanitary conditions, discomfort, immorality, and disquiet,"[13] therefore, "there appears to be nothing unreasonable in placing the restriction above set out on the use of property to the same end."[14] When presented with a revised Atlanta segregation ordinance that applied only prospectively, the Supreme Court of Georgia approved it, deciding that a local law designed to enforce residential segregation "in order to uphold the integrity of each race and to prevent conflicts between them resulting from close association ... will be upheld notwithstanding that to some extent the use of property may be somewhat restricted."[15]

As the diverging opinions in the six decisions discussed above suggest, the limits of property rights and the extent of property regulation were contested at the time and resolved in part through these segregation cases. How property rights jurisprudence evolved in the decade following the adoption of Baltimore's ordinance as these state courts considered similar segregation ordinances and weighed their encroachment on property rights against the maintenance of Jim Crow segregation shall be explored in the section to come.

II. A shifting conception of property rights in the early 1900s

In the first decade of the twentieth century, hundreds of thousands of African Americans moved from rural areas to cities, seeking access to opportunity and fleeing white supremacist terrorism, and the black population of cities in the South and the North began to increase. Between 1880 and 1910, Baltimore's

9 Carey v. City of Atlanta, 84 S.E. 456, 460 (Ga. 1915).
10 177 S.W. 472, 476 (Ky. 1917).
11 *Id.*
12 *Id.* at 477.
13 86 S.E. 139, 145 (Va. 1918).
14 *Id.*
15 Harden v. City of Atlanta, 93 S.E. 401, 402 (Ga. 1917).

black population grew from 54,000 to 85,000. As black families moved in, white neighbors sometimes sought to buy them back out. More frequently, white property owners sought to prevent this "Negro invasion" through violence. As Milton Dashiell said about the McMechens in Baltimore: "The white residents and property owners tried to buy them out at a fair profit, but they refused to sell, saying they had come there to stay."[16] Their offer rejected, the neighbors turned to violence and terror. Dashiell continued,

> Then ensued more or less lawlessness … in the neighborhood. Window-glasses of the negroes' houses were broken with stones; skylights were caved in by bricks, descending bomb-like from the sky; there were mutterings of plots to blow up the houses.[17]

After Baltimore's segregation ordinance was enacted in 1910, a new weapon was added to the arsenal whites were using to keep out black neighbors—the municipal segregation ordinance. These ordinances were justified by their proponents as necessary to prevent conflict and to preserve property values. For instance, Baltimore Mayor Mahool described the purpose of the ordinance as protecting "our people in the possession of their property":

> Its sole object and intention is to protect our people in the possession of their property and to prevent the depreciation which is of necessity bound to follow when the colored family would move into a neighborhood that had hitherto been exclusively inhabited by white people. That such depreciation does of necessity follow, we of Baltimore have learned after years of hard and sad experience.[18]

The ordinance enshrined in law an emerging view of a property owner's relationship to his neighbors and a new ability to restrict those neighbors' activities on their own property in order to avoid this feared depreciation.

In recent scholarship, Lee Anne Fennell describes this conceptualization of property as "the unbounded home" that is at once the physical property one owns as well as the meaning and value ascribed to one's home through neighborhood conditions and amenities.[19] Fennell explains the contradictions inherent in this view of property,

> Homeowners want an ironclad sphere of privacy and autonomy, but they want it wrapped in an environment that they can control in every particular.

16 *Baltimore Tries Drastic Plan of Race Segregation*, *supra* note 1.

17 *Id.*

18 *Id.*

19 Lee Anne Fennell, The Unbounded Home: Property Values Beyond Property Lines (Yale U. Press 2009).

> They want a secure and lucrative investment vehicle that doubles as an inviolable repository for subjective value.[20]

Property owners want personal autonomy when it comes to their own property, but they also want to control the conditions surrounding their property that may affect its value.

The idea that one could use public laws to limit neighbors' use of their property, however, was not as widely held in the early twentieth century as it is in the present. Through the early 1900s, courts' conceptions of property rights were driven more by a natural right theory of property than the utilitarian understanding we take for granted today.[21] A natural right conception of property treated property as inherent, prepolitical, and prelegal. Accordingly, regulations of real property were limited. Lawyers at the time

> invoked moral and political principles that *limited* the scope of "regulation" as surely as they *justified* it . . . property "regulations" were expected to "make" property rights "regular." Regulations were expected to order and encourage the free and equal use of property

not to limit it.[22] Except for limiting uses of real property that led to a physical invasion of others' property, public law restrictions on the use of property were disfavored, and emphasis was placed on the freedom to use one's own land as one saw fit.[23]

Because there was no zoning or systematic land use regulation, conflicts over the uses of a neighbor's property were resolved at the time primarily through common law nuisance actions. Blackstone defined a nuisance as an "act, in itself lawful, which yet being done in that place necessarily tends to the damage of another's property"[24] and gave the example of a smelting house situated so close to a neighbor's property that the smoke killed the neighbor's corn and damaged his cows. The examples suggest that the act sought to be addressed through the nuisance action that led to a tangible impact on the neighbor's property, akin to an invasion. Blackstone cautioned that "every man [can] do what he pleases upon the upright or perpendicular of his own soil," again implying that to constitute a nuisance, one's action on one's property must have the effect of physically invading a neighbor's property.

White property owners in the late nineteenth and early twentieth centuries went to court in an attempt to use the common law of nuisance to create and maintain

20 *Id.* at 9.

21 Eric R. Claeys, *Takings, Regulations, and Natural Property Rights*, 88 Cornell L. Rev. 1549 (2003).

22 *Id.* at 1553.

23 Eric R. Claeys, *Jefferson Meets Coase: Land-Use Torts, Law and Economics, and Natural Property Rights*, 85 Notre Dame L. Rev. 1379 (2010).

24 William Blackstone, Commentaries on the Law of England, Book III of Private Wrongs 218 (Wilfrid Prest & Thomas P. Gallantis eds., 2016).

residential segregation by race.[25] But these nuisance cases brought to prevent the sale or use of neighboring properties by African Americans were relatively unsuccessful.[26] Judges in these "race nuisance" cases expressed fidelity to existing precedent and generally refused to find that the presence of African Americans, as a class, could constitute a nuisance, without some specific conduct that impinged more directly on neighbors' enjoyment of their property. In the limited success of race nuisance cases, one can arguably see the continued influence of the natural right theory of property at the time. But the segregation ordinances initiated a shift in jurisprudence from this natural right theory to a utilitarian one.

With race nuisance cases relatively unsuccessful in the courts, white property owners seeking to enforce residential segregation were somewhat at a loss. Creating a law, like the one Dashiell proposed, that severely restricted property rights was not a self-evident solution given the presumption against the public restriction of property rights. The ordinance thus required significant justification. From property owners and real estate brokers to religious leaders and politicians, proponents of residential segregation at the turn of the twentieth century embarked on campaigns to convince white residents that their property values would depreciate with the arrival of black neighbors and that cities had a public duty to act to protect white property values, even if it required unprecedented regulation of the use of all real property. Segregation advocates facilitated this climate of fear by adopting language commonly associated with war and infectious diseases—"invasion," "protection," and "quarantine"—to mobilize white supporters. In 1910, the Reverend H. M. Wharton of Brantly Baptist Church in Baltimore cautioned, "Two things follow negro invasion: Property depreciates in value and the white people move away. The final result of this will be that the city will be given over to negroes."[27] Meanwhile, Baltimore Mayor Mahool, a member of the Progressive Movement at the time, gave credence to three major fears associated with African American residents: political dissent, disease, and declining property values. Mahool declared, "Blacks should be quarantined in isolated slums in order to reduce the incidents of civil disobedience, to prevent the spread of communicable disease into the nearby White

25 *See, e.g.*, Falloon v. Schilling, 29 Kan. 292 (1883).

26 Rachel D. Godsil, *Race Nuisance: The Politics of Law in the Jim Crow Era*, 105 MICH. L. REV. 505. (2006). Rachel Godsil groups these racial nuisance cases into "mere presence" cases and "conduct" cases. In the former set of cases, property owners initiated nuisance cases on the basis that the "mere presence" of African Americans constituted a nuisance and interfered with their right to enjoy their property. The latter set of cases were brought against "black churches, funeral homes, parks, homes for orphans and the aged, hospitals and tuberculosis sanatoriums, dance halls, crowded housing, and saloons" and contended that the nuisance was, in fact, the conduct of the African American owners and users, not their mere presence. *Id.* at 520. Whereas the "mere presence" nuisance cases were largely unsuccessful, the conduct based cases garnered some success.

27 *Strong for West Plan: Council Committee Hears Many Pleas For Segregation*, BALTIMORE SUN, Oct. 11, 1910, at 16.

neighborhoods, and to protect property values among the White majority."[28] The campaigns in favor of residential segregation ordinances eventually won out in many city halls, but it was less clear how this form of collective neighborhood control at the cost of free alienation of property might fare in the courts.

III. The collective control of property through segregation ordinances

Public opinion at the time was divided as to whether the ordinances protected or violated property rights and whether they appropriately used or inappropriately abused the municipal police power. An opinion column published in the *New York Times* in response to the segregation ordinances in St. Louis and Louisville read: "A man has a legal and constitutional right to occupy his own property! To exclude him from it on the ground of his color is a singular … abuse of the so much overworked 'police power'."[29] Another opinion from the *New York Times* expressed the same sentiment in response to the proposed ordinance in St. Louis:

> It seems a queer sort of Americanism which denies to a man the right to occupy his own property … The Missouri Constitution contains an "enjoyment of property" clause. Can an owner kept out of his own property be said to "enjoy" his property.[30]

Reporting on the hearings surrounding the Baltimore segregation ordinance, *The Baltimore Sun* reported a comment from Baltimore resident Charles Kemper:

> The last clause of the ordinance gives the whole measure the lie. It does not prohibit the buying of property by white or black. Do you think you can prevent a man from living in the house that belongs to him?[31]

Those who supported the segregation ordinances, however, expressed the opinion that, because anyone could still purchase property anywhere in the city regardless of race (most of the ordinances prohibited occupancy, not ownership), the ordinances did not impinge unduly on property rights. For example, an opinion published in the North Carolina *Twice-A-Week Dispatch* argued: "The municipal law does not affect the negro's right to hold property, but simply his right of residence …. [The] measure is designed simply and solely to preserve public order …"[32] The *Central Law Journal* reported on the decision by the

28 Dorceta E. Taylor, Toxic communities: Environmental Racism, Industrial Pollution, and Residential Mobility (N.Y.U. Press 2014).

29 *The Right to Occupy One*, N.Y. Times, Apr. 22, 1916, at 10.

30 *White and Black Blocks*, N. Y. Times, Mar. 2, 1916, at 10.

31 *Segregation Opposed: Arguments Against West Ordinance Heard by Council Committee*, Baltimore Sun, Oct. 4, 1910, at 9.

32 *Mr. Bryan and Segregation*, Twice-a-Week Dispatch, May 9, 1914, at 3.

Virginia Court of Appeals to uphold the constitutionality of the residential segregation ordinances in Richmond and Ashland and explained:

> It seems quite impossible to distinguish segregation legislation as to residence from that for separation of races in public conveyances and schools. If there is the purpose of preserving peace and order as to the latter, *a fortiori* is such a purpose legitimate as to the former and the right to use of property is certainly circumscribed in many ways as the advantage of civilized society may demand.[33]

These examples highlight the accepted view of some at the time that the use of property could be limited without violating property rights, so long as the right to own property was preserved.

IV. The state supreme court cases on residential segregation

Six cases were brought before state high courts challenging the constitutionality of segregation ordinances before *Buchanan v. Warley*, 245 U.S. 60 (1917), reached the United States Supreme Court. The first three of these cases, heard in Maryland, North Carolina, and Georgia, struck down the local segregation ordinances. The latter three, however, upheld them in Kentucky, Virginia, and Georgia.

A. A closer look at the cases striking down local segregation ordinances: **State v. Gurry; State v. Darnell;** ***and*** **Carey v. City of Atlanta**

In *State v. Gurry*, the Court of Appeals of Maryland ruled on October 7, 1913 that Baltimore's third attempt at a segregation ordinance, City Ordinance No. 692, was unlawful. The first ordinance had attempted to restrict residence for all blocks in the city based on the race predominating on the block, but lower courts had found those provisions unworkable. The third ordinance sought to sidestep the question of occupancy on mixed blocks and, instead, focused on restricting occupancy on blocks that were either all white or all black. The Court of Appeals found that this ordinance, too, constituted a confiscation of property.

The Court of Appeals accepted Baltimore's arguments about justifications for residential segregation, noting that, "[F]or years there had been more or less friction resulting from the occupancy by colored people of houses in blocks theretofore occupied wholly by white people ..."[34] Given the Jim Crow laws prevailing at the time, the Court went on to recognize that the Supreme Court had approved "the right of states to establish separate schools for white and colored children, and ... to require the separation of the white and colored races in public conveyances ..."[35] and, therefore, concluded that "we are of the opinion that the object sought to be

33 *Notes of Important Decisions*, CENT. L. J. 1874–1927, 290 (1915).
34 State v. Gurry, 88 A. 546, 551 (Md. 1913).
35 *Id.* at 552.

accomplished by this ordinance is one which properly admits of the exercise of the police power."[36] Nevertheless, the court deemed "the provisions as they were passed too unreasonable to permit us to assume that the legislature intended to confer on the municipality the power to thus affect vested rights"[37] because of their significant interference with property rights. The court presented an example of how the ordinance would work an unconstitutional taking:

> [I]t might be that a white person had a valuable and attractive house in a "block" which was otherwise occupied by colored people, yet if, at the passage of the ordinance, it happened to be unoccupied as a dwelling, he could not under the ordinance move into it or rent it to a white person. To deny him such rights would be a practical confiscation of his property … and, if he could not use it himself, he would be deprived of not only the income from it, but of the use of it as is guaranteed to every owner of property by the Constitution and laws of the land.[38]

Baltimore amended its ordinance for a fourth time, limiting its application only to those purchasing property after the ordinance was enacted. The revised ordinance was approved by the council on September 25, 1913 and struck down again by the Maryland Court of Appeals on October 7, 1913.

Inspired by Baltimore's original segregation ordinance, white residents of Winston, North Carolina pushed for an ordinance through 1911 and 1912. White residents of East Fourth Street in particular pressed the Board of Alderman to enact the ordinance because they felt "[i]ncreasingly cut off from whites elsewhere in the city and threatened by what they saw as black encroachment."[39] The Board of Aldermen convened a special session on June 13, 1912 and the same day adopted an ordinance prohibiting "any colored person to own or occupy any dwelling fronting on East Fourth Street …"[40] and prohibiting white people from residing on, but permitting them to own, property on specific sections of East Third and Depot Streets that were already occupied by black households. Upon realizing that this targeted and asymmetrical ordinance was vulnerable to legal challenge, the Board of Aldermen revised it, modeling it more closely after Baltimore's ordinance. The revised ordinance applied citywide and made it unlawful for any colored person to occupy as a residence any house on a block on which a greater number of houses were occupied as residences by white people, and vice versa. Pursuant to section 44 of the City Charter, which stated that the Board "may pass an ordinance which they may deem wise and proper for the good order, good government, or general welfare

36 *Id.*

37 *Id.* at 553.

38 *Id.* at 552.

39 Citadel Conference on the S., Warm Ashes: Issues in Southern History at the Dawn of the Twenty-First Century 258 (Winfred B. Moore et al. eds., 2003).

40 *Race Segregation*, Union Republican, June 20, 1912, at 6.

of the city, provided it does not contravene the laws and Constitution of the State,"[41] the Board of Aldermen adopted the ordinance on July 5, 1912.

After the ordinance in Winston was passed and the city combined with its neighbor, Salem, to become Winston-Salem, a local white real estate agent, Francis M. Sledge purchased a property on Highland Avenue between 11th and 12th Streets. The block was all white, but it was in a neighborhood with a growing African American population. Sledge then canvassed the block gathering signatures on a document stating that, "We, the undersigned citizens owning property on the East Side of Highland Avenue between Eleventh and Twelfth streets, do hereby agree to sell our property to colored people."[42] Reportedly, only one resident of the block refused to sign.[43] The motives for Sledge's efforts and for the support of the block's residents are not clear, but it may have been because the ordinance's prohibition on occupancy by black residents of a white block in an increasingly black neighborhood significantly reduced the values of the properties on that block. In any event, with the signatures in hand, Sledge sold the property roughly a month after purchasing it to William Darnell and his wife Lillie, and the Darnell family became the first black residents of the block. Darnell was arrested on June 10, 1913, convicted shortly thereafter of violating the segregation ordinance, and fined. Darnell appealed, and Sledge paid Darnell's bail bond. Darnell was represented by two of the leading white lawyers in Winston-Salem, Cyrus Watson, a veteran of the Confederate Army, and John Buxton, a former mayor of Winston.

In *State v. Darnell*, the North Carolina Supreme Court struck down Winston-Salem's segregation ordinance on the ground that the city government was not authorized by its charter to enact an ordinance interfering so significantly with property rights. The court stated,

> We do not think that the authority conferred by [the state] to enact ordinances for the "general welfare of the city" can justly be construed as intended by the Legislature to authorize an ordinance of this kind which establishes a public policy which has hitherto been unknown in the legislation of our state.[44]

The court went on to state that,

> [i]f the board of alderman is thereby authorized to make this restriction, a bare majority of the board could, if they may deem it "wise and proper," require Republicans to live on certain streets and Democrats on others, or that Protestants shall reside only in certain parts of the town and Catholics in another ...[45]

41 State v. Darnell, 81 S.E. 338, 339 (N.C. 1914).
42 Citadel Conference on the S., *supra* note 38, at 260.
43 *Id.*
44 Darnell, 81 S.E. at 339.
45 *Id.*

The court continued:

> Besides, an ordinance of this kind forbids the owner of property to sell or to lease it to whomsoever he sees fit, as well as forbids those who may be desirous of buying or renting property from doing so where they can make the best bargain. Yet this right of disposing of property, the *jus disponendi*, has always been held one of the inalienable rights incident to the ownership of property which no statute will be construed as having power to take away.[46]

The court relied heavily on a natural right theory of property in striking down the ordinance, emphasizing that the right to dispose of one's property as one sees fit is inalienable, and that no statute could regulate away that right.

Indeed, the court highlighted the "inalienable right to own, acquire, and dispose of property which is not conferred by the Constitution, but exists of natural right."[47] It contrasted these inalienable property rights with "suffrage, which is not an inherent right," and other social rights, asserting that

> [t]here is no question that legislation can control social rights by forbidding intermarriage of the races, and in requiring Jim Crow cars ... but none of these interfere with the fundamental right of every one to acquire and dispose of property by sale.[48]

The North Carolina court further reinforced this holding with criticism of the logic behind the segregation policy, drawing comparisons to segregative laws affecting the Irish under English rule and Jews in Russia:

> In Ireland there were years ago limits prescribed beyond which the native Irish or Celtic population could not reside. This was called the "Irish Pale," and one of the results was continued disorder and unrest in that unhappy island which had as one of its consequences that more than half its population came to this country. That policy has since been reversed. But in Russia, to this day, there are certain districts to which the Jews are restricted, with the result that vast numbers of them are emigrating to this country.[49]

The court continued, that judging by the experiences in Ireland and Russia, "the result of this policy might well be a large exodus and naturally of the most enterprising and thrifty element of the colored race ..."[50]

46 *Id.*
47 *Id.* at 340.
48 *Id.*
49 *Id.* at 339.
50 *Id.* at 340.

The City Council of Atlanta, Georgia, enacted a segregation ordinance on June 16, 1913, roughly a year after Winston. Atlanta's segregation ordinance came to be known as the Ashley Ordinance, named after Fourth Ward resident and Councilman Claude Ashley, who was its most vocal proponent. Ashley modeled the ordinance after Baltimore's and others in Virginia. The ordinance restricted the occupancy of homes by individuals of a race other than the race of the majority of the occupants of the block. Unlike prior ordinances, however, the Ashley Ordinance permitted such occupancy if the majority of owners on a street agreed that a property could be occupied by an individual of the other race. This provision allowed for the use of a covenant or agreement, similar to the one Sledge obtained from the residents of Highland Avenue in Winston-Salem, and could provide an escape for homeowners concerned that the ordinance was not protecting property values as claimed, but instead reducing them by limiting the pool of potential buyers or occupants. Also, unlike Baltimore's ordinance, Atlanta's did not include restrictions on places of assembly.

In *Carey v. Atlanta*, the Supreme Court of Georgia declared Atlanta's segregation ordinance invalid on February 12, 1915 because it unconstitutionally restricted an owner's right to sell his property. The court wrote,

> The effect of the ordinance under consideration was not merely to regulate a business or the like, but was to destroy the right of the individual to acquire, enjoy, and dispose of his property. Being of this character, it was void as being opposed to the due–process clause of the Constitution.[51]

The court distinguished the ruling in *Plessy v. Ferguson*[52] by noting that in *Plessy*, as with other segregation laws,

> [t]he most that was done was to require him as a member of a class to conform to reasonable rules in regard to separation of the races. In none of them was he denied the right to use, control, or dispose of his property, as in this case.[53]

51 Carey v. City of Atlanta, 84 S.E. 338, 460 (Ga. 1915).

52 163 U.S. 537, 544 (1896) (approving of an 1890 Louisiana statute requiring "separate railway carriages for the white and colored races" and concluding that the 14th Amendment "could not have been intended to abolish distinctions based upon color, or to enforce social, as distinguished from political, equality, or a commingling of the two races upon terms unsatisfactory to either"); see also Justice Harlan's dissent, 163 U.S. at 562, arguing that

> The arbitrary separation of citizens, on the basis of race, while they are on a public highway, is a badge of servitude wholly inconsistent with the civil freedom and the equality before the law established by the constitution. It cannot be justified upon any legal grounds.

53 84 S.E. at 459.

In short, the ordinance's interference with inherent property rights was a step too far for the regulatory power of the state, even if in the service of what the court saw as widely accepted and judicially approved goal of "separation of the races."[54]

"An owner of property," the court stated,

> could, by mere force of the ordinance and caprice of an adjoining proprietor, without any compensation or process of law, be deprived for all time of the right to reside on his property, or to substitute a tenant or grantee to do so.[55]

The court emphasized that "[o]rdinances of this character are of recent origin"[56] and that the "right of an owner of property to reside on it is inherent, and permanent deprivation of that right is in substance a taking of the property itself."[57]

These first three state high court opinions considering municipal segregation ordinances all emphasized the "inherent" or "inalienable" right to acquire, use, and dispose of property and the unconstitutionality of a regulation seeking to limit those rights so significantly. Whereas rights to vote, to association, and to marriage were described by the courts as social rights, subject to Jim Crow regulation, the right to property, conferred not only by the Constitution but "exist[ing] of natural right" seemed to represent the limit to which Jim Crow segregation laws could not extend.[58]

B. A closer look at the cases upholding local segregation ordinances: Harris v. City of Louisville; Hopkins v. City of Richmond; *and* Harden v. City of Atlanta

Then came the decision by the Court of Appeals of Kentucky in *Harris v. City of Louisville* on June 18, 1915. The Louisville ordinance was modeled after, and shared much in common with, the other segregation ordinances. The primary operative provision prohibited blacks from living on predominantly white blocks and vice versa. The notable distinction between the Louisville ordinance and its predecessors was that, whereas the others applied only prospectively to moves made subsequent to ordinance passage, the Louisville ordinance was even more narrow, applying only to moves made after the passage of the ordinance into properties purchased after the passage of the ordinance. The ordinance had been promoted by Walter D. Binford, an employee of the Louisville *Courier-Journal*, and garnered key early support from members of the Louisville Real Estate Exchange. It was marketed through an extensive campaign threatening a decline in property values without municipal action.

54 *Id.*
55 *Id.* at 458.
56 *Id.*
57 *Id.*
58 Darnell, 81 S.E. at 340.

What differed most about the ordinance compared to its predecessors, however, was its reception in the Kentucky high court, especially the court's description of its relationship to property rights. The Kentucky Court of Appeals stated:

> The *jus disponendi* has but little place in modern jurisprudence. The advance of civilization and the consequent extension of governmental activities along lines having their objective in better living conditions, saner social conditions, and a higher standard of human character has resulted in a gradual lessening of the dominion of the individual over private property and a corresponding strengthening of the regulative power of the state in respect thereof, so that to-day all private property is held subject to the unchallenged right and power of the state to impose upon the use and enjoyment thereof such reasonable regulations as are deemed expedient for the public welfare.[59]

In two sentences, the court dismissed as backward the property rights that the previous state courts had seen as inalienable. In their place was the "unchallenged right and power of the state to impose upon the use and enjoyment … such reasonable regulations as are deemed expedient." While the previous state court opinions had seen property rights as natural rights, now, to the Kentucky court, what was most natural was the "separation of the races."[60] The decision in *Harris v. Louisville* represents a significant shift from a natural right theory of property to a utilitarian one, enabled primarily by strong allegiance to white supremacist Jim Crow laws and an argument about the naturalness of segregation.

The court defended the ordinance against equal protection challenges by declaring that

> [t]he enforced separation of the races alone is not a discrimination or denial of the constitutional guaranty; and, if such separation should result in the members of the colored race being restricted to residence in the less desirable portions of the city, they may render those portions more desirable through their own efforts, as the white race has done.[61]

The decision justified the intrusion into property rights by focusing on the importance of residential segregation, which was presented as a law of nature, yet paradoxically under threat. The court continued:

> The separation of the white and black races upon the surface of the globe is a fact equally apparent. Why this is so, it is not necessary to speculate; but the fact of a distribution of men by race and color is as visible in the providential arrangement of the earth as that of heat and cold. The natural separation of

59 Harris v. City of Louisville, 177 S.W. 472, 476 (Ky. 1917).
60 *Id.* at 477.
61 *Id.* at 476.

> the races is therefore an undeniable fact, and all social organizations which lead to their amalgamation are repugnant to the law of nature. From social amalgamation it is but a step to illicit intercourse, and but another to intermarriage.[62]

The court naturalized not only racial categories, but spatial inequality more broadly. And it approved of the ordinance, and the segregation it would create and codify, as necessary for the advancement of civilization and, therefore, outweighing any costs in terms of property rights.

The Supreme Court of Appeals of Virginia upheld Richmond's and Ashland's segregation ordinances on September 9, 1915. The two challenged ordinances were again similar in form to the preceding ones, but had also been specifically authorized by the passage of a state enabling statute in the Virginia legislature. Ensuring that they would be applied prospectively only, the court held, "the ordinances [Richmond's and Ashland's] are constitutional and valid in so far as they apply to persons whose rights, either as owners or as tenants, have accrued since the enactment of the ordinance."[63]

The court emphasized that "[i]t is the declared policy of this state that close associations of the races tends to breach of the peace, unsanitary conditions, discomfort, immorality, and disquiet."[64] In view of the state segregation policies and the statewide enabling act, "there appears to be nothing unreasonable in placing the restriction above set out on the use of property to the same end."[65] Utilizing a utilitarian calculus, the court again found any intrusion on property rights outweighed by the supposed social benefit of the segregation policy. The Virginia court (quoting the Supreme Judicial Court of Massachusetts) noted that "[r]ights of property, like all other social and conventional rights, are subject to such reasonable limitations in their enjoyment as shall prevent them from being injurious."[66] In contrast to earlier cases, where property rights were seen as inalienable and contrasted against "social rights," here property rights have been recast as "social and conventional" ones subject to regulation. The court further distinguished regulations, such as the segregation ordinances, from the physical occupation or taking that would fall afoul of the Constitution's Taking Clause. The court accordingly approved of a city's right to use its police power to preserve "peace and good order,"[67] through segregation, even though it might restrict the property rights of all who purchased properties after the ordinance's passage.

62 *Id.* at 477.
63 Hopkins v. City of Richmond, 86 S.E. 139, 145 (Va. 1918).
64 *Id.*
65 *Id.*
66 *Id.*
67 *Id.* at 139.

The Supreme Court of Georgia had the opportunity to consider the issue again when Atlanta passed a revised ordinance, clarifying that it applied prospectively only. In *Carey*, the Georgia court had described the ordinance as "destroy[ing] the right of the individual to acquire, enjoy, and dispose of his property,"[68] and therefore void. Just two years later, presented with a similar, if slightly narrower, ordinance, the Georgia court in *Harden* emphasized the importance of maintaining segregation and upheld the ordinance "not withstanding that to some extent the use of property may be somewhat restricted."[69]

When the Georgia Supreme Court had struck down Atlanta's previous ordinance in 1915, it carefully distinguished *Plessy* and emphasized how different any limitations of property rights were when compared to the regulation of social rights by other Jim Crow laws. In *Harden*, the court emphasized instead the naturalness of segregation and implicitly shifted from its previous conception of the inalienability of property rights to one emphasizing their malleability. It noted that a "reasonable restraint on alienation of property by individuals not only pervades our statute law, but is found in our state Constitution" and described laws prescribing the manner of executing wills or deeds to be a restriction on the alienation of property.[70] The decision went on to argue that "the fact that police regulations may limit the use of property in ways which greatly diminish its value does not necessarily render them void."[71] The court further relied on the logic from *Plessy* and the naturalness of segregation as a justification for restricting property rights:

> Courts are not blind to the fact that by nature there are several races of people, and that the conditions of civilization compel certain regulations relating to the contact of the races. … The white and black races have been forbidden intermarriage, and have been separated in public conveyances, inns, hotels, theatres, and public schools. If it be justifiable to separate the races in the public schools in recognition of the peril to race integrity, induced by mere race association, then we cannot see why the same public policy cannot be invoked to prohibit the black and white races from living side by side. … An ordinance designed to accomplish this purpose will be upheld, not withstanding that to some extent the use of property may be somewhat restricted.[72]

Again, the maintenance of segregation was presented as fundamental to the advance of civilization. And the "right of an owner of property to reside on it"

68 Carey v. City of Atlanta, 84 S.E. 456, 460 (Ga. 1915).
69 Harden v. City of Atlanta, 93 S.E. 338, 403 (Ga. 1917).
70 *Id.* at 402.
71 *Id.*
72 *Id.*

moved from being an "inherent" right, to one subject to a utilitarian calculus balancing the perceived benefits of segregation in advancing civilization against the costs of preventing a property owner from living on his land.

The rapid shift of perspective of the Georgia Supreme Court was not without protest. Justice Atkinson dissented from the judgment, arguing that the ordinance "undertakes to deny such rights of acquisition and enjoyment of property on the mere basis of racial distinction, which the Constitution forbids."[73] He described this denial of property rights as going "beyond mere regulatory legislation."[74] "Under the Constitution and general law, any person, irrespective of race, may own or acquire land anywhere in the City of Atlanta. Such right carries with it the right to reside on land lawfully acquired."[75] While the majority maintained that the small changes to the ordinance required a different outcome, Justice Atkinson made clear that the reasons the prior ordinance had been invalidated applied equally to the remaining provisions, "namely, the denial of the right of a citizen to acquire and live in his home where he pleases, on the sole basis of racial distinction."[76]

Conclusion

The United States Supreme Court resolved this division among state courts in *Buchanan v. Warley.*[77] In the continuation of the cases involved in *Harris v. Louisville*, the Court ruled that

> [t]he right which the ordinance annulled was the civil right of a white man to dispose of his property if he saw fit to do so to a person of color and of a colored person to make such disposition to a white person.[78]

This restriction, the Court held, "is in direct violation of the fundamental law enacted in the Fourteenth Amendment of the Constitution preventing state interference with property rights except by due process of law."[79] The Supreme Court's decision, however, did not so much slow the entrenchment of segregation as direct it towards other forms. White homeowners, property developers, and public officials shifted their attention from public municipal segregation ordinances to private racially restrictive covenants, which spread rapidly across the country.[80] The segregation ordinances, however, set an important precedent for racially restrictive covenants, that protection of property values was a

73 *Id.* at 403.
74 *Id.*
75 *Id.*
76 *Id.*
77 245 U.S. 60 (1917).
78 *Id.* at 81.
79 *Id.*
80 Richard R.W. Brooks & Carol M. Rose, Saving the Neighborhood: Racially Restrictive Covenants, Law, and Social Norms (Harvard U. Press, 2013).

defensible rationale for restricting neighbors' property rights, in this case through the residential exclusion of African Americans or non-whites more broadly. As Brooks and Rose describe it, "by referring to property values, individuals can mask their own prejudice: 'it's not me, it's the market.'"[81] Although *Buchanan v. Warley* invalidated segregation ordinances just seven years after Baltimore passed its first ordinance, it would take more than thirty years for racially restrictive covenants to be struck down in *Shelley v. Kraemer*.[82]

But an even more pervasive force in maintaining racial segregation than restrictive covenants was the development of racially neutral zoning ordinances that were discriminatory in effect. The Supreme Court's approval of zoning in *Euclid v. Ambler*[83] relied on a utilitarian theory of property that was arguably enabled by the state court shift in these cases from a natural right theory of property to a utilitarian one. Although the zoning ordinance at issues was not explicitly about racial segregation, the construction of apartment houses was referred to in *Euclid* in terms not unlike the arrival of black neighbors:

> very often, the apartment house is a mere parasite, constructed in order to take advantage of the open spaces and attractive surroundings created by the residential character of the district. Moreover, the coming of one apartment house is followed by others … until finally the residential character of neighborhood and its desirability as a place of detached residences are utterly destroyed.[84]

Indeed, the popularity of zoning as a tool increased as its potential for excluding those seen as undesirable, enforcing separation, and protecting privilege was appreciated.[85] An emphasis on the freedom to acquire, use, and dispose of property associated with a natural right theory of property was at the heart of the first three state cases striking down segregation laws, and the subsequent state courts shifted to a utilitarian theory in part in order to uphold segregation. But property rights are not "natural" or inalienable. The rights of individuals with respect to resources, such as the land or housing at issue in these cases, are shaped by context-specific norms, are created fundamentally by the state, and depend on the existence of an institutional structure to enforce those rights. The shift to a utilitarian approach better reflects the

81 *Id.* at 6.

82 334 U.S. 1, 20 (1948) (holding that in granting judicial enforcement of racially restrictive covenants, "the States have denied petitioners the equal protection of the laws and that, therefore, the action of the state courts cannot stand").

83 272 U.S. 365 (1926).

84 Village of Euclid v. Ambler Realty Co. 272 U.S. 365, 390–97 (upholding the Village of Euclid's zoning ordinance "excluding from residential districts apartment houses, business houses, retail stores and shops, and other like establishments" as rationally related to health and safety and therefore within the municipality's police power, while declining to consider the effects on property rights).

85 Yale Rabin, Expulsive Zoning: The Inequitable Legacy of Euclid, in ZONING AND THE AMERICAN DREAM 101, 105 (Charles M. Haar & Jerold S. Kayden eds., Chicago: Planners Press, 1989).

ways in which property rights are created and has enabled essential equitable restrictions on those rights. But the utilitarian emphasis on a calculation of what is seen as the greatest good for the greatest number, without consideration for who benefits and who sacrifices, also enabled for a brief time these municipal segregation ordinances and may similarly contribute to the maintenance of exclusionary zoning provisions with troublesome distributional consequences today. The early twentieth century municipal segregation cases provide a warning of the need for critical reflection on the exclusionary and inequitable aspects of the social norms that prevail at a given moment and that shape urban law.

2 Privacy, participation and the city

Abigail Jackson and Julian Sidoli

Introduction

> Privacy is not something I'm entitled to. It's an absolute prerequisite.
>
> Marlon Brando

> You already have zero privacy. Get over it!
>
> Scott McNealey, CEO of Sun Microsystems

It is almost nine o' clock in the morning. The Northern Line platform at London Bridge station is crowded with commuters, dressed in a uniform of black, grey and brown. A man in an oversized trench-coat stands next to a woman checking her mobile phone, barely acknowledging her. Elsewhere, a woman listens to music on headphones, while others look at the announcement board in the hope a train will arrive soon. Yet, in spite of the crowds, there is silence. The only sounds are the shuffling of feet and the whirring of an approaching train, with the occasional interjection from the station manager telling commuters to "mind the gap." After a train pulls into the station, the doors open and a line of city workers start to disembark. Jostling against those on the platform, a man's briefcase hits another's knees, as they brush past. On the train itself, there is little space for the incomers, but as the doors start to close, a woman leaps into one of the carriages, clutching her bag and bending her head forwards to fit into the available space. The train then pulls away from the station with its passengers, ready or not for the next business day at work.

At first glance, this scene may appear to have little relevance to a chapter about privacy and participation. However, as part of our everyday life in the city, we try to achieve a balance between our public persona and our private nature. For to participate in the city, it is necessary to be a "social animal,"[1] but to be a social animal, we must understand ourselves in private first. As Sennett explained "while man *made* himself in public, he *realized* his nature in the private realm, above all,

1 Aristotle, Politics (Harris Rackham trans., 1932).

in his experiences with his family."[2] Today, the city is characterised by conflict between the public and the private. Although the neighbourhood gossip is a common stereotype in rural communities, it can still be difficult for an individual to enjoy privacy in an urban setting. Put simply, the city is uncontrollable. Space is often at a premium and the transient nature of the environment may mean that an individual does not even know her own flatmates. Likewise, technological advances that may affect an individual's privacy are tested and used more regularly in the city, rather than in smaller, local communities. By way of example, in 2013, a marketing company called Renew was criticised for embedding sensors in recycling bins in the Cheapside area of central London to monitor the movements of individuals in the area.[3]

Returning to our scene of rush hour on the London Underground, it can be seen that we regulate our privacy in an urban context through shared codes of behaviour or "rules of civility."[4] There is silence on the Northern Line platform on a weekday morning because of a common understanding that if an individual were to speak, she may be considered to be invading another's privacy. Her physical proximity to others is such that she is already far closer to them than is usually acceptable in day-to-day life. So, for her to speak is to invade another's privacy yet further, and in a way that may be intolerable according to the prevailing rules of civility. After all, it may be an intrusion into someone's private thoughts. Of course, in another city and at another time, this norm may be different. However, it has become part of London life with little thought or consideration by the commuters.

Using London as a setting and making reference to English law, this chapter aims to provide an insight into the contested relationship between privacy and participation. It will review the discourse surrounding the "right to the city" as advocated by Henri Lefebvre[5] and David Harvey,[6] looking at the way in which the increasing privatisation of urban space has affected our participation. It will also analyse how certain rules of civility have been incorporated into English law, both through the tort of breach of confidence and legislation governing electoral malpractice. To conclude, it will argue that even though there are real concerns about our ability to participate and the use of public space, urban law should take more account of the importance of the private sphere and the concept of home.[7] For a city to flourish, so, too, must its citizens, and that requires them to have a degree of privacy.

2 Richard Sennett, The Fall of Public Man, 18–19 (1st ed. 2002).

3 *See* Joe Miller, *City of London Calls Halt to Smartphone Tracking Bins*, BBC News (Aug. 12, 2013), www.bbc.co.uk/news/technology-23665490.

4 *See* Robert C. Post, *The Social Foundations of Privacy: Community and Self in the Common Law Tort*, 77 Cal. L. Rev. 957 (1989).

5 *See* Henri Lefebvre, Writings on Cities (Eleonore Kofman & Elizabeth Lebas trans., 1st ed. 1996).

6 *See* David Harvey, *The Right to the City*, 53 New Left Rev. 23 (2008).

7 *See* Lorna Fox, Conceptualising Home: Theories, Laws and Policies (1st ed. 2006).

I. The right to the city

A. Traditional conceptions of the right to the city

Traditional conceptions of rights date back to the eighteenth century, and in particular to Rousseau's theory of the social contract.[8] For Rousseau, a government could only have legitimacy in a society where citizens held and were able to exercise certain rights, such as the right to vote, the right to move and the right to representation. More recently, however, other notions of rights have emerged, with the introduction of the European Convention of Human Rights in the 1950s and Henri Lefebvre's radical reworking of urban citizenship in the 1960s. Nowadays, Lefebvre's notion of the right to the city has become an evocative call for a renewed urban democracy, particularly by those challenging social exclusion. It can be seen as the counterpoint to the "powerless" and bureaucratic model of urban government described by Gerald Frug,[9] as well as the increasing level of globalisation affecting our cities.[10] For as Lefebvre himself explained:

> The *right to the city* cannot be conceived of as a simple visiting right or as a return to traditional cities. It can only be formulated as a renewed and transformed *right to urban life*.[11]

Yet, while the right to the city may have caught both popular and academic interest, there is still a lack of clarity as to how it can transform the city, or our understanding of urban participation. In that regard, this chapter aims to provide insight into the right itself, as well as the challenges it may pose.

According to Lefebvre, the right to the city has two distinct components, namely appropriation and participation.[12] With regards to appropriation, Lefebvre argued that individuals create space where they shape their lives.[13] The nature of that space is necessarily affected by an individual's class, interests or her relationships with others. Space cannot be seen simply as a geographic form or a product of the built environment. Rather, it is a fluid concept, which is constantly produced and reproduced through the acts of individuals. Take the example of a music festival set in a park. For weeks before, the organisers may arrange for a stage to be built, or allocate areas for camping, stalls and food kiosks, while excluding visitors to the park. During the festival itself, the space will be used in the manner envisaged, before being returned to its original use as a park. Moving

8 *See* Jean-Jaques Rousseau, The Social Contract (Christopher Betts trans., 1st ed. 1994).

9 *See* Gerald E. Frug, *The City as a Legal Concept*, 93 Harv. L. Rev. 1057 (1980).

10 *See* Harvey, *supra* note 6.

11 Lefebvre, *supra* note 5, at 158.

12 Mark Purcell, *Excavating Lefebvre: The Right to the City and Its Urban Politics of the Inhabitant*, 58 GeoJournal 99 (1991).

13 *See* Henri Lefebvre, The Production of Space (Donald Nicholson-Smith trans., 1st ed. 1991).

this notion into an urban context, Lefebvre argued that an individual appropriates space by carrying out her day-to-day activities, such as living and working in the city. As such, the city becomes an "oeuvre" or a work in which all citizens participate. It can be seen as a contrast to the relative stability and homogeneity of the rural.

Turning to the right to participate in the city, this is regarded as being contingent on an individual's ability to appropriate urban space by Lefebvre. So, it follows that if an individual is able to appropriate urban space, she should have the right to determine how that land is used. In short, she should be able to participate in all decisions affecting urban space. At first, there may seem to be nothing surprising in this aspect of Lefebvre's right to the city. Yet, it represents a rejection of traditional concepts of enfranchisement and participation. More specifically, enfranchisement is no longer based on an individual's membership of a national political community. Instead, it is concerned with whether she is an urban inhabitant, or "citadin" to use Lefebvre's terminology.

Likewise, Lefebvre's notion of participation does not simply refer to an individual's right to elect government officials or vote in a referendum. To the contrary, he envisaged that citadins should play a central and direct role in all decisions affecting urban space, having the "majority and hegemonic voice."[14] In London, for example, citadins would be able to participate in decisions about the location of an office block, or a new railway station. However, they would also be able to participate in the decision-making process of other nation states that affect the production of space in the city, such as the French government's decision to demolish a refugee camp in Calais, known as the "Jungle."[15] Since many of the refugees in the camp were attempting to reach the United Kingdom and in particular, London, this decision could have real effect on the production of space in the city.

Despite its initial attractiveness, Lefebvre's right to the city remains problematic and difficult to define. Even though Lefebvre perceived the right to the city to be transformative, there is little evidence that it would operate in this way in practice.[16] Applying his theory, however, the nature of the city would depend on the political leanings of its inhabitants at the time the right was invoked. Take the example of Notting Hill and Shepherds Bush in London. In the 1950s and 1960s, the area was associated with immigration from the Caribbean, where

14 *See* Purcell, *supra* note 12.

15 *See* Robert Booth, *Calais Camp Demolitions "Forcing More Refugees to Make Crossing to UK,"* GUARDIAN (Mar. 24, 2016), www.theguardian.com/world/2016/mar/24/calais-refugee-camp-demolitions-increase-uk-asylum-seekers.

16 In Lefebvre's theory, he does not address whether any checks and balances are required to prevent citadins from introducing exclusionary and discriminatory measures, such as racially restricted covenants. This has led to the continued and ongoing residential segregation of certain racial groups in America. *See* Kevin Fox Gotham, *Urban Space, Restrictive Covenants, and the Origin of Racial Residential Segregation in a U.S. City, 1900–1950*, 24 INT'L J. URB. & REGIONAL RES. 616 (2000).

individuals would live in poor quality housing that was administered by slum landlords, such as Perec Rachman. If Lefebvre's right to the city had operated in that area at that time, this could have had a real effect on the way in which that part of London developed. It may have affirmed the rights of the Afro-Caribbean community against other marginalised groups or more powerful communities. By contrast, Notting Hill is now an affluent neighbourhood, with many of the properties being owned by an international elite. If those inhabitants were to exercise Lefebvre's right to the city, this would lead to a very different urban environment and style of governance. In this regard, Lefebvre is notably vague about the definition of a city, whether it requires a certain population or if it should include the suburbs.[17] Moreover, Lefebvre does not consider how the right to the city would operate where two or more cities have an interest in a particular measure. So, returning to our example of the French government's decision to demolish the "Jungle" refugee camp in Calais, it is inevitable that this will affect nearby cities, such as Lille and Paris. If those cities have competing interests, it is unclear whose interests will take precedence and how that will be determined. By way of example, would the decision be made by the city where there is the greatest effect on the production of space? Or should it be the city with the largest population? How can a decision be reached on the production of space in the city, when there is no general consensus amongst the citadins?

Finally, and perhaps in the context of this chapter, most importantly, some commentators have argued that the right to the city fails to take proper account of the importance of the private sphere, or the way in which they are interrelated. So, while Lefebvre argued that all citadins had the right to live in the city, he gave little thought to housing conditions or the space that an individual requires to flourish. Instead, he simply rejected the notion of property rights, denouncing them as part of a "bureaucratic society of urban consumption."[18] Looking at this matter from a feminist perspective, it should be noted that Lefebvre does not consider how a woman's rights within her home may affect her enjoyment of the city, or the possibility that she may be excluded from certain public spaces through fear of harassment and unwelcome attention.[19] That same criticism may be made with regards to certain racial groups, or other disadvantaged members of society, such as the disabled and homeless.[20] After all, to participate in the city, an individual must have access to a space where she can express herself fully and without fear of recrimination. If she lives in an environment controlled by others, be it a home, prison or on the streets, this may not be possible.

17 *See* Purcell, *supra* note 12.

18 Mustafa Dikeç, *Justice and the Spatial Imagination*, 33 ENV'T & PLAN. A 1785, 1789 (2001).

19 *See* Tovi Fenster, *The Right to the Gendered City: Different Formations of Belonging in Everyday Life*, 14 J. GENDER STUD. 217 (2005).

20 DON MITCHELL, THE RIGHT TO THE CITY: SOCIAL JUSTICE AND THE FIGHT FOR PUBLIC SPACE (1st ed. 2003).

B. The private city or a public space?

In the context of the debate over the privatisation of urban space, it is notable there has been a growing interest in the right to the city, as well as the notion of the "commons." In cities across the world, shopping malls are being privatised, together with large areas of open space.[21] Even shelters in public parks are becoming high-end coffee kiosks, serving hot drinks at a price only a few residents can afford.[22] As Klein commented:

> There are oppositional threads taking form in many different campaigns and movements. The spirit that they share is a radical reclaiming of the commons. As our communal spaces disappear – town squares, streets, schools, farms, are being displaced by the ballooning marketplace, a spirit of resistance is taking hold around the world. People are reclaiming bits of nature and culture and saying "this is going to be public space."[23]

If the commons is understood as land or resources that are managed by a community and to which we all have access,[24] it can be seen in housing cooperatives, village greens[25] or even informal settlements that have been built outside the city.[26] Using London as an example, the River Thames can be seen as an urban commons. Since the city was established by the Romans, the river has been used by inhabitants for both trade and leisure pursuits, while in 1989, the Thames Path was granted the status of being an official National Trail. As a result of this designation, members of the public are able to walk approximately 200 miles from the river's source in the Cotswolds to the Thames Barrier. However, that right has been curtailed by property developers, who have built large residential complexes or apartment blocks by the banks of the river. This has meant that it is increasingly difficult for ramblers to walk along the Thames Path, without passing through private developments where access is controlled by a security guard or locked gate.[27] Once again, this highlights the conflict between an individual's right to enjoy the city and another's right to privacy. Put simply,

21 Antonia Layard, *Shopping in the Public Realm: A Law of Place*, 37 J. L. & Soc'y 412 (2010).

22 Take the example of the Kiosk Café in Bethnal Green Gardens in London. Until recently, this was a unique Art Deco style public shelter, designed by the London Passenger Transport Board architect, Charles Holden. *See* Planning Application no. PA/14/02366 from the London Borough of Tower Hamlets.

23 Naomi Klein, *Reclaiming the Commons*, 9 New Left Rev. 81, 82 (2001).

24 *See* Nicholas Blomley, *Enclosure, Common Right and the Property of the Poor*, 17 Soc. & Legal Stud. 311 (2008).

25 Commons Act 2006, § 15 (U.K.).

26 *See* Boaventura de Sousa Santos, *The Law of the Oppressed: The Construction and Reproduction of Legality in Pasargada*, 12 L. & Soc'y Rev. 5 (1977).

27 *See* Jack Shenker, *Privatised London: The Thames Path Walk That Resembles a Prison Corridor*, Guardian (Feb. 24, 2015), www.theguardian.com/cities/2015/feb/24/private-london-exposed-thames-path-riverside-walking-route.

the owner of a waterside apartment may wish to exclude members of the public from the space outside her building to protect her own quiet enjoyment of the land. Yet, in doing so, the property owner is limiting the right to the city enjoyed by another individual.

At this juncture, it is perhaps pertinent to consider Gray and Gray's conception of "quasi-public" property.[28] In terms of land, Gray and Gray have argued that "notions of 'public' and 'private' operate not dichotomously, but continuously across a spectrum in which adjacent connotations shade easily into one another."[29] By way of explanation, many of the public services that we use on a regular basis, such as parks, libraries and civic buildings, operate on privately owned land, even if the title is held by a local authority or government department. Given the nature of the land and the character of its owner, it is arguable that any exclusion from these places could be challenged on proportionality grounds under the Human Rights Act 1998, with the users invoking either Article 8, Article 10 or Article 11 of the European Convention on Human Rights. Yet, the complexity of property arrangements in the city means that disputes over access are rarely so simple. For example, if a local authority had an office in a privately owned building, could the freeholder exercise her discretion to refuse entry to certain individuals? Is it reasonable for the owner of a riverside property to impose conditions on when and how part of the Thames Path can be used? Should the owner of a shopping centre be able to exclude members of the public from the property on a permanent and ongoing basis for acts of nuisance and anti-social behaviour?

In fact, the last question was answered in the affirmative by the Court of Appeal in *CIN Properties Ltd v. Rawlins.*[30] Although there was an implied permission for members of the public to enter a shopping centre, this was an equitable right that could be revoked with immediate effect.[31] Moreover, there was no obligation on the landowner to act rationally, or consider whether the exclusion was proportionate to the aim that she was trying to achieve. Interestingly, that decision was upheld by the European Court of Human Rights in *Appleby v. United Kingdom*,[32] where a landowner was able to exclude an individual from a shopping mall for collecting signatures to protest against a local development. This did not represent a breach of the applicant's rights to freedom of assembly or expression, and neither could the government be expected to take any responsibility for the applicant's human rights.

More recently, however, there has been a move by the courts towards restricting a landowner's ability to evict individuals from her property. In a minority

28 *See* Kevin J. Gray & Susan F. Gray, *Private Property and Public Propriety in* PROPERTY AND THE CONSTITUTION (Janet McClean ed., 1999); *see also* Kevin J. Gray & Susan F. Gray, *Civil Rights, Civil Wrongs and Quasi-Public Space*, 4 Eur. Hum. Rts. L. Rev. 46 (1999).

29 *See* Gray & Gray, *Private Property and Public Propriety, supra* note 28.

30 CIN Properties Limited v. Rawlins, 2 EGLR 130 (1995) (UK).

31 *See* Wood v. Leadbitter, 13 M. & W. 838 (1845).

32 Appleby & Others v. United Kingdom, ECHR 222 (2003).

opinion in *Malik v. Fassenfelt*,[33] Sir Alan Ward held that Article 8 of the European Convention on Human Rights was engaged where squatters had established a settlement and used the property as their home. As a result, the squatters could only be evicted if the eviction was a legitimate means of achieving proportionate aim. At first glance, this may appear to be an affirmation of the right to the city and an individual's ability to take part in all aspects of urban life. After all, by allowing an individual to remain on another person's land, she may be able to participate fully in the life of the community as an active citizen. Nevertheless, that decision is necessarily limited. Referring to the jurisprudence on evictions from social housing,[34] Sir Alan Ward accepted that the circumstances that would prevent the eviction of a squatter or an occupier would have to be "exceptional." Indeed, it is difficult to envisage a case where the squatter's rights would take precedence over those of the owner. Further, it fails to take account of other legislation, which may exclude an individual from certain parts of the city. For instance, under the Anti-Social Behaviour, Crime and Policing Act 2014, a local authority is able to obtain an "injunction to prevent nuisance and annoyance" against an individual whose behaviour is likely to cause alarm, harassment or distress, for what could be an indefinite period of time. Had that law been in force at the time of the judgment in *CIN Properties Ltd v. Rawlins*,[35] the young men may have found themselves subject to such an injunction that permanently excluded them from the shopping centre in question. In short, although the law that is used may be different, the consequences remain the same.

As we have seen before, the right to the city demands the right to use urban space, both for an individual's day-to-day activities and her participation in political life. In other words, a citadin needs to have a space where her voice can be heard without any undue restrictions, as well as gain access to the political process.[36] Nevertheless, a balance needs to be struck between our right to public space and private property rights. Writing on the plight of the homelessness, Waldron explains:

> there is no place governed by a private property rule where he is allowed to be whenever he chooses, no place governed by a private property rule from which he may not at any time be excluded as a result of someone else's say-so.[37]

Put simply, a person who is homeless has nowhere to carry out her private functions, such as cooking, washing, sleeping and eating. She is allowed to live

33 Malik v. Fassenfelt, EWCA Civ. 798 (2013).

34 *See* Manchester City Council v. Pinnock, UKSC 45 (2010); *see also* London Borough of Hounslow v. Powell, UKSC 8 (2011).

35 *See* CIN Properties Limited v. Rawlins, 2 EGLR 130 (1995) (UK).

36 *See* Jürgen Habermas, *The Public Sphere: An Encyclopaedia Article*, 3 New German Critique 49 (1974).

37 Jeremy Waldron, *Homelessness and Freedom*, 39 UCLA L. Rev. 295, 299 (1991).

on the streets or under bridges, but only in the manner that society allows her to do so. Extrapolating Waldron's argument further, the same problem could arise if all land was common or publicly held. For instance, where in a warzone or a dystopian wasteland could an individual go to carry out her daily routine, without any unnecessary interference from others? Once again, she may be allowed to live in a refugee camp or a deserted building, but only in the manner that society allows her to do so. In these circumstances, it is necessary for us to examine the notion of privacy and how that can be achieved in the city, both through property rights and other laws. For the private sphere is not only where an individual lives the most intimate parts of her life, but it is also the place in which she develops her ideas and associations with others. It is the place where an individual becomes a fully developed citadin.

C. *Ideas and understandings of privacy*

As a legal concept, privacy is notoriously difficult to define. Traditionally seen as "the right to be let alone,"[38] it has more recently been described by Daniel Solove as a "relief from ... social friction. It enables people to engage in worthwhile activities that they would otherwise find impossible."[39] In England and Wales, the courts have refused to recognise a general right to privacy.[40] Yet, notions of privacy are present elsewhere in the law. Take landlord and tenant law for example. It is almost a truism that every residential tenancy agreement contains the implied covenant of quiet enjoyment.[41] This allows a tenant to use the rental property without any unreasonable interference from others, and in particular, her landlord. If a landlord enters a property without the tenant's consent or cuts off any essential services, this will be deemed to be a breach of contract and possibly even a criminal offence.[42] Meanwhile, harassment is a criminal offence,[43] as is sending grossly offensive, indecent or obscene messages.[44] There is also legislation governing the dissemination of personal information[45] and perhaps, most importantly, a restitutionary claim for breach of confidence has been developed.[46] This provides an individual with a remedy where there is an unauthorised disclosure of her confidential information to her detriment.

38 *See* THOMAS COOLEY, COOLEY ON TORTS 29 (2nd ed. 1888).
39 Daniel J. Solove, *A Taxonomy of Privacy*, 154 U. PA. L. REV. 477, 484 (2008).
40 *See* Kaye v. Robertson, EWCA Civ. 21 (1990). This position was later affirmed in Wainwright v. Home Office, UKHL 53 (2003).
41 *See* Jenkins v. Jackson, 40 Ch. D. 71 (1888). *See also* Kenny v. Preen, 1 QB 499 (1963).
42 *See* Protection from Eviction Act 1977 § 5 (UK).
43 *See* Protection from Harassment Act 1997 § 2 (UK).
44 *See* Communications Act 2003 § 127.
45 *See* Data Protection Act 1998.
46 *See* Douglas v. Hello!, 2 WLR 992 (2001).

Nevertheless, even though privacy has been described as a concept in "disarray,"[47] there is often something instinctive about any breach. From a young age, we are able to recognise when there has been an unacceptable intrusion into our personal space, be it a parent entering a bedroom or a teacher looking at messages on a student's mobile phone. We can also identify when another person's right to privacy has been breached. So, for instance, most individuals would agree that a woman's privacy has been invaded if she sees a peeping tom at the window, or learns that an embarrassing photograph of her has been published in the press without her consent. The common theme in these examples is that others were involved, and have behaved towards us in a manner that we consider to be unacceptable. As such, privacy can be seen as a set of social norms that govern our relationships with others, and regulate any interactions.[48] To that end, there may be little need for privacy laws on a deserted island with only one or two inhabitants, but by way of contrast, the privacy of a citadin is likely to be challenged on a day-to-day basis, in view of the large, diverse and transient population of the city.

II. Privacy in the city

To understand how privacy operates in the city, it is necessary for us to examine how the law strikes a balance between an individual's right to be let alone, and the rights of others to freedom of expression and assembly. Often, these cases can be difficult and fact-dependent. Nevertheless, in part, that can be explained by the contradictory nature of an individual herself. On one hand, she may have a desire to be part of a community, but at the same time, she may wish for privacy. In her study of social ordering in four urban neighbourhoods, Sally E. Merry observed such a contradiction in how middle-class Americans perceive society.[49] Individuals would often express a desire to have distance from their neighbours, but if there was any anti-social behaviour, they would look to the police for assistance. Even though Merry's study is over twenty years old, the conflict between an individual's need for privacy and community continues to exist. Indeed, it has become even more contested, given that the population of towns and cities is ever-increasing and space is more limited.

Despite the continued challenges to an individual's privacy, the English courts have failed to regulate our interactions with others in urban life adequately. Although the character of the neighbourhood may be a factor in determining whether certain conduct amounts to a nuisance,[50] this only discriminates in favour of individuals living in the countryside, to the detriment of those in the city. More

47 *See* Solove, *supra* note 39.

48 *See* Post, *supra* note 4.

49 Sally E. Merry, *Mending Walls and Building Fences: Constructing the Private Neighbourhood*, 33 J. Legal Pluralism 71 (1993).

50 *See* Sturges v. Bridgman, LR 11 Ch. D. 852 (1879).

specifically, the law will not offer an individual any protection against her neighbour's reasonable use of land, even if it has a real and lasting effect on her wellbeing. In short, we must tolerate what our neighbours do, even if that hurts us. In *Southwark Borough Council v. Mills*,[51] for example, the House of Lords expressed sympathy for a tenant living in the inner city, who could hear "not only the neighbours' televisions and their babies crying but their comings and goings, their cooking and cleaning, their quarrels and their love-making."[52] However, she had no viable nuisance claim in respect of the reasonable daily activities of those living nearby. As a citadin, she was *expected* to know that she may have to endure the behaviour of her neighbours, before taking up residence in the apartment.

To that end, it is notable that many of the laws governing privacy in England and Wales apply an objective test, looking at the breach from the perspective of the "reasonable man" or "the man on the Clapham omnibus."[53] As Post argued, such a test can be seen as an extrapolation of the community's moral judgment on whether certain behaviour is acceptable, or if it is an invasion of privacy.[54] Yet, there may be particular issues with placing the reasonable man in the context of the city. By its very nature, the city is diverse in terms of age, culture, religion and ethnic background. In London, for instance, is the reasonable man a bearded hipster, city worker or lifelong resident? In addition, the use of an objective test means that little consideration is given to the way in which an individual's surroundings affect her behaviour towards others. That is to say, the conduct of the reasonable man is not considered from a spatial perspective. Rather, he is deemed to be a "legal fiction," which arises by the application of an impersonal standard.[55] Taking into account the above considerations, the objective standard may be better seen as the moral judgement of a small number of individuals within the legal system, rather than as reflective of the interests of those living in the city. Against that background, this chapter will conclude by examining two instances where the court has attempted to balance privacy and our right to participate in the city.

A. *Public interest in a private life*

Ever since lawyers have contemplated an action for breach of privacy, there has been debate over the level of privacy that should be enjoyed by an individual in public life. As Warren and Brandeis explained:

> The design of the law must be to protect those persons with whose affairs the community has no legitimate concern, from being dragged into an

51 *See* Southwark Borough Council v. Mills, UKHL 40 (1999).
52 *Id.* at 41 (quoting Lord Hoffman).
53 McQuire v. Western Morning News, 2 KB 100, 109 (CA) (1903) (citing test articulated by Sir Richard Henn Collins MR).
54 *See* Post, *supra* note 4.
55 Healthcare at Home Ltd. v. Common Serv. Agency, UKSC 49 (2014) (at para. 2).

> undesirable and undesired publicity and to protect all persons, whatsoever … their position or station, from having matters which they may properly prefer to keep private, made public against their will. It is the unwarranted invasion of individual privacy which is reprehended, and to be, so far as possible, prevented.[56]

So, for instance, to establish a claim for breach of confidence in England and Wales, a claimant must demonstrate that the information in question is private, and that the interests in keeping it private outweigh those in favour of publication.[57] Further, in deciding whether to allow publication, the judge will consider whether an individual is performing an official function, or is simply in the public eye. Using that analysis, the courts have allowed personal information to be published about Sir Fred Goodwin, the former Chief Executive of the Royal Bank of Scotland,[58] and Boris Johnson, a prominent Conservative politician.[59]

Looking at this matter in the context of privacy and urban participation, a number of questions still remain. By way of example, what protection should be afforded to an individual who participates in the political life of the city, but to a lesser degree, such as a local councillor or an elected police commissioner? Likewise, the city contains a number of organisations that carry out a public function, but are run by private enterprises, such as housing associations and academy schools. How much privacy should the headmaster of such a school enjoy? Is there a legitimate public interest in the behaviour of a chief executive of a housing association, if he has acted recklessly in his private life?

Returning to Lefebvre's notion of the right to the city, it could be argued that all of these individuals make decisions that affect the production of urban space. Therefore, any relevant information about their private lives should be disclosed. Put simply, it affects a citadin's participation in the city, as well as any decisions she makes. Nevertheless, that fails to address how the publication of private information may affect the wellbeing of an individual and her family. It could deter her from participating fully in urban life, or even from carrying out her usual daily activities. More importantly, however, there is a risk that this could deter other members of the community from participating in the city, particularly women or those from minority groups.[60] For the city to operate effectively, there

56 Samuel D. Warren & Louis D. Brandeis, *The Right to Privacy*, 4 Harv. L. Rev. 193, 214–15 (1890).

57 *See* McKennitt v. Ash, QB 73 (2008).

58 *See* Goodwin v. News Grp. Newspapers Ltd. (No. 3), EWHC 1437 (QB) (2011).

59 *See* AAA v. Associated Newspapers Limited, EWCA Civ 554 (2013).

60 *See* Shalailah Medhora, *Julia Gillard Backlash Puts Woman with Traditional Gender Beliefs off Politics – Study*, Guardian (Jan. 13, 2015), www.theguardian.com/world/2015/jan/13/julia-gillard-backlash-puts-women-with-traditional-gender-beliefs-off-politics-study; *see also* George Eaton, Why Chukka Umunna Withdrew from the Labour Leadership Race, New Statesman (May 15, 2015), www.newstatesman.com/politics/2015/05/why-chuka-umunna-withdrew-labour-leadership-race.

needs to be participation at grass-roots level and across all ages, races, genders and cultures. Without this, the interests of certain groups of citadins will not be adequately represented, and in some cases, may not be represented at all.

B. Public participation in a private decision

Aside from claims for breach of confidence, the law governing the conduct of elections regulates privacy and participation in the city, both through domestic legislation in the Representation of the People Act 1983 and the European Convention on Human Rights. Although it is a qualified right,[61] Article 1, Protocol 3 of the European Convention on Human Rights provides that elections shall be held at regular intervals and by secret ballot, under conditions that ensure the free expression of members of the public. Of course, if an election is not conducted properly, it cannot be said to be democratic or represent the will of the people. In that regard, there are obligations on the candidates and their supporters, as well as public officials,[62] the returning officer,[63] broadcasters[64] and the police.[65] By way of example, it is an illegal practice to publish any false statement about a candidate's personal character or conduct, unless the publisher has reasonable grounds for believing it to be true. Likewise, it is a criminal offence to procure votes in exchange for money, a financial benefit[66] or hospitality.[67]

In recent years and in particular under the Blair Government, there has been a move towards the devolution of power to regional governments and local authorities, with the London Assembly and the elected position of Mayor of London being established in the Greater London Authority Act 1999. Further, the Local Government Act 2000 gave local authorities the ability to adopt a governance structure with a directly elected mayor, if that was approved by the electorate in a referendum. As a consequence, this has renewed interest in local democracy, but it has also meant that elections are bitterly fought between different interest groups, each seeking control of the authority in question. Given the contested nature of the city, these developments have proved to be problematic in London, and nowhere more so than in the London Borough of Tower Hamlets. The London Borough of Tower Hamlets can perhaps be best described as one of the most diverse and heavily populated areas of London. At one time, the borough had a reputation for poverty and crime,[68] with an underlying

61 *See* Hirst v. United Kingdom (No. 2*)*, 19 BHRC 546 (2006).
62 *See* Representation of the People Act 1983 § 99 (UK).
63 *Id.* at § 28.
64 *Id.* at § 93.
65 *Id.* at § 100.
66 *Id.* at § 113.
67 *Id.* at § 114.
68 ARTHUR MORRISON, TALES OF THE MEAN STREETS (1st ed. 1894); *see also* ARTHUR MORRISON, A CHILD OF THE JAGO (1st ed. 1896); SARAH WISE, THE BLACKEST STREETS: THE LIFE AND DEATH OF A VICTORIAN SLUM (1st ed. 2009).

narrative of "waves of foreign immigration,"[69] dating back to the arrival of French Huguenots in the seventeenth century. Nowadays, there are still areas of real deprivation, but it is also home to the Tower of London, Canary Wharf, Spitalfields Market and Brick Lane. Moreover, Tower Hamlets has had a history of electoral problems, as well as political conflicts with central Government.[70] So, perhaps it is pertinent to examine the most recent judgment involving electoral malpractice in the borough, namely *Erlam v. Rahman*.[71]

The judgment in *Erlam* concerned a petition by four voters in the London Borough of Tower Hamlets, alleging that the election of Lutfur Rahman as Mayor in 2014 should be set aside on the basis of corrupt and illegal practices.[72] The petition contained numerous instances of alleged electoral malpractice, including personation, treating, bribery, making unlawful payments to canvassers, tampering with ballot papers and misleading voters as to the political affiliation of Mr. Rahman. Most importantly, however, the petition alleged that there had been undue influence on the part of Mr. Rahman and his supporters, involving both spiritual injury and intimidation at polling stations.

With regards to the allegation of intimidation at polling stations, the petitioners adduced evidence of voters being harassed by the jeering and cat-calling of Mr. Rahman's supporters. Some spoke of having to "run the gauntlet" into the polling station.[73] One woman even told the court that Mr. Rahman's supporters besieged her car, banging on its windows with leaflets from his campaign.[74] Arguably, this demonstrates that proper consideration should be given to both the spatial and temporal aspects of our participation in the city, as well as the privacy that this requires. As Timothy Zick has claimed, many accounts of participation fail to address the importance of place.[75] In part, the conduct of Mr. Rahman's supporters was objectionable because they were based at the polling station on an election day. Had this campaigning taken place in a different place or on a different day, an individual may not have felt intimidated by the supporters' behaviour, or obligated to vote in a certain way. On an election day, an individual needs to have privacy to be able to cast her vote freely, while a candidate's supporters may wish to canvass at every opportunity. As a result, participation in urban life can lead to greater and ever-increasing challenges to privacy. To that end, it is notable that when the mayoral election was re-run in Tower Hamlets in 2015, there was a greater police presence at

69 Spitalfields, *Spitalfields History*, www.spitalfields.co.uk/spitalfields-history (last visited Mar. 24, 2016).
70 Erlam v. Rahman [2015] EWHC 1215, [56]-[57] (Eng.).
71 *Id.*
72 *See* Representation for the People Act 1983 § 158 (UK).
73 Erlam v. Rahman [2015] EWHC 1215, [590].
74 *See id.* at 178.
75 Timothy Zick, *Speech and Spatial Tactics*, 84 Tex. L. Rev. 581 (2006).

polling stations.[76] In addition, zoning was used to protect voters from unreasonable interference by candidates and their supporters in a manner that was reminiscent of the bubbles surrounding abortion clinics in the USA.[77]

Turning to the allegation of undue spiritual injury, the election commissioner summarised the petitioners' case in the following terms:

> Mr. Rahman … was determined to play the religious card. The campaign would be targeted at Tower Hamlets' Muslim population with a stark message. Islam is under threat: it is the duty of all devout Muslims to vote for Mr. Rahman and his party.[78]

In support of that allegation, the petitioners cited two occasions during the election campaign where Mr. Rahman had shared a platform with Mr. Hoque, the Chairman of the Council of Mosques. From a video and a contemporaneous newspaper article that was written by one of Mr. Rahman's supporters, it was evident that Mr. Hoque enthusiastically endorsed Mr. Rahman's candidature, and had encouraged voters to elect him as Mayor of Tower Hamlets. Further, a letter was sent to a local Bangladeshi newspaper, the Weekly Desh, by 101 Muslim clerics and scholars, in support of Mr. Rahman. Rightly or wrongly, the election commissioner characterised this letter as a call by influential religious leaders to the faithful, informing them that it was their duty to vote for Mr. Rahman.

At first glance, this allegation may appear to have little relevance to an individual's privacy in the city. Yet, there are certain private matters that are so fundamental to ourselves and our personhood that to refer to them in an election campaign could be seen as unfair and even undemocratic. Take the example of a candidate who threatens to assault a voter, if she fails to cast her vote in a certain way. That is a simple case where an individual is unable to exercise her democratic right for fear of harm. By way of analogy, is there any real difference if a voter is told that it is her religious duty to elect a certain candidate? If she is devout in her religion, she may believe that any failure to comply with the teachings of a religious leader could lead to grave consequences. To argue otherwise is to fail to take account of the strength of an individual's religious beliefs. However, it is that same devoutness that may encourage an individual to participate in the city. Indeed, supporters of Mr. Rahman have argued that the judgment could be regarded as being discriminatory and even racist.[79] They may contend that by placing restrictions on the content of a

76 *See* Catherine Neilan, *Tower Hamlets Mayoral Election: Police Will Be Monitoring Voting Tomorrow to Curb "Fraudulent Activity,"* City A.M. (June 10, 2015), www.cityam.com/217626/tower-hamlets-mayoral-election-police-will-be-monitoring-voting-tomorrow-curb-fraudulent.

77 *See* Madsen v. Women's Health Ctr. Inc., 512 U.S. 753 (1994).

78 Erlam v. Rahman [2015] EWHC 1215, [160].

79 *See* Nadine El-Enany, *Why Muslims Can't Trust the Legal System: The Lutfur Rahman Judgment and Institutional Racism*, Critical Legal Thinking (May 16, 2015), www.criticallegalthinking.com/2015/05/16/why-muslims-cant-trust-the-legal-system.

candidate's election campaign, the law does not adequately consider the interests of different communities or the way in which they may wish to participate in the city. Given these competing interests, it may be appropriate to consider urban participation from a utilitarian perspective. In other words, participation in the city should be regulated in such a way that the greatest number of citadins are able to take part in urban life with as few restrictions as possible, so long as the privacy of others is respected. Here, it is notable that in *Erlam v. Rahman*, the election court held that there was no undue intimidation at polling stations, even though the conduct of Mr. Rahman's supporters may have been unacceptable to some voters.[80]

Conclusions

To summarise, it is difficult to see how a consensus can be reached as to the balance that should be struck between an individual's right to privacy and her ability to participate in urban life. Such a conflict is inherent in the contested nature of the city, as well as the wider incongruity between social capital and diversity.[81] One approach, however, may be to view the relationship between privacy and participation as the operation of a social norm. As such, this necessarily depends on the nature of the city itself, as well as the expectations of its citadins and any shared codes of behaviour. Returning to our original example of the London Underground, there is an implicit understanding amongst commuters that a train journey during rush hour may involve physical intrusions in the personal space of others. To prevent further intrusion into an individual's private space, there is silence. Of course, that conduct is a social norm, and may be particular to London. It may not be replicated on the Paris Metro, New York Subway or Berlin U-Bahn.

Nevertheless, there is still a circularity to the arguments surrounding both privacy and participation. Put simply, an individual should be encouraged to participate in all aspects of city life, and that requires the wider community to respect her privacy. Yet, to participate, an individual must relinquish certain aspects of her right to a private life and accept that her acts may intrude on the privacy of others. Perhaps this circularity is why the conflict between privacy and urban participation has not been considered in greater detail in the academic literature. Even so, without privacy or a private space, an interest group would not be able to organise its members. An individual would not be able to develop her sense of self in a way that allows her to participate in public life. The city has been developed both through privacy and participation, and that should be given due consideration in any account of urban law.

80 *See* Erlam v. Rahman [2015] EWHC 1215, [56]-[57] (Eng.).

81 *See* Robert D. Putnam, Bowling Alone: The Collapse and Revival of American Community (2000); *see also* Stephanie Stern, *The Dark Side of Town: The Social Capital Revolution in Residential Property*, 99 Va. L. Rev. 811 (2013).

3 Discrepancy between legal approaches and policy goals

A case study of subsidized housing in Hong Kong

Alice Lee and Phoebe Woo

Introduction

More than a densely populated concrete jungle, Hong Kong is also known as "the world's priciest home market."[1] Faced with a heating property market and increasing public demand for affordable housing units, the Hong Kong government has implemented a number of housing schemes and policies including the Home Ownership Scheme (HOS), the Tenants Purchase Scheme and the Home Purchase Loan Scheme to cater to the needs of different income groups.

This chapter focuses on HOS, exploring how the application of equitable principles in the context of HOS presents a dilemma between serving justice for persons who contribute to the purchase of HOS flats and upholding the policy objectives of HOS. Recent Hong Kong cases involving families disputing over ownership of HOS flats will be cited as illustrations.

HOS offers flats at a concessionary price to existing public rental housing (PRH) tenants and members from the lower middle income class who may not be able to afford private housing units. In order to ensure that HOS flats are only allocated to people in need, there are statutory restrictions regarding the transfer of ownership of HOS flats under the Housing Ordinance.[2] The Hong Kong Housing Authority (HKHA), a statutory body established in 1973 under the Housing Ordinance, has also set stringent conditions of eligibility. As will be shown, such conditions and transfer restrictions are in potential conflict with equitable doctrines that confer beneficial ownership on those who made direct or indirect financial contributions towards the purchase of property.

The Court of Final Appeal (CFA), the highest court in Hong Kong, in the consolidated appeal of *Cheuk Shu Yin v. Yip So Wan & Lo King Fai*[3] and *Ling Wing Fai Billy v. Ling Shui Fai*[4] (collectively cited as *Cheuk Shu Yin v. Yip So*

1 Peggy Seto & Sandy Li, *Hong Kong the World's Priciest Home Market for the Seventh Year*, S. China Morning Post (Jan. 23, 2017), www.scmp.com/business/article/2064554/hong-kong-named-most-expensive-housing-market-world-seventh-straight-year.

2 *See* Housing Ordinance, (1973) Cap. 283 (H.K.).

3 F.A.C.V. 9/2011 (C.F.A.).

4 F.A.C.V. 11/2011 (C.F.A.).

Wan[5]), ruled that the creation of beneficial interests in HOS flats under resulting trusts or common intention constructive trusts did not amount to an alienation forbidden by Section 17B of the Housing Ordinance. Accordingly, the CFA recognized that the plaintiffs in both cases, who were family members of the HOS applicants (the defendants) and who contributed to the purchase of the HOS flats in question, were able to acquire beneficial interests proportionate to their financial contributions. It is a purely legal analysis, focusing on the meaning of the word "alienation" without further consideration of whether the aforesaid eligibility conditions are met. The CFA's decision is final and has been followed in subsequent cases such as *Lee Kin Wai v. Lee Kin Chuen and Another.*[6] Yet, whether its approach is correct or desirable is another question. With hindsight, the CFA should have questioned the plaintiffs' eligibility for HOS interests. This chapter explains why it was a missed opportunity to redraw the balance between law and policy. Part I gives an overview of the policy and statutory framework under HOS. Part II examines the legal principles for determining beneficial ownership. Parts III and IV analyze court cases involving family disputes over HOS properties. It will be shown that there are blind spots in judicial reasoning. A more holistic and pragmatic approach is called for.

I. Hong Kong's home ownership scheme

HOS has been an important housing source in Hong Kong since it was launched in 1976 to provide permanent homes to existing PRH tenants and the less affluent class at discounted prices. It was so successful that within two years, in 1978, the HOS was supplemented by an ancillary scheme called the Private Sector Participation Scheme[7] which engaged private sector developers in the construction of HOS flats. The social good it served was emphasized by Sir Murray MacLehose, the then Governor, at the opening session of the Legislative Council on October 6, 1976:

> In this year's budget speech, the Financial Secretary announced the Government's intention of boosting production by building an additional 30,000 flat for sale at an average rate of 5,000 flats a year to provide additional accommodation for some 180,000 people. The original intention was to sell them only to persons already in housing estate so as to make room in rented accommodation for other in more need. However, after careful thought, I reached the conclusion that promotion of home

5 [2012] 15 H.K.C.F.A.R. 344 (C.F.A.).

6 [2017] H.C.A. 212/2014 (C.F.I.).

7 *See Background Information on the Development of Public Housing of the Housing Authority Since its Establishment in 1973*, Legis. Council Secretariat (IN08/01–02), www.legco.gov.hk/yr01-02/english/sec/library/0102in08e.pdf (last visited Feb. 3, 2018).

ownership is such a desirable social objective in its own right that the scheme needed broadening.[8]

At present, HOS has already become a regular part of the Hong Kong government's housing policy, achieving its dual purpose, namely:

(a) to encourage better off public rental housing (PRH) tenants to upgrade to home ownership so that public rental flats released by them could be allocated to other families in need of assisted housing; and
(b) to provide an avenue to home ownership for middle income households who were not eligible for public rental housing, and are unable to buy private sector housing.[9]

In 2016, subsidized sale flats[10] made up 14.8% of Hong Kong's total stock of residential flats.[11] The Long Term Housing Strategy Steering Committee[12] has praised HOS as a core component of the government's long term housing strategy, being "an essential element of the housing ladder which helps promote social mobility."[13] Accordingly, HOS has strict conditions of eligibility, and allotment is only open to applicants meeting those criteria.

A. Conditions of eligibility

There are two forms of application under HOS, namely "Green Form" application and "White Form" application. Green Form applications aim at current PRH

8 *The Legislative Council Debates Official Report*, from The Session of the Legislative Council of Hong Kong in the Twenty-fifth Year of the Reign of Her Majesty Queen Elizabeth II, at 12 (Oct. 6, 1976), www.legco.gov.hk/yr76-77/english/lc_sitg/hansard/h761006.pdf.
9 *Housing Authority 1996 Report on the Review of the Home Ownership Schemes*, at 3 § 2.2(a)-(b) www.cityu.edu.hk/hkhousing/pdoc/HOS96.pdf (last visited Feb. 3, 2018).
10 "Subsidized sale flat" is a term used by the HKHA in its statistics report, encompassing flats under HOS, the Private Sector Participation Scheme and other housing schemes administered by the HKHA and the Housing Society (a non-governmental organization that serves the housing needs of the Hong Kong community). Flats that can be traded in the open market (including flats in which premium had been paid, for they have been classified as private housing units) are excluded.
11 By the end of March 2016, there were 399,000 subsidized sale flats out of a total 2,707,000. *See* the Table "Stock of flats by type of permanent housing" in *Housing in Figures 2016*, H.K. Hous. Auth., www.housingauthority.gov.hk/en/about-us/publications-and-statistics/index.html (last visited Mar. 5, 2018), at 3.
12 The Long Term Housing Strategy Steering Committee is a committee under the Transport and Housing Bureau that serves to review and formulate long-term housing strategies for Hong Kong. It is led by the Secretary of Transport and Housing and is made up of members and ex-members of the HKHA, the Housing Society, academics and professionals.
13 *Long Term Housing Strategy 2014; Chapter 5 – Subsidised Home Ownership*, H. K. Transport & Hous. Bureau, www.thb.gov.hk/eng/policy/housing/policy/lths/LTHS201412.pdf (last visited Feb.3, 2018), at 27.

tenants whose family members have not received any form of housing subsidies.[14] Green Form applicants are required to "return their PRH units in vacant possession"[15] in exchange for a flat under HOS. On the other hand, White Form applicants and their family members as listed on the application form are subject to income and asset tests.[16] Other than satisfying the tests, they should not have ownership in any other properties and should not be receiving any housing subsidies.[17]

Both Green Form and White Form applicants are required to provide in the application forms the names of their family members who would be residing with them. Under Green Form application, such family members should be those who would move out of the PRH unit with the applicant; under White Form application, the financial positions of those family members would be considered for the income and asset tests. All HOS flats should be used only for residential purposes and for occupation by the purchaser and his/her family members as listed in the application form. Only the owner's spouse and child/children under the age of 18 may be added to the household register of the HOS flat subsequently.[18] Staff members of the Housing Department[19] are empowered under Section 22 of the Housing Ordinance to require owners or occupiers of HOS flats to provide particulars about the use and occupation of the flat, with rights of entry and inspection.

Given that current PRH tenants are the primary targets of HOS, it is puzzling that the term "authorized occupant," which is commonly used in the context of PRH, is omitted in the Green and White Forms. "Authorized occupants" are persons listed on the PRH tenancy agreement; they are the only persons authorized by the HKHA to reside in the PRH unit allocated. Should there be any change in the number of tenants living in a PRH unit, the HKHA must be notified.[20] In particular, there are stringent criteria regarding the categories of

14 *See Hong Kong Housing Authority "Sale of Home Ownership Scheme Flats 2016" and Hong Kong Housing Society "Subsidised Sale Flats Project" – Application Guide for Green Form Applicants*, H. K. Hous. Auth., http://hos.housingauthority.gov.hk/mini-site/hos2016/common/pdf/application-form/hos_2016_app_guide_green_e.pdf (last visited Feb. 3, 2018), at para. 1.

15 *Id.* at para. 3(a)–(b).

16 *See Hong Kong Housing Authority "Sale of Home Ownership Scheme Flats 2016" and Hong Kong Housing Society "Subsidised Sale Flats Project" – Application Guide for White Form Applicants*, H. K. Hous. Auth., http://hos.housingauthority.gov.hk/mini-site/hos2016/common/pdf/application-form/hos_2016_app_guide_white_e.pdf (last visited Feb. 3, 2018), at para. 2.5.

17 *Id.* at paras. 2.6–2.7 and 4.1.

18 *See supra* note 14 at, para. 18.4; *and see supra* note 16 at para. 18.4.

19 The Housing Department is the executive arm of the HKHA.

20 Through an application form "Amendment of Public Rental Housing (PRH) Application Information (Application for Addition of Family Member)," www.housingauthority.gov.hk/en/common/pdf/global-elements/forms/flat-application/HD10-1.pdf (last visited Feb. 3, 2018); or through an application form "Amendment of Public Rental Housing (PRH) Application Information for Deletion of Family Member)," www.housingauthority.gov.hk/en/common/pdf/global-elements/forms/flat-application/HD10-2.pdf (last visited Feb. 3, 2018).

persons who can be added to the tenancy.[21] Biennial inspection would be carried out by the Housing Department to verify the occupancy position of PRH units.[22]

A former executive of the Housing Department expressed in a private interview that "authorized occupants" in the context of HOS would mean persons listed on the HOS application form, or those being subsequently added as members of the owner's family. Strangely, such an important label is not even used in the HOS application process. In the absence of express stipulation or mechanism for verification, the requirement of occupation by authorized persons is only in name. It was recalled that at the early stage of HOS, the HKHA did make an effort to carry out biennial checks for HOS flats, and later, even required biennial declaration from owners that the occupants were the same as those who were present at the time of purchase. Nonetheless, it was soon proved to be meaningless as HOS flats were self-owned properties and the HKHA did not enjoy any power of entry or enforcement as in the case of PRH units.

B. Restrictions on change of ownership

Generally speaking, change of ownership of HOS flats is restricted except for a sale to existing PRH residents, disposal in the HOS Secondary Market,[23] or disposal in the open market upon payment of a premium. The HKHA may, however, based on the merits of each case, exercise its discretion by giving its consent to an HOS owner's request for change of ownership under special circumstances.[24] These special circumstances include:

(A) Inclusion of spouse as joint owner;
(B) Transfer to spouse owing to divorce or separation;
(C) Transfer to other family member(s) owing to marriage and moving out … to join his/her spouse;
(D) Transfer to other family member(s) owing to owner's emigration or long-term working abroad;

21 *See Application Form for Addition of Household Member(s)*, H.K. Hous. Auth. www.housingauthority.gov.hk/en/common/pdf/global-elements/forms/public-housing/HD962.pdf?formref=HOU-F002 (last visited Feb. 3, 2018).

22 *See Changes of Household Particulars*, H.K. Hous. Auth., www.housingauthority.gov.hk/en/public-housing/tenancy-matters/changes-of-household-particulars/index.html (last visited Feb. 3, 2018).

23 The HOS Secondary Market is operated by the HKHA under the Housing Ordinance, Schedule, para. 4(c). It allows eligible persons to purchase HOS flats without requiring the owner to pay a premium. *See supra* note 2.

24 *See Information for Applicants on Application for Transfer of Ownership*, H.K. Hous. Auth. (revised in April 2017), www.housingauthority.gov.hk/en/common/pdf/global-elements/forms/home-ownership/HD7.pdf (last visited Feb. 3, 2018), at para. 1.

(E) Owner or spouse or authorized occupant eligible for civil service housing benefits or housing package provided by the employer;
(F) Change of ownership reflecting financial contribution towards down payment/mortgage repayment by authorized occupant;
(G) Transfer of ownership owing to death of owner;
(H) Old age of owner (i.e. 65 years old or above);
(I) Owner suffering from terminal disease e.g. cancer;
(J) Bankruptcy of owner; or
(K) Reasons other than (A) – (J) will be considered only in exceptional circumstances.[25]

Besides falling within any of the grounds listed above, for a transfer to be valid, the change of ownership must be by Deed of Assignment at nil monetary consideration (except in bankruptcy cases). With the exception of deceased causes, the proposed assignee must be an authorized occupant of that property.[26]

There are also provisions under the Housing Ordinance that serve to prevent HOS owners from making short-term profit or investment returns through disposing of or leasing HOS flats. Anyone purporting to transfer ownership of HOS flats is subject to statutory restrictions under paragraph 1 of the Schedule to the Housing Ordinance:

> Subject to paragraph 4 of this Schedule, the purchaser shall not at any time alienate, convey, charge or part with possession or purport to alienate, convey, charge or part with possession or enter into any agreement to alienate, convey, charge or part with possession of the land sold other than to the Authority, or such person as the Authority may nominate, unless
>
> (a) either
>
> (i) a period of 5 years has elapsed from the date of first assignment of the land – (A) from the Authority to any purchaser; or (B) to any purchaser nominated by the Authority, whichever is earlier; or . . .[27]; and
>
> (b) the purchaser has first paid to the Authority . . . [a] premium . . . .[28]

25 *Id.* at para. 2.
26 This additional requirement is called "Pre-requisite for the Application" in Transfer of Ownership, H.K. Hous. Auth., www.housingauthority.gov.hk/linear/en/home-ownership/information-for-home-owners/ownership-matters/transfer-of-ownership/index.html (last visited Feb. 3, 2018).
27 (ii) before that period has lapsed, the purchaser has offered to assign the land to the Authority and the Authority or its nominee (other than a prescribed nominee) has declined to accept the assignment. *See supra* note 2 at Schedule, para. (1)(a).
28 *See id.* at para. A(1)(b). The premium is calculated under a formula stipulated in para. 1(b).

There are serious consequences to non-compliance. Under Section 17B of the Housing Ordinance, any non-compliant mortgage, charge, assignment or other alienation, or any agreement to do so, shall be void. Anyone who purports to enter into such a transaction commits an offence under Section 27A and is liable to a fine of HK$500,000 and to one-year imprisonment.

The legislative intent behind the stringent requirements is to ensure that only qualified persons (i.e. those who meet the conditions of eligibility) benefit from HOS; this social objective has been reiterated by Lord Hoffmann NPJ, one of the CFA judges in *Cheuk Shu Yin v. Yip So Wan*:

> As the primary purpose of the scheme was to provide qualified purchasers with a permanent home, the HOS contained restrictions on alienation or parting with possession, intended to prevent the purchasers from realizing an immediate profit by the sale of the flat or an income from letting it to someone else. The objective was both to prevent the purchasers from making a cash profit from having received a discount at the public expense and to ensure that the effect of a sale on the public housing stock was more or less neutral, that is to say, that those who had been sold a flat would not again be candidates for social housing, at least until a substantial period of time had elapsed.[29]

Bokhary PJ (as he then was) made similar observations in the same judgment:

> [HOS] was introduced in 1978 to serve the social purpose of assisting eligible persons to acquire a home when they cannot otherwise afford to do so. An applicant is required to disclose in his or her application the persons with whom he or she would occupy the flat and the total income and assets of the applicant and these occupants which must not exceed a certain limit. The disclosure on the identity of the occupants together with the restrictions imposed under the Schedule and sections 17B and 27A are aimed at ensuring that after acquisition, the flat will actually be occupied as a home for the applicant and his or her family members (although change of the composition of this "household" after acquisition is clearly permitted). The disclosure on this household's combined income and assets at the time of acquisition is to ensure that the applicant, together with whatever financial support he or she may get from family members (if necessary), is eligible for such home purchase. (In the case of a Green Form applicant, while there is no eligibility requirement, upon a successful application, he or she has to give up the public housing unit he or she is occupying and to stay in the HOS flat and the same statutory restrictions on alienation apply.)[30]

29 Cheuk Shu Yin v. Yip So Wan & Lo King Fai, *supra* note 5 at para. 18.
30 *Id.* at para. 4.

II. Legal principles on beneficial property interest

Following the celebrated cases of *Stack v. Dowden*[31] and *Jones v. Kernott*,[32] which have been affirmed by Hong Kong courts in cases such as *Chan Chui Mee v. Mak Chi Choi*[33] and *Liu Wai Keung v. Liu Wai Man*,[34] there has been an ongoing debate about whether the trust under which a person can acquire beneficial interest in land by virtue of his or her contribution to the purchase should be a resulting trust or a common intention constructive trust.[35] When a real or personal property is conveyed to a purchaser jointly with others, or to one or more persons other than the purchaser, a resulting trust will be presumed in favor of the person who is proved to have paid the purchase money in the character of purchaser (as opposed to that of donor or lender).[36] A common intention constructive trust, on the other hand, is to prevent inequitable conduct. When there is a common intention that B is to have a beneficial interest in the property assigned to A, and B has relied on that intention to his or her detriment, then it is inequitable for A to claim sole beneficial ownership.[37] A common intention constructive trust will be imposed so that A will hold the legal title on trust for B.

While the U.K. Law Commission critically evaluated both doctrines in its 2002 Discussion Paper,[38] and considered alternatives from other jurisdictions,[39] the majority of the House of Lords and the U.K. Supreme Court have a clear preference for common intention constructive trust in what they call the "domestic" context.[40] In the most recent Hong Kong Court of Appeal decision *Primecredit Limited v. Yeung Chun Pang Barry*,[41] Lam VP also opined that "at least in a domestic context, if it is possible to resolve the matter by reference to common

31 [2007] 2 AC 432 (HL).
32 [2012] 1 AC 776 (UKSC).
33 [2009] 1 H.K.L.R.D. 343.
34 [2013] 5 H.K.L.R.D. 9.
35 *See, e.g.* Martin Dixon, *The Never-Ending Story – Co-Ownership after Stack v Dowden*, CONV. & PROP. LAW. 456 (2007); Simon Gardner, *Family Property Today*, 124 L.Q.R. 422 (2008); Simon Gardner & Katherine M. Davidson, *The Future of Stack v Dowden*, 127 L.Q.R. 13 (2011); Martin Dixon, "*The Still Not Ended, Never-Ending Story*, CONV. & PROP. LAW. 83 (2012); Simon Gardner, *Heresy – or not? – in Family Property*, CONV. & PROP. LAW. 332 (2015); *and* Simon Gardner, *The Ongoing Evolution of Family Property Constructive Trusts* 132 L.Q.R. 373 (2016).
36 *See* ARTHUR UNDERHILL ET AL., LAW OF TRUSTS AND TRUSTEES 317 (15th ed. 1995), cited in Lam So Yuk Hang Minnie and Others v. Superyield Holdings Ltd. and Others [2000] H.C.M. P. 6440/1998 (C.F.I.). *See also* S.H. GOO & ALICE LEE, LAND LAW IN HONG KONG (4th ed. 2015), at para. 4.42.
37 *See* Grant v. Edwards [1986] Ch 638. *See* S.H. GOO & ALICE LEE, LAND LAW IN HONG Kong (4th ed. 2015, LexisNexis), at para. 4.87.
38 Law Commission Discussion Paper 278 Sharing Homes (Nov. 2002), www.lawcom.gov.uk/app/uploads/2015/04/lc278.pdf.
39 Such alternatives from other jurisdictions include Australian "unconscionability," Canadian "unjust enrichment" and New Zealand's "reasonable expectation." *Id.* at part IV.
40 *See* Stack v. Dowden [2007] 2 AC 432 (HL); *and* Jones v. Kernott [2012] 1 AC 776 (UKSC).
41 [2017] 4 H.K.L.R.D. 327.

intention, there is no need to report to resulting trust."[42] Kwan JA, on the other hand, decided the case on the basis of a resulting trust while Cheung JA held that the same outcome could be achieved by resulting and constructive trusts.[43] Given the modern view that a common intention may be inferred from conduct other than direct financial contribution,[44] there is much to be said for Cheung JA's insightful approach.

While the "domestic" context was singled out in the aforesaid cases, none of them touched upon ownership issues of subsidized housing. All the landmark property ownership cases, whether in the U.K. or Hong Kong or other common law jurisdictions, are concerned with private properties. When it comes to cases where HOS flats are at stake, taking into account the stringent eligibility conditions and resale restrictions, should courts apply the legal principles in a different manner? As will be seen in cases discussed below, Hong Kong courts have embarked on varied approaches when faced with disputes over ownership of HOS flats.

III. Judicial decisions involving home ownership scheme properties

The appeals from *Cheuk Shu Yin v. Yip So Wan & Lo King Fai*[45] and *Ling Wing Fai Billy v. Ling Shui Fai*[46] were heard together by the CFA as they both concerned family disputes over HOS properties. They centered on the issue of whether the creation of beneficial interests under a resulting trust or constructive trust amounts to an "alienation" prohibited by the Housing Ordinance, hence rendering it void under Section 17B.

A. Factual background for the Ling and Cheuk cases

In *Ling Wing Fai Billy v. Ling Shui Fai*,[47] Ling Wing Fai Billy (P1) and Ling Shui Fai (D1) were brothers. P1 and his wife (P2) sought a declaration that they

42 *Id.* at para. 1.3.
43 *Id.* at para. 2.9.
44 In Lloyds Bank v. Rosset [1991] 1 AC 107, Lord Bridge, in explaining the basis of an inferred common intention, said that "it is at least extremely doubtful whether anything less [than direct financial contribution] will do." In a subsequent Hong Kong case, Ip Man Shan Henry v. Ching Hing Construction Co. Ltd. [2003] 1 H.K.C. 256, Lam J. (as he then was) did not regard Lord Bridge's statement as precluding the inference of common intention from conduct other than direct financial contribution. In the U.K., Lord Walker and Lady Hale also revisited Lord Bridge's judgment and said in Stack v. Dowden [2007] 2 AC 432 that "the law has moved on."
45 F.A.C.V. 9/2011 (C.F.A.).
46 F.A.C.V. 11/2011 (C.F.A.).
47 [2007] H.C.A. 6853/1999; (C.F.I.) [2010] 5 H.K.L.R.D. 247 (C.F.A.). There was actually a third defendant, Tam Kwok Chiu, who had signed a provisional sales and purchase agreement with respect to the HOS flat in question with D1 and D2 in January 1997 for a consideration

were the beneficial owners of the HOS flat in question, and that D1 and his wife (D2) were holding the flat on trust for them. The flat was purchased in 1983 with D1 and D2 as registered joint owners. The down payment and initial expenses were provided by the mother of the brothers (P1 and D1), Madam Siu, who had passed away by the time of the court hearing and was represented by P1, who was then her estate's administrator. A mortgage of HK$200,000 was made in the names of D1 and D2.

The dispute arose in 1997 when the defendants purported to sell the flat. The plaintiffs commenced the action in April 1999, claiming that when Madam Siu intended to apply for a HOS flat in 1983, a family arrangement was made, *inter alia*, in that:

(a) to increase the chance of success in the draw, two applications would be lodged, one in the name of Madam Siu, and the other in the names of D1 and D2;
(b) down payment and initial expenses would be borne by Madam Siu;
(c) the purchase price would be financed by a mortgage over the flat;
(d) members of the family who were to occupy the HOS flat would repay the mortgage and be responsible for household expenses; and
(e) family members would have a pro-rata beneficial interest according to their monetary contributions.

It is the plaintiff's case that they occupied the flat after D1 and D2 left it in March 1985. The plaintiffs also alleged that they took up the rest of the mortgage repayment after Madam Siu had paid for the first five to six installments, and that they have incurred expenses totaling about HK$90,000 for decorating the flat. The plaintiffs therefore claimed that they should therefore be entitled to a proportionate beneficial interest in the property. The defendants, on the other hand, denied the existence of any family arrangement. They admitted that Madam Siu had paid for the deposit and the expenses for the purchase of the property and that the plaintiffs repaid the mortgage since they moved into the property; that said, they claimed that Madam Siu's contribution to the purchase was her gift to them. D1 further claimed that he was the one paying for the mortgage from February 1984 until he and his wife moved out in March 1985. In the alternative, the defendants argued that even if the alleged family arrangement did exist, it should be rendered void under Section 17B of the Housing Ordinance.

of around HK$1.2 million. The provisional sale and purchase agreement was registered but both parties have not taken any step to further perform or complete the agreement. The plaintiffs brought a claim against the third defendant, seeking a declaration that the provisional sale and purchase agreement was void, the third defendant also brought counterclaims against the plaintiffs. As such claims were only dealt with in the CFI and were not put forward to the CA and the CFA, they would not be discussed here.

In *Cheuk Shu Yin v. Yip So Wan & Lo King Fai*,[48] Yip So Wan (D1) was the wife of Lo King Fai (D2). Their son Lo Yeuk Wai, then deceased, married Cheuk Shu Yin (the plaintiff) in 1994, but later divorced. The plaintiff initiated the proceedings in relation to a HOS flat that had been her residence since it was purchased by D1 and D2 in 2000. She sought a declaration that the defendants held the property on trust for her and an order that the defendants transfer the legal title to her. The defendants counterclaimed for vacant possession and sought a declaration that they were both the legal and beneficial owners of the property.

The HOS flat at stake was purchased in April 2000 by the defendants as legal joint tenants through Green Form application. Soon after the application was successful, the defendants returned their PRH unit to the HKHA. The purchase price was fully paid by the plaintiff and Wai with no mortgage financing. The plaintiff and Wai moved into the flat immediately after the purchase in 2000; the defendants primarily lived in Shenzhen in the Mainland. The plaintiff continued to live in the flat after her divorce with Wai in 2006 and Wai passed away in 2010. While there were different allegations concerning the defendants' periodical stays in the HOS flat, both parties agreed that the plaintiff and Wai had been staying in the flat for a continuous period.

The parties also had different recollections of events with respect to the funding of the purchase. The plaintiff claimed that prior to the completion of the sale and purchase, she had a discussion with Wai regarding the interests of the property, and that Wai had agreed to ask the defendants to sign a declaration of trust. The plaintiff also claimed that she and the defendants subsequently went to a law firm under Wai's arrangement to sign the declaration. She was able to produce as evidence a copy of an unsigned declaration purportedly prepared by a law firm on its letterhead. Although the defendants acknowledged that the plaintiff had brought them to a law firm, they claimed that they had no idea why they were brought there at that time. The defendants also denied that they had wanted to give the property to the plaintiff and Wai. The court after considering these different versions of the facts accepted that the plaintiff and Wai had contributed to the purchase of the property, and ruled that the defendants held the property on trust for the plaintiff and Wai.

However, it is worth noting that Wai had in fact bought another HOS flat back in 1992, and that the plaintiff and Wai had stayed there until 2000 when they moved into the HOS flat in question. Ownership of a HOS flat would have rendered the plaintiff and Wai ineligible for another application under HOS, or as a family member of the applicants (the defendants) whether under Green Form or White Form at that time. This issue had been raised at the Court of First Instance (CFI) and Court of Appeal (CA) but was not taken up by the CFA. The courts could have also enquired and explored more deeply whether the plaintiff

48 H.C.A. 2700/2006 (C.F.I.); [2011] 4 H.K.L.R.D. 514 (C.A.).

and Wai might not have passed the means test under HOS given the fact that they managed to pay the purchase price of HK$1,214,000 in one go without the aid of a mortgage.

B. The Court of First Instance (CFI) decisions

The CFI in both cases ruled that the plaintiffs have acquired beneficial interests in the HOS flats in question under resulting or constructive trusts. In coming to a decision in favor of the plaintiffs, the CFI discussed whether the creation of beneficial interests constituted an "alienation" under paragraph 1 of the Schedule and Section 17B of the Housing Ordinance.

The trial judge, Caryle Chu J, in *Ling Wing Fai Billy and Ors. v. Ling Shui Fai and Ors.*[49] held that "what is prohibited is alienation by the purchaser," meaning the HOS flat owner. Since the plaintiffs acquired beneficial interests by operation of law, not by any positive act or alienation by the defendants, no unlawful alienation had taken place:

> It is clear from the wordings of the previous Section 17B and the current Section 17B(1) and the successive versions of paragraph 1 of the Schedule to the Ordinance that what is prohibited is alienation by the purchaser. On the facts of this case, it is not a case of the 1st and 2nd defendants purporting to alienate or alienating the beneficial interest in the Property.
>
> Plainly, the statutory restriction against alienation was to prevent abuses of the HOS, which is to enable certain sectors of the community to acquire residences at reasonably affordable prices, by ensuring that only those eligible could benefit from the scheme. It would not have been the legislative intent to nullify genuine family arrangements between husband and wife and among family members.[50]

While referring specifically to the HOS objective of benefiting eligible persons, it was surprising that Chu J did not go on to explore whether the plaintiffs would have met the eligibility conditions under HOS.

Barnabas Fung J in *Cheuk Shu Yin v Yip So Wan & Lo King Fai*[51] noted from the evidence a possible violation of the HKHA's HOS policies. The learned judge adjourned the determination of the plaintiff's application and required her to write to the HKHA. In a subsequent judgment,[52] with reference to the HKHA's reply, Fung J made the declaration that the plaintiff was the sole owner of the HOS flat in question and that the defendants were holding the property as

49 [2007] H.K.C.U. 2029 (C.F.I.), at para. 42.
50 *Id.* at paras. 42–43.
51 [2009] H.C.A. 2700/2006 (June 25, 2009) (translated in English).
52 [2009] H.C.A. 2700/2006 (October 22, 2009) (translated in English).

trustees. He held that purchasing a HOS flat through Green Form application with a third party being the flat's beneficial owner does not contravene any public policy.[53]

C. *The Court of Appeal (CA) decisions*

The CFI decisions in both cases were overturned by the CA, with the same judges (Tang Ag CJHC, Yeung JA and Kwan JA) sitting on the bench. In the CA judgments, there were substantial discussions on the definition of "alienation" under the Housing Ordinance.

For the case of *Ling Wing Fai Billy and Ors. v. Ling Shui Fai and Ors.*,[54] Tang Ag CJHC ruled that the CFI had overlooked the positive acts done by the defendants, which included making the family arrangement with respect to application of the HOS flat (presuming that the arrangement was intended to be legally binding), using Madam Siu's money to pay the deposit, and permitting the plaintiffs to reside in the flat and make installment payments. He also emphasized that arrangements which have been made among family members should not be treated differently from those made among friends and strangers. Tang Ag CJHC cited[55] the following paragraph from Keith JA's judgment in *Re A Solicitor*[56] when discussing the meaning of the word "alienation":

> The fact that the word "alienation" is grouped together with the words "conveyance" and "parting with possession" is also an indication of what it was intended to cover. The sale of a Housing Authority flat would amount

53 *Id.* at para. 10 (citing the HKHA's reply (original in Chinese)):

> (a) Owners of the Fanling property [HOS flat in question] were originally PRH tenants, they met the conditions of eligibility to apply for a PRH flat at that time.
> (b) Owners of the Fanling property applied for a HOS flat through Green Form application, they were thus exempted from the income and means test and were not bound by the requirement that they cannot own any other property. However, as soon as they purchased a HOS flat, they shall return the PRH unit, which the owners of the Fanling property did.
> (c) HOS flats are sold below the market price to households, and transfer of ownership is subject to restriction. Generally speaking, unless a premium has been paid, ownership cannot be transferred freely.
> (d) If the ownership of the HOS flat is to be transferred to a family member in the household register, and that the transfer does not involve monetary consideration, the HKHA may exercise its discretion based on the merits of the case.
> (e) If the transferee is not a family member in the household register, even though s/he is a beneficial owner of the property, the HKHA will not allow an application for transfer of ownership without a premium being paid.

54 [2010] 5 H.K.L.R.D. 247 (C.A.).
55 *Id.* at para. 27.
56 [2008] C.A.C.V. 117/2000 (C.A.).

> to its conveyance. The grant of tenancy or an exclusive license in respect of such a flat would amount to parting with possession of the flat. The word "alienation" must have been included for a reason, and it must therefore have been intended to cover something other than the sale of the flat or the grant of a tenancy or exclusive license in respect of the flat. That "something" must have related to the creation and grant of rights over the flat, which did not involve either its sale or the grant of a tenancy or exclusive license in respect of it, but which impinged upon the most important features of ownership.[57]

Re A Solicitor was concerned with disciplinary proceedings against a solicitor in which it was necessary for the court to decide whether the creation of an unauthorized legal charge amounted to an alienation of the property within the meaning of Section 17B. Tang ACJHC considered the explanation of "alienation" in *Re A Solicitor* applicable and wide enough to cover the instant case since the defendants were involved in a family arrangement that gave rise to the creation and grant of rights over the flat in favor of the plaintiffs. Such creation of beneficial interests hence amounted to an alienation under paragraph 1 of the Schedule, rendering it void under Section 17B of the Housing Ordinance.

As for *Cheuk Shu Yin v. Yip So Wan & Lo King Fai*,[58] Yeung JA after examining the purpose of HOS and relevant case law on the meaning of "alienation" found the plaintiff's position no different from that of the plaintiffs in *Ling Wing Fai Billy v. Ling Shui Fai* and ruled that the family arrangements as alleged were void under the Housing Ordinance and hence unenforceable.

D. The Court of Final Appeal (CFA) decision

As both cases concerned the scope of restriction imposed on ownership of HOS flats under the Housing Ordinance, they were heard together in one hearing and dealt with in one judgment.[59] At the end of the day, the CFA unanimously concluded that the creation of beneficial interest under resulting or constructive trusts was not an alienation, but the approaches it adopted were slightly different. While Chan PJ (as he then was) decided to give effect to the meaning of "alienation" in the context of HOS, Lord Hoffmann NPJ, with whom the other judges concurred, focused on whether it was necessary to interpret "alienation" widely to give effect to the Housing Ordinance.

Chan PJ held that the family arrangements in the two cases were not the kind of mischief targeted by the Housing Ordinance for two reasons. First, the restrictions under HOS "are not intended to frustrate or outlaw genuine family arrangements of pooling the financial resources of family members together to acquire the HOS flat," but "are intended to prevent the owner from taking

57 *Id.* at para. 14.
58 [2011] 4 H.K.L.R.D. 514 (C.A.).
59 Cheuk Shu Yin v. Yip So Wan, [2012] 15 H.K.C.F.A.R. 344 (C.F.A.) (consolidated appeal).

advantage of [the] discount and making a quick profit by any unauthorized re-sale or transfer or parting with possession of the flat after acquisition."[60] This is because, in his Lordship's opinion, the pooling of family resources is a factual reality that is recognized by the HKHA, which permits the change of ownership to reflect the financial contributions of authorized occupants, and does not contravene the HKHA's policy or offend against the purpose of the Scheme. It is clearly different from any subsequent resale that is made without satisfying the prescribed requirements or the approval of the HKHA.[61] Second, in order to fall within the Schedule and Sections 17B and 27A, the alienation must be "a transfer or divesting *by the owner* of his or her rights and interests in the flat and this supports the argument that a positive act by the owner is required."[62] The type of alienation caught by the provisions "does not include the situation of a constructive or resulting trust as alleged in the present cases which usually arises by operation of law."[63]

It is undeniable that a constructive or resulting trust comes into existence by operation of law, but that is not the question Lord Hoffmann NPJ sought to address in his judgment.

> The reason why the creation of a beneficial interest does not come within Section 17B is not because the trust arises by operation of law rather than by an intentional act but because the creation of an equitable interest is not in my opinion an alienation of the land assigned to the purchaser. It is the creation of a new interest in that land.[64]

In other words, the alienation of a pre-existing interest is categorically different from the creation of a new interest. Only the former is caught by the statutory restrictions. While Chan PJ decided the case on the natural and ordinary meaning of the word "alienation,"[65] Lord Hoffmann NPJ did not think that the current appeal could or should be reduced to a linguistic point. In his Lordship's view, the CA was right to concentrate on the question whether it was necessary to give "alienation" a wide meaning in order to give effect to the policy of the Housing Ordinance.[66] His Lordship deduced the policy of including the alienation restriction in four key ways analyzed below.

First, with reference to the words used by the Secretary for Housing in moving the second reading of the 1978 Bill, "a 5-year restriction on resale is necessary, in order to discourage speculation on the part of the purchaser" and "to provide homes for people eligible for them."[67]

60 *Id.* at para. 6.
61 *Id.* at para. 5.
62 *Id.* at para. 8 (emphasis original).
63 *Id.* at para. 8.
64 *Id.* at para. 36.
65 *Id.* at para. 7.
66 *Id.* at para. 25.
67 *Id.* at paras. 26–27.

Second, in principle, it would be difficult to distinguish a case in which an outsider obtained the entire beneficial interest by paying the whole of the purchase price from a case which involved members of the family.[68]

Third, it is unlikely that the creation of equitable interests in HOS flats can give rise to abuses that Section 17B is intended to prevent. Unlike a typical beneficiary, who is entitled to terminate the trust and require the trustee to convey to him the legal estate, the holder of an equitable interest in a HOS flat cannot have the flat sold (because this would be unlawful under Section 17B) or require the property be let to provide him with an income (because the statutory terms and conditions in Schedule 4 to the Housing Ordinance contain a covenant against parting with possession).

> Until the expiration of the restriction period, all the equitable owner's normal means of realizing the value of his interest are barred. So there is nothing which he can do which would interfere with the occupation of the flat by the eligible purchasers to whom it was sold.[69]

Fourth, it is in the public interest that persons with incomes so low that they are not only eligible for a HOS flat but unable to pay the deposit or keep up the mortgage payments out of their own resources should be able to buy a flat with the assistance of their family or friends, on the basis that the latter will have beneficial interests which they can realize when the restriction period has expired.[70]

In his Lordship's view, the denial of a remedy to a person who paid all or part of the purchase price on the understanding that he would acquire a beneficial interest can be very unjust.[71]

IV. Unresolved questions of eligibility and equitability

While it is settled by the CFA for the time being that the creation of beneficial interests under trust principles does not amount to unlawful alienation under the Housing Ordinance, there remain questions that even judges cannot answer.

The first mystery concerns the interplay between HOS eligibility and equitable ownership. Judges at all levels have acknowledged that the objective of HOS is to provide permanent homes for eligible persons. It is only reasonable to go one step further and explore whether the plaintiffs in both cases would have satisfied the conditions of eligibility under HOS. As understood, under White Form applications, family members whose names are included in the application forms would be subject to income and asset tests. In *Ling Wai Fai Billy v. Ling Shui*

68 *Id.* at para. 29.
69 *Id.* at para. 30.
70 *Id.* at para. 33.
71 *Id.* at para. 35.

Fai, the plaintiffs alleged that the family had agreed to lodge two separate White Form applications, one by Madam Siu and the other by the defendants. When the defendants' application succeeded, the plaintiffs contributed to part of the purchase price. The CFA accordingly recognized that the plaintiffs had acquired beneficial interests in the flat under constructive trust, but no issue was raised as to whether the plaintiffs were eligible to apply for HOS through a White Form in the first place. If only one White Form application had been lodged, in the names of both the plaintiffs and the defendants, would they have met the conditions of eligibility under HOS? This point was actually touched upon by Litton NPJ in his passing remark that the family arrangements in question might have contained elements of deception:

> That is to say, deception of the Housing Authority in that lies might have been told in the application forms as regards the households intended to be benefited under the Home Ownership Scheme. This might then in turn have brought into play the principle that a resulting or a constructive trust cannot be enforced by a contributor if he or she had to rely on such an arrangement to succeed.[72]

There was, however, not a chance for his Lordship to go further on this since the matter came to the CFA on preliminary issues, upon the presumption that the bare facts pleaded in the statement of claim were true.[73] Similarly, in *Cheuk Shu Yin v. Yip So Wan & Lo King Fai*, despite the fact that Wai (the plaintiff's deceased ex-husband) owned a HOS flat back in 1992, the court did not look into the possibility that had the plaintiff, Wai and the defendants applied for a HOS flat as a family through a Green Form in 2000, they would likely have been found ineligible. The family by not including the plaintiffs in the HOS application form in return for better chances to obtain HOS flats might in fact have deceived the HKHA as to who would benefit from the HOS flat. The HKHA's reply as cited in the CFI judgment[74] actually did not address the eligibility of the plaintiffs. If the plaintiffs themselves were in fact not eligible to apply for HOS, but ended up acquiring beneficial interests in a HOS flat by virtue of the CFA decision, the objective of HOS would be undermined. As the eligibility issue has not been discussed in-depth in both cases, it is open to debate whether the CFA decision adheres to the objectives and restrictions of HOS, and whether it is fair to other HOS applicants.

Other than the eligibility issue, the CFA apparently was not aware of the potential practical difficulties faced by beneficial owners of HOS flats when they seek to realize their interests. Beneficial owners of private properties have the right to use, possess and enjoy the properties. They may even seek a declaration

72 Cheuk Shu Yin, *supra* note 59 at para. 11.
73 *Id.* at para. 12.
74 *See supra* note 53 at para. 10.

to terminate the trust arrangement and request the trustee to either revert the legal title to them or sell the property and hand in the sale proceeds. Yet, it is unclear from the CFA's judgment whether beneficial owners of HOS flats enjoy the same rights as those of private properties. In *Chuek Shu Yin v. Yip So Wan & Lo King Fai*,[75] while the CA dismissed the plaintiff's request for an order that she had the right to apply to the Housing Department upon the defendants' death for transferring the property to her without a premium, the CFA did not follow up on the issue. Land searches of the disputed properties in the two cases reveal that there is no change in their legal or beneficial ownership. There is no practical difference to the winning parties, who have no right to enforce their paper titles.

Subsequent to the CFA decision, in a recent CFI case *Lee Kin Wai v. Lee Kin Chuen*,[76] Deputy Judge Keith, while granting a declaration that the defendants held the HOS flat in question on trust for the plaintiff, the sole beneficial owner, declined to make a vesting order as requested by the plaintiff:

> However, I decline to make an order under Section 45 of the Trustee Ordinance (Cap 29) vesting the Flat in Kin Wai [the plaintiff]. I acknowledge that it might have been expedient to do that to make it less likely that Kin Wai's title to the Flat as its sole owner will be disputed when he comes to sell the Flat. But I do not know whether there are any restrictions in the Scheme relating to the transfer of the legal title of a flat acquired under the Scheme. In any event, it would not be right to make a vesting order until such time as it is known whether the Housing Authority will take any steps to unpick things on the basis that it was misled.[77]

To that effect, the plaintiffs in the cases discussed above, despite being beneficial owners of HOS flats, are unable to realize their rights unless the legal owners sell the flat. The question as to whether the HKHA should and would allow the transfer of legal title without payment of a premium on the strength of a court order has remained unresolved. Accordingly, the sense of justice that Lord Hoffmann wishes to serve,[78] to persons who have contributed to the purchase price on the understanding that they would acquire a beneficial interest to actually obtain and enjoy the interest they deserve, does not seem to have been fully upheld. That said, the eligibility issue remains: what if these persons who acquire beneficial interests in HOS flats are actually ineligible to apply for HOS, wouldn't the policy goal of HOS, to assist underprivileged families in obtaining permanent homes, be hindered?

In fact, shortly after the CFA judgment was handed down on November 13, 2012, a news reporter from the Hong Kong Economic Times interviewed a

75 *See supra* note 59.
76 *See supra* note 6.
77 *Id.* at para. 41.
78 *See supra* note 59 at para. 35.

member of the Long Term Housing Strategy Committee.[79] This member opined that if the HKHA agreed with the CFA's interpretation on statutory restrictions, the Housing Ordinance should be amended. To date the HKHA still has not taken any action.

One way to deal with persons who have already made such contributions is for the HKHA to clarify two matters: whether a person who is not eligible to apply for a HOS flat but contributes to its purchase price should be recognized as a beneficial owner of the flat; and whether payment of premium is necessary for requests of transfer of title to HOS flats pursuant to a court order. Further, to tackle the problem presented in recognizing beneficial interest for persons who contributed to the purchase of HOS flats at the expense of hindering the policy goals of HOS, the HKHA may introduce new policies to prevent or discourage any common intention to acquire beneficial interest on the basis of financial contributions in the future. For instance, the HKHA may make it a rule that HOS applicants should indicate in the application form, be it White Form or Green Form, the names of those who will reside with them in the HOS flat if they succeed in the application; tactics such as duplicate HOS applications by individual family members may be expressly forbidden. As a matter of clarification, the rule does not prohibit the pooling of financial resources among families and friends – instead it expressly nullifies any understanding formed by persons other than those being mentioned in the application forms that they would acquire ownership of HOS flats simply by contributing to the purchase price. In other words, these people, be they family members or friends of the HOS applicants or moneylenders, who contribute to the purchase price, would only be treated as having had the intention to enter transactions with the HOS applicant for something other than one that involves ownership of the HOS flat. Instances as such can be an intention to form private loan agreements with the HOS applicants, or present monetary gifts to the HOS applicants. In this way, Lord Hoffmann's concern about the injustice in denying these people of a remedy and criminalizing their contribution can be resolved, as there can no longer be a legally enforceable understanding that financial contribution to purchase will translate into beneficial interests.

Conclusion

While public sentiments for an increase in housing supply have been calmed down following the implementation of HOS, the housing scheme has imposed a new set of challenges for the development of property law and trusts law with respect to ownership of subsidized housing units in Hong Kong. The CFA no doubt reached the correct legal decision in *Cheuk Shu Yin v. Yip So Wan*.[80] It is

79 *Hong Kong Home Ownership Scheme Property Dispute: CFA Granted Ownership to Those Who Contributed* ("港居屋爭議案: 有份供款 終院判擁業權"), H. K. ECON. TIMES (Nov. 14, 2012), www.hkcna.hk/content/2012/1114/167414.shtml.

80 *See supra* note 59.

trite that monetary contribution can give rise to beneficial interests under a resulting or constructive trust, which arises by operation of law and is thus not an "alienation." The further question of the individual plaintiff's eligibility and/or the entire family's eligibility to apply for a HOS flat is just a natural follow-up. Given that the key objective of HOS is to assist PRH tenants or the lower middle income class in obtaining home ownership, if ineligible family members or friends of the HOS applicants or even moneylenders can get around restrictions of ownership under the scheme to become beneficial owners of HOS flats, this objective will be hindered. Nor did the CFA make it clear how beneficial owners of HOS flats may exercise their rights or realize their interests. Without any real means to actualize their remedies, it is hard to see how justice can be served to these people who, according to Lord Hoffmann, have paid all or some of the purchase price on the understanding that they would acquire a beneficial interest.

Although it remains unknown how common it is for Hong Kong families to employ tactics as in the two cases discussed to apply for HOS flats, or to pool their financial resources for the purchase of HOS flats in the face of spiraling property prices, it is not inconceivable that following this CFA decision, more disputes over the ownership of HOS flats would arise. Family members who are not eligible to apply for HOS flats but have financially supported the legal owners of HOS flats, and have been quiet all along, might argue that they have acquired beneficial interests especially when the legal owners pass away, or when priority issues come into place. They may also make applications to the HKHA requesting for transfer of ownership without the need to pay a premium. The uncertainties and problems identified in this chapter therefore call for action by the HKHA in reviewing its existing HOS policies, in particular, regarding the possibility that HOS be exploited in such a way that ineligible persons may acquire ownership of HOS flats through trust agreements with eligible persons, and considering whether transfer of legal title without payment of a premium on the strength of a court judgment should be permitted. It is hoped that with the HKHA's clarification and counter-actions, there is a way out of the dilemma between serving justice through recognizing beneficial interests created under resulting or constructive trusts and pursuing the policy goals of HOS in the near future.

4 Eviction as a tool for crime control

Fighting drug-related crime in the Netherlands and the United States

L. Michelle Bruijn and Michel Vols

Introduction

Over the last decade, the body of research literature on evictions has grown steadily.[1] The topic attracts scholarly attention in various continents and from scholars of various academic disciplines such as medical sciences, political science and urban planning.[2] Moreover, a significant part of the literature on eviction resolves around legal issues.[3] Recently, eviction research received an impulse through the innovative and Pulitzer Prize winning work of the North-American scholar Matthew Desmond. In his book *Evicted: Poverty and Profit in the American City* he describes that in the United States (US) eviction is often a cause of poverty instead of a consequence and a frequent source of economic hardship and (mental) health problems. His other research shows, inter alia, that especially women and mothers are at high risk of eviction.[4]

In this chapter, we assess the use of eviction as a legal tool for crime control in the US and the Netherlands. Over the last decades, literature on crime control

1 In this chapter, the term eviction refers to the permanent or temporary removal of individuals, families or communities from their homes against their will (UN Committee on Economic, Social and Cultural Rights, 1997).

2 *See, e.g.*, Geographies of Forced Eviction Brickell (Katherine Brickell et al. eds., 2017); Michel Vols & Julian Sidoli del Ceno, *Common Threads in Housing Law Research: A Systematic and Thematic Analysis of the Field, in* People and Buildings: Comparative Housing Law (2018).

3 *See* Andries Johannes van der Walt, Property in the Margins (2009); Padriac Kenn et al., Pilot Project – Promoting Protection of the Right to Housing – Homelessness Prevention in the Context of Evictions (2016); Sarah Fick & Michel Vols, *Best protection against eviction? A Comparative Analysis of Protection against Evictions in the European Convention on Human Rights and the South African Constitution*, 3 Eur. J. Comp. L. & Governance 40 (2016); Tenancy Law and Housing Policy in Europe: Towards Regulatory Equilibrium (Christoph Schmid ed., 2018).

4 *See* Matthew Desmond & Nichol Valdez, *Unpolicing the Urban Poor: Consequences of Third-Party Policing for Inner-City Women*, 78 Am. Soc. Rev. 117 (2013); Matthew Desmond & Rachel Tolbert Kimbro, *Eviction's Fallout: Housing, Hardship, and Health*, 94 Soc. Forces 295 (2015); Matthew Desmond, *Unaffordable America: Poverty, Housing, and Eviction*, 22 Fast Focus: Inst. Res. Poverty 1 (2015); Matthew Desmond, Evicted: Poverty and Profit in the American City (2016).

shows strong signs for an exponential growth in the use of eviction as a tool to fight crime. Due to a perceived enforcement deficit in criminal law, law and policy makers decided to decentralize crime control and involve a variety of actors other than criminal justice officials in the fight against crime.[5] This 'new crime control establishment' is known by a mixture of terms such as third-party policing, responsibilization and community-based law enforcement, and results in blurring lines between criminal law and other areas of law.[6] The aim of this chapter is to show that eviction is one of the most widespread and powerful instruments used at the disposal of local authorities and private parties such as property owners and landlords to control and prevent crime.

Although some researchers – including Desmond – have studied the role of eviction in crime control,[7] this research area is far less developed compared to other eviction research. Most literature on eviction and crime is relatively old, does not include comparative research or focuses on relatively minor offences such as neighbor nuisance and other incivilities. This chapter corrects this oversight by focusing on a type of crime often combatted by eviction – drug-related crime – and providing a comparative and detailed overview of the use of evictions. More specifically, we 1) analyze to what extent eviction is used to combat drug-related crime in the US and the Netherlands; 2) show the extent to which the law provides protection against drug-related evictions; and 3) provide an explanation for the use of eviction to fight drug-related crime.

Accordingly, the chapter presents new insights on the use of eviction as a tool to control drug crime on three different levels: an exploratory level, a legal level and a theoretical level. The exploratory level analyzes the landscape of drug evictions in the Netherlands and the US, including the key characteristics of the housing context, the relevant policy documents and the extent to which eviction is used to fight drug-related crime. The legal level conducts a doctrinal and comparative analysis of the relevant legal frameworks and legal safeguards that protect evictees in the Netherlands and the US. Finally, the theoretical level analyzes the collected

5 *See* Roger Matthews, Realist Criminology (2014).

6 *See* David Garland, The Culture of Control: Crime and Social Order in Contemporary Society 124 (2001); Lorraine Mazerolle & Janet Ransley, Third Party Policing (2006); Wim Huisman & Monique Koemans, Administrative Measures in Crime Control, 1 Erasmus L. Rev. 121 (2011); Ellen Devroe, A Swelling Culture of Control (2012); Desmond & Valdez, *supra* note 4; L. Michelle Bruijn et al., *Home Closure as a Weapon in the Dutch War on Drugs: Does Judicial Review Function as a Safety Net?*, 51 Int'l J. Drug Pol'y 137 (2018).

7 *See* Caroline Hunter et al., *Neighbours Behaving Badly: Anti-social Behaviour, Property Rights and Exclusion in England and Australia*, 5 Macquarie L. J. 149 (2005); Housing, Urban Governance and Anti-Social Behaviour: Perspectives, Policy and Practice (John Flint ed., 2006); John Flint & Hal Pawson, *Social Landlords and the Regulation of Conduct in Urban Spaces in the United Kingdom*, 9 Criminology & Crim. Just. 415 (2009); Desmond & Valdez, *supra* note 4; Lahny Silva, *Criminal Histories in Public Housing*, 5 Wis. L. Rev. 375 (2015); Michel Vols & Sarah Fick, *Using Eviction to Combat Housing-related Crime and Anti-social Behaviour in South Africa and the Netherlands*, 134 S. African Law Journal 327 (2017).

empirical and legal data through the lens of the third-party policing theory.[8] This meso-level or middle range theory functions as an explanatory framework to understand and explain certain aspects and legal issues with regard to the use of evictions in the fight against drug-related crime.[9] Besides using the theory to make sense of the collected data we contribute to theory building by discussing examples of third-party policing in the Netherlands and the US.

Throughout the chapter, we apply different research methods. First, we use doctrinal legal research methods to establish and analyze the relevant legal frameworks. This means that we read and analyze literature, legislation, case law and policy documents to establish the nature and parameters of the law and legal issues involved.[10] Second, we conduct a comparative legal analysis between the US and the Netherlands,[11] specifically focusing on the role of private landlords and the role of public authorities. The comparison is initially focused on the US as a whole, since drug evictions are for a great part organized by federal governments such as the U.S. Department of Housing and Urban Development. Yet, we focus on New York City (NYC) in particular when discussing drug evictions from other types of housing, specifically private (non-subsidized) housing.[12] Although drug evictions from private housing play an important role throughout all states, analyzing the existing legal frameworks in all states, counties and cities will inevitably result in a cursory overview, which has never been our intention. Focusing on one jurisdiction only enables us to provide a comprehensive analysis of how the law reads and works. The reason to focus on NYC is the Narcotics Eviction Program (NEP), which led the charge in employing 'one strike' evictions in both public and private housing by creative use of nuisance abatement laws.

This chapter is divided into four sections. The first focuses on drug-related crime and eviction in the Netherlands. The second section discusses drug-related crime and eviction in the US. The third section conducts the comparative analysis and discusses our findings on an exploratory, a legal and theoretical level. The chapter concludes with some final remarks.

8 Mazerolle & Ransley, *supra* note 6.

9 On the diffuse meaning of the term theory *see, e.g.*, JOHN W. CRESWELL, RESEARCH DESIGN: QUALITATIVE, QUANTITATIVE, AND MIXED METHODS APPROACHES (2nd ed. 2014); LEE EPSTEIN & ANDREW MARTIN, AN INTRODUCTION TO EMPIRICAL LEGAL RESEARCH (2014).

10 Terry Hutchinson & Nigel Duncan, *Defining and Describing What We Do: Doctrinal Legal Research*, 17 DEAKIN L. REV. 83 (2012).

11 Ralf Michaels, *The Functional Method in Comparative Law, in* THE OXFORD HANDBOOK OF COMPARATIVE LAW (Mathias Reimann & Reinhard Zimmerman eds., 2006); MATHIAS SIEMS, COMPARATIVE LAW (2014).

12 The US housing stock contains owner-occupied housing units and rental housing units. Within the rental housing unit federal assitance programs exist such as public housing, but also privately owned subsidized housing.

I. Drug evictions in the Netherlands

In this section we analyze how authorities in the Netherlands use eviction to combat drug-related crime in residential areas. We first describe the Dutch policy on drugs (A) and then assess how local authorities (B) and private landlords (C) use eviction to tackle drug-related crime.

To truly understand the Dutch approach, some key characteristics of the Dutch housing market bear discussion. In 2017, the housing stock in the Netherlands included 7,686,178 premises.[13] In the last few decades, it has been government policy to promote home-ownership and this policy has been successfully implemented. Whereas in 1986, the minority of the housing units were owner-occupied (43%), in 2017 the majority of all units are occupied by the owners (56.2%). Nearly all other housing units are rental premises. Housing associations (semi-public landlords) own nearly 70% of the rental housing units. This is 29.5% of the total housing stock. According to the Housing Act 2015, housing associations are non-profit landlords that are legally obliged to rent the majority of their premises to people with a relatively low annual income. Private landlords own 13% of the housing stock, which is roughly 30% of the rental housing units. Research shows that most of the private rental housing units are owned by private investors (77%), and the other premises are owned by institutional landlords such as insurance companies. The vast majority of private investors own less than ten premises.[14]

A. Drug policy and drug-related crime in the Netherlands

In the Netherlands, the use of illegal narcotics became a serious public order and health issue in the late 1960s. Around that time, a public debate started on the rapid increase of drug misuse, the criminal approach and the subsequent criminalization of large parts of the population.[15] As early as the 1970s, the Dutch started to create alternatives to the punitive prohibition approach. This caused in 1976 the distinction between cannabis (soft drugs) and drugs with unacceptable risks for public health (hard drugs), followed by the decision to officially tolerate the sale and possession of cannabis to prevent cannabis from becoming a gateway drug.[16] At the time, cannabis was the only 'soft drug' under Dutch law. Today, the Opium Act includes more than 250 different soft drugs.

13 *Voorraad woningen; eigendom, type verhuurder, bewoning, regio.* STATLINE CENTRAAL BUREAU VOOR STATISTIEK (Nov. 3, 2017), http://statline.cbs.nl/Statweb/publication/?VW=T&DM=SLNL&PA=82900NED&D1=a&D2=a&D3=0,6–18&D4=a&HD=180, 223–1114&HDR=T&STB=G1,G2,G3.

14 MARIEKE JONKER-VERKAART & FRANK WASSENBERG, KANSEN VOOR PARTICULIERE HUUR IN NEDERLAND 14 (2015).

15 Henk Jan van Vliet, *The Uneasy Decriminalization: A Perspective on Dutch Drug Policy*, 18 HOFSTRA L. REV. 717, 721 (1990).

16 *See* Van Vliet, *supra* note 15; MARGRIET VAN LAAR & MARIANNE VAN OOYEN-HOUBEN, EVALUATIE VAN HET NEDERLANDSE DRUGSBELEID (2009).

The Dutch drug policy is commonly known as the 'tolerance policy': cannabis sale and possession are tolerated as a matter of government policy, but are officially still criminal offences.[17] In the early days of the tolerance policy, few rules regulating the upcoming drug market existed and the number of tolerated cannabis outlets – better known as 'coffeeshops' – grew exponentially. In 1980, the first guidelines for small retail in cannabis came into force.[18] Over the years, the guidelines were adapted and formalized by the Public Prosecution Service. As long as coffeeshops comply with the following rules, coffeeshops avoid closure and the owners avoid criminal prosecution: coffeeshop owners may neither advertise; nor sell hard drugs; nor cause public disturbance; nor sell to minors nor allow them in; nor stock up more than 500 grams of cannabis; nor sell to anyone other than residents of the Netherlands nor allow them in.[19]

While a formal non-enforcement policy exists towards possessing five grams of cannabis and the sale from coffeeshops, coffeeshop owners may neither cultivate more than five plants nor purchase cannabis.[20] This situation is known as the 'backdoor problem': transactions at the backdoor have always remained unregulated and hence illegal.[21] Due to this gap in the tolerance policy, organized crime is controlling the supply-side of coffeeshops.[22] As long as five cannabis plants remains the maximum tolerated amount and the backdoor stays unregulated, growers and coffeeshop owners and employees are forced into the underworld to supply coffeeshops.

Growing cannabis for the purpose of coffeeshops is not only excluded from the tolerance policy, the government started a forceful fight against cannabis cultivation, especially in housing units. Previous research found that cannabis is predominantly cultivated indoors instead of out in the open air.[23] In 2007, it was found that 78–90% of the discovered growing facilities were found inside housing units, and the vast majority were rental units.[24] Similar results were presented in another study.[25]

The governmental fight against cannabis cultivation received a boost in 2003 and has been intensified ever since. In that year, an influential criminological study was published that called for a more forceful fight against cannabis growing.[26] Accordingly, the Dutch government published plans in 2004 (the *Cannabisbrief* 2004) with a 'comprehensive approach' as the key element. This means that all public and

17 Opium Act (1976), art. 3.
18 Richtlijnen voor Het Opsporings- en Strafvorderingsbeleid Inzake Strafbare Feiten van de Opiumwet 137, *Staatscourant* (1980).
19 Aanwijzing Opiumwet 5391, *Staatscourant* (2015).
20 Opium Act, art. 3.
21 Marianne Van Ooyen-Houben, *Hoe Werkt Het Nederlandse Drugsbeleid? Een Evaluatieve Verkenning van Een Decennium Drugsbeleid*, 32 JUSTITIËLE VERKENNINGEN 24 (2006).
22 Wim Huisman & Hans Nelen, *The Lost Art of Regulated Tolerance? Fifteen Years of Regulating Vices in Amsterdam*, 41 J. L. & SOC'Y 604 (2014).
23 MARIJE WOUTERS ET AL., HARDE AANPAK, HETE ZOMER 8 (2007).
24 A.C.M. SPAPENS ET AL., DE WERELD ACHTER WIETTEELT 111 (2007).
25 WOUTERS ET AL., *supra* note 23, at 102–103.
26 *See* FRANK BOVENKERK & W. HOGEWIND, HENNEPTEELT IN NEDERLAND. HET PROBLEEM VAN DE CRIMINALITEIT EN HAAR BESTRIJDING (2003). *See also* Spapens et al., *supra* note 24, at 23.

private stakeholders should be involved to address the problem of cannabis cultivation. Especially the housing associations were named as key stakeholders. The government encouraged local authorities[27] to make detailed agreements with these semi-public landlords and to document these in so-called cannabis covenants. In 2006, the government even created a Cannabis Covenant template. This template cited, for example, that a housing association should cancel the lease and evict the tenant if a growing facility is discovered in a rental premises.[28] As such, landlords became important players in the fight against drug-related crime.[29]

In 2009, five years after the *Cannabisbrief* was published, 205 municipalities had developed cannabis covenants.[30] Yet, research shows regional differences, especially among housing associations. In Eindhoven, for example, housing associations opposed the idea that housing providers should focus on 'catching criminals'.[31] At the same time, police officers from that area complained about the indifference of housing associations towards controlling drug-related crime.[32]

Several scholars declare the success of the comprehensive approach: eviction or the threat of eviction seems an effective measure to curb cannabis cultivation.[33] Spapens and others[34] use interviews and news articles to show the success of the comprehensive approach. They hold that homegrowers fear the risk to be removed from their social environment, their neighborhood, their community and 'extended families'. With the threat of eviction, the fear to use the own (rental) home as a growing facility increases.[35] Spapens and others refer to news articles in which people beg for a second chance after being evicted due to cannabis cultivation. Yet, the researchers acknowledge the lack of reliable data to truly measure the effectiveness of the 'comprehensive approach'.[36]

27 Throughout the chapter, the term 'local authority' will be used to describe the authority entitled with this power while it is officially the (in Dutch:) *burgemeester*. In the Netherlands, a *burgemeester* is a non-elected administrative authority appointed by the national government. The burgemeester chairs both the executive board and legislative council of a municipality, and is responsible for safety and public order. The title for burgemeester is sometimes translated as 'mayor' or as 'burgomaster' to emphasize the significant difference between the Dutch mayor and the British mayor. However, unfamiliarity of the Dutch concept burgemeester in international context and the – in our view – lack of proper translation induced us to use the term local authority.

28 *See* Spapens et al., *supra* note 24, at 23–25, 106–107; Marc Schuilenburg & Wytske van der Wagen, *Samenwerking in de Criminaliteitsbestrijding: Kwalitatief Onderzoek Naar de Integrale Aanpak van Illegale Hennepteelt*, 10 Tijdschrift voor Veiligheid, 10 (2011).

29 Spapens et al., *supra* note 24, at 25.

30 Van Laar & Van Ooyen-Houben, *supra* note 16; Schuilenburg & Van der Wagen, *supra* note 28, at 13.

31 Schuilenburg & Van der Wagen, *supra* note 28, at 15.

32 *Id.*

33 Wouters et al., *supra* note 23, at 114, 118.

34 Spapens et al., *supra* note 24, at 113.

35 *Id.*

36 *Id.* at 126, 138.

Although data are scarce, we were able to collect data on the number of discovered and dismantled growing facilities between 2003 and 2017. Between 1999 and 2003, about 1,000 and 2,000 growing facilities were dismantled each year.[37] This increased significantly after 2003, the starting point of the 'comprehensive approach', with about 5,000 to 6,000 dismantled growing facilities per year.[38] Although, the researchers acknowledge that the data in the early 2000s might be incomplete, the numbers clearly indicate a strengthened approach towards growing facilities over the years.

In 2007, two studies suggest that the increased fight against growing facilities in rental housing units triggered cannabis growers to use other premises such as owner-occupied homes, empty buildings or commercial buildings. One of the main reasons for the shift to owner-occupied housing units was the lack of a legal instrument to evict an owner-occupier.[39] This changed at the end of 2007 when the legislature decided to extend the scope of the already existing administrative closure power with homes and other non-public premises (Article 13b Opium Act).[40] Before the extension, local authorities were already entitled to close down public premises used for illegal drug trades, including coffeeshops if they fail to comply with the rules under which they are tolerated.[41] As of November 2007, local authorities are entitled to close down public premises, such as restaurants and companies, and non-public premises, including owner-occupied housing units, if illicit drugs are sold, delivered, provided, or present for one of these purposes at or near a property.[42] The latter use of the closure power evidently results in eviction.

The start of the comprehensive approach in 2003 and the extended scope of the administrative closure power in 2007 represent the mounting concentration on eviction to control drug-related crime in the Netherlands. Without bringing criminal law into play, drug activities can be fought by local authorities and private landlords who both have the instrument of eviction at their disposal. The following two sections concentrate on administrative drug evictions by local authorities and drug evictions by private landlords, respectively. Both sections present the available data on the number of drug evictions, examine the applicable legal frameworks and discuss key issues in case law.

B. *Administrative law evictions by local authorities*

Drug evictions by local authorities in the Netherlands are subject to administrative law. Unlike evictions initiated by landlords, drug evictions initiated by

37 Magriet Van Laar et al., Nationale Drugsmonitor Jaarbericht 171 (2004).

38 *Id.* at 354.

39 Spapens et al., *supra* note 24; Wouters et al., *supra* note 23.

40 Kamerstukken II. *Staatscourant*, 30,515(3) (2005/2006).

41 Richtlijnen voor het opsporings- en strafvorderingsbeleid inzake strafbare feiten van de Opiumwet 187, *Staatscourant* (1996); Aanwijzing Opiumwet, *Staatscourant* (2000).

42 Opium Act, art. 13b.

local authorities are not based on a breach of the lease but on a violation of the law. Local authorities are entitled to issue a closure order if drugs are sold, delivered, provided, or present for one of these purposes at or near a property.[43] Although the closure power goes beyond just eviction, closing a housing unit evidently results in eviction of the household. As such, closing a housing unit falls under our definition of eviction.[44]

Under Dutch law, the owner, owner-occupier, business owner or tenant may file a notice of objection with the local authority who issued the closure order (Article 7:1 General Administrative Law Act, hereafter: GALA). The local authority reviews the objection notice and reconsiders the order. If the local authority considers the objection unfounded, the party may appeal to the district court (i.e., the court of first instance).[45] The district court can dismiss the appeal or rule that the closure order is unlawful. In the latter case, the court will annul the order and instruct the local authority to issue a new order.[46] Rulings of district courts are open to higher appeal at the Administrative Jurisdiction Division of the Council of State (the Council of State).

To provide insights into the number of drug-related evictions conducted by local authorities, we surveyed fifty municipalities – the forty largest and ten other municipalities – in 2015 and 2016 about the total number of premises they closed because of drug activities.[47] In 2015, forty-six municipalities responded to the survey (92%). The respondents issued a total of 593 drug-related closure orders. In 2016, the number of drug-related closures significantly increased: the respondents closed 793 buildings involved in drug-related crime (88% response rate). In 2016, the news site *The Post Online* conducted a similar survey among all municipalities in the Netherlands (N=388). With a response rate of 68.8%, this study reveals that the respondents closed 988 buildings due to drug-related crime in 2016.[48] These findings show that local authorities use their closure power on a regular basis and that administrative closure and subsequent eviction most often occur in larger municipalities.

We analyzed case law to uncover the main legal issues in applying the drug-related closure power.[49] The first legal issue is proving that drugs are being sold,

43 *Id.*

44 *Id.*

45 General Administrative Law Act (1992), art. 8:1.

46 *Id.* at art. 8:51(a).

47 Michel Vols et al., De Aanpak van Malafide Pandeigenaren & de Handhaving van de Woningwet 55–58 (6th ed. 2017).

48 Tom Kiel, *Gemeenten Sloten in 2016 Met Wet Damocles Duizend Panden*, Post Online (Oct. 05, 2017), http://politiek.tpo.nl/2017/10/05/tpo-onderzoekt-gemeenten-sloten-2016-wet-damocles-duizend-panden/.

49 We used the online database of the Dutch judiciary, www.rechtspraak.nl, to gather relevant published Dutch case law, using the following search terms: 'Article 13b Opium Act', 'eviction' and 'drug-related closure'. Throughout this chapter, all Dutch case law is referred to using the European Case Law Identifier (ECLI). ECLI is an identifier for case law in Europe and consists of five components. The first part is the acronym 'ECLI', the second part is the country code, followed by the code of the court, year of the decision, and unique identifying number.

delivered, provided, or are present for one of these purposes at or near a property. Initially, the closure power was primarily introduced to close premises involved in illegal drug trade and to tackle coffeeshops that violate the tolerance conditions.[50] For a number of years, courts and local authorities were uncertain whether the mere presence of a large quantity of drugs in the property is sufficient evidence to prove drug dealing.[51] Eventually, the Council of State decided that possessing drugs for 'commercial purposes' is sufficient to prove that drugs are being sold at the premises.[52]

To determine whether someone possess drugs for 'commercial purposes', local authorities use the guidelines from the Public Prosecution Service. These guidelines presume that any amount up till 0.5 grams of hard drugs, five grams of soft drugs or five cannabis plants are for personal use.[53] Any amount that exceeds these limits is presumably used for sale. In other words, a quantity of drugs larger than the tolerated amount for personal use is conclusive evidence of sale and therefore sufficient ground for eviction. It is up to the tenant or owner-occupier to prove otherwise.

Similar to drug possession, case law reveals the scope of the closure power is extended to cannabis cultivation. While the parliamentary history of the Opium Act unambiguously shows that the closure power should not be used to close growing facilities,[54] courts find a 'large' quantity of cannabis plants (i. e., more than five plants) conclusive proof of drugs sale and hence justifies eviction.[55]

The second legal issue represents indistinctness about the possibility to immediately close a housing unit after someone committed a drug crime for the first time. With the introduction of the closure power, the legislature clarified that the closure power should be used as a last resort. Less intrusive measures, such as a warning or a penalty payment, should always precede eviction. Only 'extreme situations' could be exemptions to this rule (Kamerstukken, 2006/2007b; Kamerstukken, 2006/2007c).

Courts quickly characterized any activity involving hard drugs as such exemption, including possession.[56] In cases involving soft drugs, ambiguity exists about the quantity of discovered soft drugs that should indicate an 'extreme situation'. In one case, the court ruled that possessing 191 cannabis plants without any

50 Kamerstukken II, *Staatscourant*, 25,324(3) (1996/1997); Kamerstukken, *supra* note 40.

51 Rechtbank Noord-Nederland, Jun. 12, 2014 (Neth.) (ECLI:NL:RBNNE:2014:2850); Rechtbank Haarlem, Dec. 4, 2012 (Neth.) (ECLI:NL:RBHAA:2012:BY5942).

52 ABRvS, Jan. 21, 2015 (Neth.) (ECLI:NL:RVS:2015:130).

53 Aanwijzing, *supra* note 19.

54 Kamerstukken, 2005/2006 *supra* note 40; Kamerstukken II, *Staatscourant*, 30 515(6) (2006/2007); Kamerstukken II, *Staatscourant*, 30,515(14) (2006/2007a).

55 ECLI:NL:RVS:2015:130, *supra* note 52.

56 ABRvS, van Nov. 28, 2012 (ECLI:NL:RVS:2012:BY4412); ABRvS, Jul. 29, 2015 (ECLI:NL:RVS:2015:2388); ABRvS, May 4, 2016 (ECLI:NL:RVS:2016:1174); ABRvS, Jun. 15, 2016 (ECLI:NL:RVS:2016:1676); ABRvS, Mar. 10, 2017 (ECLI:NL:RVS:2017:634).

other indication of drug dealing did not justify the closure.[57] Yet, in another case, 467 grams of cannabis together with a large sum of money was sufficient to close the home.[58] Yet, in the latter case, the Council of State mentioned the geographical location of the municipality near the German border as an important factor for its decision. According to the Council of State, the closure power should be enforced more stringently in municipalities close to the international borders and/or with high coffeeshop density as these municipalities suffer from more drug-related crimes than others.[59] However, in another case, the Council of State approved the policy of the municipality of Groningen, which was neither coffeeshop dense nor located near the international border. Groningen has a written policy that defines drug possession for commercial purposes as an extreme situation. According to this policy, the quantity of discovered drugs is sufficient to prove commercial activities when the quantity exceeds 0.5 grams of hard drugs or 30 grams of soft drugs. The Council of State approved this policy, as long as the local authority reviews each case on its own and includes the circumstances of every case, and investigates whether a less intrusive measure is more appropriate.[60] In other words, the relevance of the rule that eviction is only justifiable in extreme situations has almost relaxed to the point of no importance.

The third legal issue deals with the review of circumstances. The power to close premises used for drug-related crime is a discretionary power. Under Dutch law, discretionary powers are subject to a limited judicial review that mainly focuses on the procedural standards.[61] In many cases, local authorities did not apply a contextual approach, but just referred to their policy rules to substantiate their decision to dismiss the objection of the residents.[62] According to local authorities, all possible circumstances surrounding a drug-related activity and all possible consequences of eviction are already considered while drafting the policy rules. As such, they held they are not required to apply a contextual approach to each case as long as their policy rules are in line with the law.[63] Prior quantitative research supports these findings and shows that legal defenses focusing on the disproportionate consequences of the closure for the residents are barely accepted in court.[64]

Yet, in 2016, the Council of State held – in contrast to its earlier interpretation – that all circumstances of a case should be taken into account, irrespective of whether the possible circumstances were considered while writing the policy

57 ABRvS, Jul. 30, 2014 (ECLI:NL:RVS:2014:2859).

58 ABRvS, Mar. 30, 2016 (ECLI:NL:RVS:2016:950).

59 ECLI:NL:RVS:2014:2859, *supra* note 61.

60 ABRvS, Feb. 8, 2017 (ECLI:NL:RVS:2017:294).

61 A.T. Marseille et al., Bestuursrecht deel 2: Rechtsbescherming tegen de overheid (2016).

62 L. Michelle Bruijn & Michel Vols, *Case note: ECLI:NL:RVS2016:2840: JG 2017/18, No. ECLI:NL:RVS:2016:2840, Oct 26, 2016*, Jurisprudentie voor Gemeenten 2 (2017).

63 *Id.*

64 Bruijn et al., *supra* note 6.

rules. According to the Council of State, local authorities cannot foresee whether certain circumstances will lead to disproportionate consequences in a particular case. As such, instead of focusing just on the procedural standards, the Council of State ruled that courts should also review whether local authorities sufficiently considered all circumstances of a case before they issued the closure order.[65]

An analysis of case law shows that since this Council of State ruling, local authorities indeed consider the circumstances of each case in more detail.[66] Nevertheless, case law shows no signs that courts annul the closure order more often because of the disproportionate consequences for the household. If a court decides to annul the closure procedural reasons are still most influential. In fact, courts still rule that certain consequences of a closure, such as a cancellation of the lease, are irrelevant for the lawfulness of the eviction or they acknowledge the effect of the eviction on children or future housing, but simply rule that the consequences are not disproportionate.[67]

C. *Landlord–tenant law evictions by landlords*

As discussed above, landlords are heavily involved in the fight against drugs related crime. Since the introduction of the comprehensive approach in 2003, eviction seems to be their main instrument to tackle drug crime. This section first assesses the applicable legal framework, then presents data on the number of drug-related evictions under landlord–tenant law, and lastly, discusses case law concerning such drug-related evictions.

Under Dutch law, the legal framework of landlord–tenant law evictions is relatively simple. The overwhelming majority of leases are open-ended contracts, even if parties concluded a temporary contract. If a landlord wants to terminate the lease unilaterally and evict the tenant, he or she should go to court.[68] The court uses a strict basic rule to assess the landlord's claim: every breach of the lease allows the court to terminate the lease and, consequently, issue an eviction

65 ABRvS Oct. 26, 2016 (ECLI:NL:RVS:2016:2840).

66 Brouwer & Bruijn, *supra* note 57.

67 *See, e.g.*, Rechtbank Zeeland-West-Brabant van Jan. 23, 2017 (ECLI:NL:RBZWB:2017:418); Rechtbank Amsterdam van, Apr. 3, 2017 (ECLI:NL:RBAMS:2017:2086); Rechtbank Limburg van, 29 maart 2017 (ECLI:NL:RBLIM:2017:2853); ABRvS, Apr. 19, 2017 (Neth.) (ECLI:NL:RVS:2017:978); ABRvS, May 22, 2017 (ECLI:NL:RVS:2017:1329); Rechtbank Midden-Nederland, Dec. 13, 2016 (ECLI:NL:RBMNE:2016:7439); ABRvS, Nov. 30, 2016 (Neth.) (ECLI:NL:RVS:2016:3167); Rechtbank Oost-Brabant, Nov. 14, 2016 (Neth.) (ECLI:NL:RBOBR:2016:6267); Rechtbank Rotterdam, Apr. 6, 2017 (Neth.) (ECLI:NL:RBROT:2017:3323).

68 Still, the relatively new Act on Movement in the Housing Market 2016 allows that private landlords' temporary contracts can be terminated unilaterally if the contract's period has expired. As a result, private landlords do not need to go to court to terminate the lease. Yet, this option is not available for housing associations, which rent out the vast majority of rental premises in the Netherlands. See arts. 7:231, 7:274 BW.

order.[69] Drug-related activities in a rental premises, such as selling drugs or using the property as a location to grow cannabis or create a drug lab, will usually be a breach of the lease.[70] Consequently, the court should first assess whether the landlord provided sufficient proof of the accused drug-related activity. If this evidence is persuasive, the court will usually conclude that the lease is breached, that the lease should be terminated and that the tenant should vacate the apartment.[71] This standard procedure is more complicated if a tenant puts forward a proportionality defense. According to the Dutch Civil Code, the court does not have to terminate the tenancy if the breach of the lease does not justify the termination given the nature or minor importance of the drug-related activity.[72] A court may also conclude that the termination and eviction have disproportional consequences for the tenant and other residents.

There are no exact data on the number of landlord–tenant law eviction proceedings.[73] For the private rental sector there are no data available at all, yet, for the social rental sector we found data on the number of eviction judgments. An eviction judgment is a court verdict that requires a tenant to vacate the building. In other words, we do know the number of court cases in which a housing association won the case. Figure 4.1 shows the number of eviction judgments over the last thirteen years.

Figure 4.1 shows that the total number of eviction judgments declined over the last years. In 2014 the courts delivered 23,500 eviction judgments, in 2015 there were 22,000 eviction judgments and in 2016 the number declined to 18,500.[74] Unfortunately, the data available on the eviction judgments do not reveal the reason for the proceeding. In other words, the number of cases that involved drug-related crime remains unknown.

Yet, the data do show how many eviction judgments are executed. When a judgment is executed, the tenant did not leave the home after the eviction period and a bailiff had to execute the court order. Figure 4.1 shows that over the last few years roughly 25% of all eviction judgments were executed. In 2016, 4,800 eviction judgments were executed. We know that over the last few years roughly 4–5% of the eviction judgments were related to drug crime (this was only 3.6% in

69 Art. 6:265 BW. Michel Vols, *Artikel 8 EVRM en de Gedwongen Ontruiming van de Huurwoning Vanwege Overlast*, 2 WR Tijdschrift Voor Huurrecht 55 (2015).

70 *See* Michel Vols et al., *Courts and Housing Related Anti-Social Behaviour. A First Statistical Analysis of Legal Protection Against Eviction*, Int'l J. L. Built Env't 148 (2015).

71 *See* Michel Vols et al., *Human Rights and Protection against Eviction in Anti-Social Behaviour Cases in the Netherlands and Germany*, 2 Eur. J. Comp. L. & Governance 156; Michel Vols & Marvin Kiehl, *Balancing Tenants' Rights While Addressing Neighbour Nuisance in Switzerland, Germany and the Netherlands*, 4 Eur. Prop. L. J. 1 (2015).

72 *See* Supreme Court Oct. 22, 1999, *Nederlandse Jurisprudentie* 1999, 179. Art. 6:265 BW.

73 Michel Vols, *Evictions in the Netherlands in* Evictions in Europe (P. Kenna ed., 2018).

74 *See* Corporatiemonitor, Aedes (July 1, 2016), www.aedes.nl/artikelen/aedes/vereniging/kennisproducten-aedes/corporatiemonitor/corporatiemonitor.html; Vols, *supra* note 77.

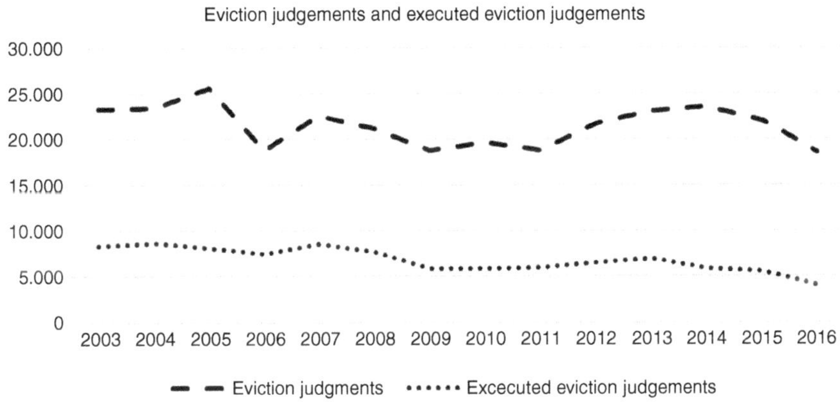

Figure 4.1 Eviction judgments and executed eviction judgments
Sources: Aedes, 2017; Vols, 2018.

2016). In approximately 270 cases in 2015 and 173 cases in 2016 the drug-related eviction judgments were executed by a bailiff.[75]

An analysis of recent published case law concerning drug-related evictions under landlord–tenant law reveals two main legal issues.[76] The first issue concerns the amount of drugs (usually cannabis) that will lead to a breach of the lease.

A quantitative analysis of eviction case law found that courts generally consider drug-related activities a convincing reason for the court to award the landlord's claim and issue an eviction order.[77] Vols and others show that courts issue eviction orders significantly more often in cases concerning drug-related activities than in cases concerning other types of anti-social behavior or crime, such as noise nuisance or violence. These findings confirm the growing importance of landlord–tenant law in the fight against drug-related crime in the Netherlands.

Still, an analysis of recent case law reveals disparity among courts regarding the amount of drugs that qualifies as a breach of the lease. On the one hand there are very strict courts. For example, the District Court Noord Nederland issued an eviction order after eight cannabis plants were found.[78] In another case, the District Court Rotterdam ordered a tenant to vacate the housing unit after growing five cannabis plants.[79] Other courts are less strict. The District Court Midden

75 *Id.*
76 H.J. TER MEULEN, HENNEPKWEEK WR TIJDSCHRIFT VOOR HUURRECHT 288 (2004); H.J. TER MEULEN, HENNEPKWEEK, DE STAND VAN ZAKEN. WR TIJDSCHRIFT VOOR HUURRECHT (2007); Vols *supra* note 73.
77 Vols et al., *supra* note 74.
78 Rechtbank Noord-Nederland, Sep. 19, 2017 (ECLI:NL:RBNNE:2017:4158).
79 Rechtbank Rotterdam, Sep. 2, 2016 (Neth.) (ECLI:NL:RBROT:2016:6752).

Nederland, for example, ruled that the presence of eight cannabis plants in a premise does not necessarily constitute a breach of the lease.[80] The Court of Appeal's-Hertogenbosch and the District Court Amsterdam decided that possessing five cannabis plants does not breach the lease and hence does not justify eviction.[81]

The second issue is the question of proportionality.[82] If the tenant breached the lease because of drug-related activities in the housing unit, does this breach justify the eviction of the tenant? A quantitative analysis of case law shows that a proportionality defense is raised in nearly three-quarters of the cases concerning drug-related activities. Nevertheless, the court dismisses the proportionality defense in the vast majority of cases.[83]

Yet, in a small number of cases we noticed that courts are more lenient and allow a proportionality defense and dismisses the landlord's eviction claim. For example, the Court of Appeals-Hertogenbosch held that the presence of one cannabis plant could breach the lease, but ruled that termination of the tenancy and subsequent eviction are disproportional.[84] Similarly, the District Court Noord Nederland ruled that small amounts of cocaine and heroin in the housing unit did breach the lease, but did not justify the termination of the lease and the subsequent eviction.[85] The same conclusion was reached in a case in which roughly 8 grams of cocaine were found. According to the court, the breach of the lease was not serious enough to justify eviction.[86]

These previous sections on drug evictions in the Netherlands not only reveal how immersed local authorities and landlords are in the War on Drugs, but also that the legal issues encountered in case law are fairly identical. The next sections conduct a similar analysis for drug evictions in the US.

II. Drug evictions in the United States

In this section we analyze how public and private landlords and governmental agencies in the US use eviction to fight drug-related crime. In the first part of this section, we describe the drug-related crime problems in the US and the development of eviction as a tool to rid housing units from drug activities. In the next section, we discuss how Public Housing Authorities (PHA) use eviction to curb drug-related crime from public housing. In the third part, we examine the Narcotics Eviction Program in NYC as an example of how landlords in private housing use eviction to fight drug-related crime. To provide the necessary urban

80 Rechtbank Midden-Nederland, Nov. 16, 2016 (ECLI:NL:RBMNE:2016:6099).

81 Gerechtshof s-hertogenbosch, Jul. 11, 2017 (ECLI:NL:GHSHE:2017:3143); Rechtbank Amsterdam, Mar. 6, 2017 (ECLI:NL:RBAMS:2017:1331).

82 *See* Fick & Vols, *supra* note 3; Vols & Fick, *supra* note 7.

83 *See* Vols et al., *supra* note 74.

84 Gerechtshof's-Hertogenbosch, Aug. 8, 2017 (ECLI:NL:GHSHE:2017:3557).

85 Rechtbank Noord-Nederland, Mar. 8, 2017 (ECLI:NL:RBNNE:2017:807).

86 Rechtbank Noord-Nederland, Aug. 29, 2017 (ECLI:NL:RBNNE:2017:3288).

context we first discuss the key characteristics of the US housing market, and NYC in particular.

In the third quarter of 2017, the US housing market included over 136,684,000 housing units.[87] Table 4.1 shows that owner-occupied housing units make up the largest part of the total housing stock in the US.

Rental premises accounted for 36.1% of the housing stock in the USA in 2017. The vast majority (74%) of the rental housing units are owned by individual investors (Fernald, 2017, p. 14).[88] The federal government provides housing assistance to low-income renters through programs administered by the U.S. Department of Housing and Urban Development (HUD). In 2017, 5,018,939 rental housing units fell under such HUD program. This is 11.7% of the rental housing stock. Within the rental housing sector, federal rental assistance programs provided under HUD programs subsist. For the US as a whole and NYC in particular, public housing, one such federal rental assistance program, constitutes only a small portion of the rental housing stock. Table 4.1 shows the number of public housing units in the United States declined over the years. In 2000, the national housing stock accounted for 1,282,099 public housing units. This number declined to 1,168,503 public housing units in 2010 and to 1,040,888 in 2017. This is a decline of 18.8% over seventeen years. Yet, the overall percentage of public housing units as part of the renter-occupied housing shows a small decrease.

Table 4.1 also shows the housing market in NYC. While most Americans own their home, the table shows that most New Yorkers live in rental housing. In NYC, the public housing stock dropped severely between 2010 and 2016. The most recent data show that in NYC 172,765 public housing units account for 8.1% of the occupied rental housing in 2016. Similar to the housing stock in the US as a whole, in NCY the overall percentage of public housing units among renter-occupied units shows a small decline.

A. *Drug-related crime in the United States*

In the 1970s and 1980s, crime and in particular drug-related crime was plaguing the US. Traditional law enforcement tools such as criminal prosecution were inadequate to tackle drug dealers.[89] Citizens' fear of testifying, along with long procedures and the high standard of proof made criminal law slow and cumbersome in quickly dealing with drug crime.[90] As such, the War on Drugs established a 'shadow system' outside the traditional criminal law procedures.[91]

87 HUD PD&R. *National Housing Market Summary*. (2017) www.huduser.gov/portal/sites/default/files/pdf/NationalSummary_3Q17.pdf.

88 Marcia Fernald. America's rental housing 2017. (2017).

89 *See* Peter Finn, *The Manhattan District Attorney's Narcotics Eviction Program*, U.S.D.O.J., Nat'l Inst. Just. 2 (1995).

90 *See* Lisa Weil, *Drug Related Evictions in Public Housing: Congress' Addiction to a Quick Fix*, 9 Yale L. & Pol'y Rev. 161 (1991); Finn, *supra* note 93, at 2.

91 Silva, *supra* note 7.

Table 4.1 Housing characteristics: US national and NYC

Subject	*US*				*NYC*		
	2000	*2010*	*2016*	*2017*	*2000*	*2010*	*2016*
All housing units	115,904,641	130,038,080	134,054,899	136,684,000	3,200,912	3,371,062	3,436,084
Owner-occupied	69,815,753 (66.2%)	76,089,650 (66.6%)	74,881,068 (63.6%)	76,146,000 (63.9%)	912,296 (30.2%)	962,892 (31.0%)	1,000,242 (32.0%)
Renter-occupied	35,664,348 (33.8%)	38,146,346 (33.4%)	42,835,169 (36.4%)	42,939,000 (36.1%)	2,109,292 (69.8%)	2,146,892 (69.0%)	2,128,004 (68.0%)
Public housing units	1,282,099 (3.6% of renter-occupied units)	1,168,503 (3.1% of renter-occupied units)	1,074,437 (2.5% of renter-occupied units)	1,040,888 (2.4% of rental housing stock)	180,247 (8.5% of renter-occupied units)	185,000 (8.6% of renter-occupied units)	172,765 (8.1% of renter-occupied units)

Note: Percentage owner-occupied and renter-occupied units represent the percentage of all *occupied* housing units.
Sources: HUD User, 2000; Daniels & Schill, 2001; NYU Furman Center, 2010, p. 34; HUD PD&R, 2017; HUD User, 2018.

Without bringing criminal law into play, officials target people involved in drug activities using civil penalties that affect public benefits and housing in particular. Especially eviction seems to provide a relatively quick fix to rid premises of drug dealers.[92] One scholar even argued that 'evictions are being used to compensate for the ineffectiveness of the criminal justice system'.[93]

Due to the (drug-related) crime plague, most apartment complexes in inner-city neighborhoods were undesirable to live in, poorly managed and maintained and had inadequate security which resulted in problems with drug-related and violent crime.[94] According to Congress, drug-related criminal activities and violence led to deterioration of the physical environment of public housing developments.[95] In response to the problem, Congress passed the Anti-Drug Abuse Act of 1988. Congress was of the opinion that the Federal Government should provide public housing 'that is decent, safe, and free from illegal drugs' and the Anti-Drug Abuse Act was the solution. The Act was supposed to address the increasing 'reign of terror' inflicted on public housing residents.[96]

Part of the Act was the 'one strike'-eviction policy, which requires each PHA to include a provision in the lease allowing the termination of the tenancy if a tenant, a member of the tenant's household, guest, or other person under the tenant's control engaged in drug-related criminal activity on or near the premises.[97] Drug-related activity is defined as 'the illegal manufacture, sale, distribution, use or possession with intent to manufacture, sell, distribute, or use a controlled substance (as defined in Section 802 of Title 21)'.[98]

With the introduction of this one strike eviction policy, the focus of the federal War on Drugs turned towards public housing communities.[99] The Anti-Drug Abuse Act of 1988, the Cranston-Gonzalez National Affordable Housing Act of 1990, the Housing Opportunity Program Extension Act of 1996, and the Quality Housing and Work Responsibility Act of 1998, form the basis of the US drug policy in public housing. These four pieces of federal

92 Weil, *supra* note 94; Finn, *supra* note 93, at 2.

93 Regina Austin, *Step on a Crack, Break Your Mother's Back: Poor Moms, Myths of Authority, and Drug-Related Evictions from Public Housing*, 14 Yale J. L. & Feminism 273, 288–89 (2002).

94 Sarah Kelly, *Separating the Criminals from the Community Procedural Remedies for Innocent Owners in Public Housing Authorities*, 51 N.Y.L.Sch. L. Rev. 379, 384–85 (2006).

95 42 U.S.C. § 11,901 (1988).

96 *Id.*

97 42 U.S.C. § 1437d(1)(5) (1990). The current version is found at 42 U.S.C. § 1437d(l)(6) (2018).

98 42 U.S.C. § 1437d(1)(9) (2018).

99 Paul Stinson, *Restoring Justice: How Congress Can Amend the One-Strike Laws in Federally-Subsidized Public Housing to Ensure Due Process, Avoid Inequity, and Combat Crime*, 11 Geo. J. on Poverty L. & Pol'y, 11, 435, 440–43 (2004); Silva, supra note 7, at 789.

legislation together create the authority and discretion for PHAs to evict public housing residents.[100]

To increase community safety, similar one strike policies have been adopted in the private housing sector through creative use of nuisance abatement laws.[101] Nuisance abatement is a civil process to sanction property owners for public nuisance occurring on their property to compel the end of these activities.[102] By labelling drug-related activities as public nuisance, nuisance statutes and ordinances can be used to combat drug crimes occurring in the private housing sector. Individuals, attorneys and officials may bring a civil suit seeking abatement of the nuisance and landlords risk fines, revocation of licenses, closure or forfeiture of the property and even imprisonment if they fail to abate the nuisance.[103] This way, landlords become responsible for the drug activities occurring at their premises. Often, the threat of civil remedies is for most landlords enough incentive to evict the problem tenant. In many jurisdictions across the US, landlords may avoid penalties, or curb the suit by evicting the problem tenant household.[104] Some nuisance abatement laws recommend or even require eviction of the tenant's household if the nuisance constitutes (drug-related) criminal activities.[105] As such, landlords have often the feeling that they have no other choice but to evict the problem tenants.[106]

NYC was one of the first jurisdictions to use one strike eviction strategies in private housing. In 1988, the Manhattan District Attorney created the Narcotics Eviction Program (NEP) that uses nuisance abatement laws to evict tenants and occupants who

100 Silva, *supra* note 7, at 789–91.

101 *See* John Eck & Julie Wartell, *Improving the Management of Rental Properties with Drug Problems, in* Civil Remedies and Crime Prevention: Crime Prevention Studies (Lorraine Mazerolle & Jan Roehl eds., 1998); Arthur Lurigio et al., *More Effective Place Management: An Evaluation of Cook County's Narcotics Nuisance Abatement Unit, in* Civil Remedies and Crime Prevention: Crime Prevention Studies (Lorraine Mazerolle & Jan Roehl eds., 1998); Lorraine Mazerolle et al., *Controlling Social Disorder Using Civil Remedies: Results from a Randomized Field Experiment in Oakland, California, in* Civil Remedies and Crime Prevention: Crime Prevention Studies (Lorraine Mazerolle & Jan Roehl eds., 1998).

102 *See* Desmond & Valdez, *supra* note 4; Theresa Langley, *Living without Protection: Nuisance Property Law Unduly Burden Innocent Tenants and Entrench Divisions between Impoverished Communities and Law Enforcement*, 52 Hous. L. Rev. 1255 (2015).

103 *See, e.g.*, Wis. Stat. § 113.823; Tex. Civ. Prac. & Rem. Code art. 6.125 §§ 2 & 15 (1963); Ark. Code § 16–105-403 (2016). Cari Fais, *Denying Access to Justice: The Cost of Applying Chronic Nuisance Laws to Domestic Violence*, 108 Colum. L. Rev. 1181 (2008); Desmond & Valdez, *supra* note 4; American Civil Liberties Union, Silenced: How nuisance ordinances punish crime victims in New York (2015), www.aclu.org/sites/default/files/field_document/equ15-report-nuisanceord-rel3.pdf (last visited, Apr. 10, 2018).

104 Emily Werth, *The Cost of Being Crime Free: Legal and Free Rental Housing and Nuisance Property Ordinances*, Sargent Shriver Nat'l Ctr. on Poverty L. 2–4, 18–19, App. A (2013); Hous. Apartment Ass'n, *Ordinance Guide – Forfeiture Abatement Support Team*, www.haaonline.org/Display.aspx?ID=257 (last visited Apr. 3, 2018).

105 Werth, *supra* note 108.

106 Desmond & Valdez, supra note 4, at 131.

deal drugs and who knew or should have known that illegal-drug dealing was conducted from the premises. Many states followed suit and NEP is frequently heralded as a model for community-based prosecution of drug crimes and third-party policing.[107]

With the introduction of the 'one strike you are out' policy in public housing and the use of nuisance abatement laws in the private housing sector, a 'shadow system' of the War on Drugs is created in which drug-related crime is fought using eviction instead of the traditional criminal law measures. In the following two sections, we concentrate on drug evictions in public housing and private housing, respectively. Both sections examine the applicable legal frameworks, present the available data on drug evictions and discuss key issues in case law. In the latter section on drug evictions in private housing, we primarily focus on NYC's Narcotics Eviction Program as an example of using nuisance abatement laws to fight drug-related crime.

B. One-strike evictions from public housing

Following the passing of the Anti-Drug Abuse Act of 1988, PHAs had still significant discretion in deciding whether or not to evict a tenant because of drug-related criminal activity. It was not mandatory to evict a tenant that was connected to drug crime. The Federal Department of Housing and Urban Development (HUD) even published guidelines that encouraged PHAs to include the context of the individual case in the decision whether to evict or not.[108]

In 1996, this contextual approach to eviction was replaced by a far stricter approach. In that year, in his State of the Union Address, President Clinton challenged local housing authorities and tenant associations. He argued that criminal gang members and drug dealers were destroying the lives of decent tenants and that 'from now on, the rule for residents who commit crime and peddle drugs should be one strike and you're out'.[109] Later that year, a special One Strike Policy symposium was organized. At that symposium, Clinton held that PHAs are legally entitled to evict tenants involved in drug-related crime, yet

107 *See, e.g.*, Scott Levy, *The Collateral Consequences of Seeking Order Through Disorder: New York's Narcotics Eviction Program*, 43 Harv. Civ. Rts.-Civ. Liberties L. Rev. 539, 547 (2008). *See also*, L.A. Cal. Mun. Code § 47.50 (2017); LA Citywide Nuisance Abatement Program (CNAP), www.lacp.org/2003-Articles-Main/CNAPprogram.html (last visited Nov. 12, 2017); Shelby County District Attorney, Drug dealer Eviction Program, www.scdag.com/preventingcrime/eviction (last visited Nov. 12, 2017); Albany County District Attorney, Narcotics Eviction Program, http://albanycountyda.com/Bureaus/StreetCrimesUnit/Initiatives/SafeHomesSafeStreets/NarcoticsEvictionProgram.aspx (last visited Nov. 12, 2017); Jackson County Prosecutor Drug Abatement Response Team (DART), www.jacksoncountyprosecutor.com/161/Drug-Abatement-Response-Team-DART (last visited Nov. 12, 2017); Anti-Crime Covenant, Minn. Stat. §§ 609.5317 & 504B.171, https://jux.law/landlord-tenant-rights-the-anti-crime-covenant/ (last visited Nov. 12, 2017).

108 Kelly, *supra* note 98, at 386–87.

109 President Bill Clinton, State of the Union Address (Jan. 23, 1996).

'in most places in this country, one strike has not been carried out'.[110] President Clinton argued that PHAs should adopt a strict One Strike Policy:

> this policy today is a clear signal to drug dealers and to gangs: If you break the law, you no longer have a home in public housing. One strike and you're out. That should be the law everywhere in America.[111]

After President Clinton's speeches, HUD published new guidelines that embraced the new One Strike Policy. The guidelines hold that by refusing to evict 'problem tenants, we are unjustly denying responsible and deserving low-income families access to housing and are jeopardizing the community and safety of existing residents who abide by the terms of their lease'.[112] In that same year, the geographic scope of the eviction policy broadened. Instead of 'on or near the premises', PHAs' power to evict applies to any drug-related activity 'on or off the premises'.[113]

Although the One Strike Policy was supposed to introduce a law and order approach to drug-related crime in public housing communities, the HUD guidelines still provide some discretion for PHAs to apply a more contextual approach towards drug-related evictions.[114] Nonetheless, most PHAs decided to impose a 'strict-liability eviction policy', which resulted in the eviction of tenants who were not the offending party, had no knowledge of the drug-related activity nor foresaw that activity.[115]

Federal funding policy clearly gave an incentive to PHAs to adopt this strict approach. It was decided to tie federal funding of PHAs to increased crime-related evictions, which encouraged PHAs not to assess the context of each individual case but to evict tenants connected to drug-related criminal activity regardless the circumstances.[116] In the six months after the One Strike Policy was adopted, the number of evictions increased significantly: from 9,835 to 19,405.[117]

An analysis of case law on the one-strike eviction reveals that this strict-liability eviction policy is controversial. Various courts across the US allowed an 'innocent

110 President Bill Clinton, Remarks by the President at One Strike Symposium (Mar. 28, 1996).

111 *Id.*

112 'One Strike and You're Out' Screening and Eviction Guidelines for Public Housing Authorities (HAs), 1996.

113 Housing Opportunity Program Extension Act of 1996, Pub. L. No. 104–120. *See also* the current 42 U.S.C. § 1437d (1)(9) (2018).

114 *See* Gerald Dickinson, *Towards a New Eviction Jurisprudence*, 23 Georgetown J. on Poverty L. & Pol'y 1 (2015).

115 *Id.*

116 *See* Kelly, *supra* note 98. *See* John Harris, *Clinton Links Housing Aid to Eviction of Crime Suspects*, Wash. Post (Mar. 29, 1996), www.washingtonpost.com/archive/politics/1996/03/29/clinton-links-housing-aid-to-eviction-of-crime-suspects/fd81a5bb-a407-4f85-b427-5a6d2754da5f/.

117 Kelly, *supra* note 98, at 387). See also, American civil liberties Union, Collateral Consequences of the War on Drugs (2003), www.aclu.org/sites/default/files/field_document/final%20brochure.pdf at 2.

tenant defense'. This defense states that eviction is a violation of the tenants' 'due process rights by holding them accountable even if they did not know of or have control over the person engaging in the drug-related criminal activity'.[118] The tenants hold that PHAs do not have the right to evict owners that have no involvement or knowledge of the commission of the drug-related crime.[119] The U.S. Supreme Court, however, eliminated the innocent tenant defense in the case of *The Department of Housing and Urban Development v. Rucker*.[120]

In this *Rucker* case, the Oakland Housing Authority (OHA) initiated eviction proceedings against a number of public housing tenants based on a violation of the lease that obliges the tenants to assure that guests or another person under his/her control shall not engage in any drug-related activity on or near the premise. First, the OHA held that the grandsons of the tenants Lee and Hill were caught in their grandparents' apartment complex parking lot smoking marijuana.[121] Second, OHA alleged that the daughter of tenant Rucker was found with cocaine and a crack cocaine pipe three blocks from the apartment.[122] Third, the OHA held that tenant Walker's caregiver and two others were found with cocaine in Walker's apartment on three instances.[123] All these tenants objected to the eviction and advanced the innocent tenant defense.

The Supreme Court dismissed their defenses and held that 'any drug-related activity engaged in by the specified persons is grounds for termination, not just drug-related activity that the tenant knew, or should have known, about'.[124] The Supreme Court found that it is 'not "absurd" that a local housing authority may sometimes evict a tenant who had no knowledge of the drug-related activity'.[125] It held that a strict-liability eviction policy 'maximizes deterrence and eases enforcement difficulties'.[126]

In the same *Rucker* case, however, the Supreme Court emphasized that PHAs are not obliged to evict every tenant that fails to assure that guests or another person under his/her control shall not engage in any drug-related activity on or near the premise.[127] The Anti-Drug Abuse Act of 1988

> entrusts that decision to the local public housing authorities, who are in the best position to take account of, among other things, the degree to which the housing project suffers from "rampant drug-related or violent crime," . . ., "the seriousness of the offending action," . . . and "the extent to which the

118 Dickinson, *supra* note 118, at 21.
119 Kelly, *supra* note 98, at 387–88.
120 *Id.* at 382.
121 Dep't of Hous. v. Rucker, 535 U.S. 125, 128 (2002).
122 *Id.*
123 *Id.*
124 *Id.* at 131.
125 *Id.* at 134.
126 *Id.*
127 *Id.* at 133–34.

> leaseholder has ... taken all reasonable steps to prevent or mitigate the offending action."[128]

Although the *Rucker* case can be characterized as a clear victory for the strict One Strike policy and no fault evictions, it does not prohibit PHAs to exercise their discretion and adopt a more contextual approach to evictions.[129] HUD's response to the Supreme Court's judgment was not very clear.[130] At the one hand, the Assistant Secretary of HUD urged PHAs in June 2002 to 'consider a wide range of factors in deciding whether, and whom, to evict as a consequence of such a lease violation' and 'balance them against the competing policy interest that supports the eviction of the entire household'.[131] These factors include

> among many other things, the seriousness of the violation, the effect that eviction of the entire household would have on household members not involved in the criminal activity, and the willingness of the head of household to remove the wrongdoing household member from the lease as a condition for continued occupancy.[132]

On the other hand, HUD's Associate General Counsel for Litigation confirmed in August 2002 'that as a matter of law, a PHA may evict all members of a household any time the relevant lease provision is violated'.[133] The Associate General Counsel holds that there is 'no legal authority for the proposition that a PHA cannot adopt a policy of maximum deterrence pursuant to which every violation of the lease provision required by Section 6(l)(6) results in lease termination and household-wide eviction'.[134] However, under the Obama administration, HUD issued a notice encouraging PHAs to exercise their discretion and not to strictly enforce the one strike eviction policy.[135]

Research has shown that the strict-liability eviction policies can be limited by state landlord–tenant law.[136] For example, the Pennsylvania Legislature adopted the Expedited Eviction of Drug Traffickers Act 1995. This Act allows courts to

128 *Id.* at 134.

129 Kelly, *supra* note 98, at 391.

130 Anne Fleming, *Protecting the Innocent: The Future of Mentally Disabled Tenants in Federally Subsidized Housing After HUD v. Rucker*, 40 Harv. Civ. Rts.-Civ. Liberties L. Rev. 197, 206–07 (2005); Kelly, *supra* note 98, at 391.

131 Letter from Michael Liu, Asst. Secretary, HUD to Public Housing Directors (June 6, 2002) https://portal.hud.gov/hudportal/documents/huddoc?id=DOC_10888.pdf.

132 *Id.*

133 *See* Letter from Carole Wilson, Associate Gen. Council for Litigation, HUD to Charles Macellaro P.C. (Aug. 15, 2002), https://portal.hud.gov/hudportal/documents/huddoc?id=DOC_11426.pdf.

134 *Id.*

135 U.S. Dep't of Hous. and Urban Dev., HUD Notice PIH 2015–9 (Nov. 2, 2015), https://www.hud.gov/sites/documents/PIH2015-19.PDF.

136 Dickinson, *supra* note 118.

take into account the context of the individual case when deciding to issue an eviction order:

> If the grounds for a complete eviction have been established, the court shall order the eviction of the tenant unless, having regard to the circumstances of the criminal activity and the condition of the tenant, the court is clearly convinced that immediate eviction or removal would effect a serious injustice the prevention of which overrides the need to protect the rights, safety and health of the other tenants and residents of the leased residential premises.[137]

Dickinson holds that this Act and landlord–tenant law from other states can be the foundation of new eviction jurisprudence. This new doctrine 'would not bar One-Strike evictions; it would effectively restrict them when involuntary removal would clearly be unjust as determined by the trial court'.[138] It entitles courts to consider a 'carefully calibrated matrix of factors' such as circumstances surrounding the incident of criminal activity and the condition of the tenant when deciding to permit the tenant's eviction.[139]

C. Narcotics eviction program in New York City

Private housing encountered similar drug problems as public housing.[140] For long, landlords in NYC encountered difficulties in ridding their housing units of drug-related crime. They had no legal access to police reports, and tenants were often too afraid to testify against drug dealers. As such, they were unable to prove that illegal businesses were conducted in their premises.[141] This situation changed with the case *Kellner v. Cappellini* in 1986. For the first time the Real Property Actions and Proceedings Law (RPAPL) was used in a case concerning the eviction of tenants who sold drugs from a housing unit.[142] The RPAPL permits the District Attorney (DA) to share police reports with landlords to ensure that landlords will have enough evidence to present their eviction case.

The *Kellner* case marked the beginning of the Narcotics Eviction Program (NEP). In 1988, the Manhattan District Attorney established the NEP to remove drug dealers from residential and commercial premises, using the RPAPL as a legal basis along with New York's Real Property Law (RPL). The three relevant provisions (§715, §711 RPAL and §231 RPL) are generally known as the nuisance abatement laws and were originally used to abate 'bawdy house'

137 35 PA. CONS. STAT. § 780–157(b).
138 Dickinson, *supra* note 118, at 50.
139 Dickinson, *supra* note 118, at 7, 53.
140 *See* Finn, *supra* note 93.
141 *Id.*
142 Kellner v. Cappellini, 135 Misc. 2d 759 (N.Y. Civ. Ct. 1986).

activities (i.e., prostitution).[143] Yet, similar to other nuisance abatement laws, these statutes can be used against many other activities, such as gambling, weapon trafficking, or any other illegal operation. As the name suggests, the primary focus of the NEP is evicting for drug crimes.

We divide the eviction proceeding under the NEP into three main steps. The first step is serving the landlord a written notice stating that the housing unit is used to conduct illegal drug business. The DA and any other duly authorized enforcement agency as well as residents living within 200 feet of the property can serve such notice (RPAPL §715). Generally, the DA will notify the landlord and will ask to initiate eviction proceedings to remove the tenants and occupants conduct drug business from the building.[144] If the landlord fails to make an application of eviction within five days after receiving the notice, the DA's office has the authority to initiate eviction proceedings as though it were 'the owner or landlord of the premises' (RPAPL §715(1)).[145] Subsequently, not only the tenants and occupants, but also the landlord will be defendant in the eviction proceedings (RPAPL §715).[146]

The second step is commencing a drug eviction proceeding. Landlords are generally not required to serve the tenants with a notice of termination as the lease is deemed void (§231 RPL); instead of a violation of the lease, NEP cases are based on a violation of the law.[147] In fact, these statutory eviction proceedings can be brought even if the lease has no clause prohibiting illegal activities.[148] NEP cases are heard by the special Narcotics Eviction section in the NYC Civil Court. The judge conducts these cases as summary proceedings due to the immediate action needed. It can be seen as a fast-track program in which trials are rarely delayed or postponed.

The third step is proving that the housing unit is used for illegal purposes. The burden to prove that the building is being used for illegal business lies with the petitioner (i.e., landlord, property owner or DA).[149] Instead of the criminal burden of proof – beyond a reasonable doubt – the petitioner needs to establish evidence that the premises is used as illegal drug business by a preponderance of evidence.[150] What is more, the petitioner should prove that the use of the housing unit for such

143 *See* Jan Roehl, *Civil Remedies for Controlling Crime: The Role of Community Organizations*, 9 Civ. Remedies & Crime Prevention 241 (1998); Levy, *supra* 111, at 539–543.

144 *See* Finn, *supra* note 93, at 5–6; D. J. Seidman & G. Lebovits, *Drug Holdover Proceedings: An Overview from 'Knew,' to 'Should Have Known,' to 'Strict Liability,'* 28 NYSBA 33 (2007); Levy, *supra* note 111, at 544.

145 The written notice – which is also sent to the landlord's attorney – informs the landlord about the evidence found and requests the landlord to start eviction proceedings against the tenants.

146 City of New York v. Rodriguez, 140 Misc. 2d 467, 468 (N.Y. Civ. Ct. 1988).

147 *Id.* at 471; Jackson Terrace Assocs. v. Patterson, 159 Misc.2d 637, 611 N.Y.S.2d 430, 430 (N.Y. App. Term. 1994); Kings County Dist. Attorney's Office v. Underwood, 543 N.Y.S.2d 247, 249 (N.Y. Civ. Ct. 1989).

148 NYC Housing Authority v. Grillasca, 18 Misc. 3d 524, 528 (N.Y. Civ. Ct. 2007).

149 Normandy Realty v. Boyer, 773 N.Y.S.2d 186 (N.Y. Civ. Ct. 2003).

150 Rodriguez, 140 Misc. 2d 467; Normandy Realty v. Boyer, 773 N.Y.S. 2d 186 (N.Y. Civ. Ct. 2003).

drug activities was conducted with the participation, knowledge or at least acquiescence of the tenant.[151] This standard of proof will be discussed in more detail below.

If the evidence is sufficient, the judge signs a judgment of possession, which returns the housing unit to the control of the landlord.[152] Next, the landlord should arrange for a city marshal to execute the eviction. If a landlord refuses to remove the tenant, the landlord risks a fine of up to $5,000 (RPAPL §715(4)) or forfeiture of the property.[153]

Unfortunately, we do not know the number of evictions under the NEP for each year. Yet, we do know that more than 6,000 drug evictions under the NEP have been made in Manhattan from the start of the program, 1988, to 2009.[154] Further quantitative research has been done for the first six years of the program: June 1988 – August 1994. This study shows that eviction proceedings have been initiated in 2,150 cases.[155] Of these 2,150 cases, only 2% of the eviction requests were dismissed by the court or withdrawn by the petitioner. This suggests that few successful legal challenges have been made to these drug eviction proceedings in the first six years of the program. In 5% of all cases, the court and parties agreed to settle the case and allowed the tenant to remain. The court ordered eviction in 38% of the cases. However, in more than half of the cases (55%), the tenants left the property already before the court ordered eviction. As a result, most of the evictions under the NEP can be seen as informal evictions that happen 'beyond the purview of the court'.[156] Such informal evictions stay out of court records and do not result in any legal data that can be analyzed by legal scholars.

An analysis of case law involving formal evictions reveals a number of legal issues. Here, we discuss two of them. The first main legal issue is the burden to prove the use of the housing unit for illegal drug businesses. To prove this, the petitioner should demonstrate 1) that the activity constitutes a commercial activity, 2) that the activity is ongoing and continuous, and 3) a nexus between the activity and the premises.

First, the petitioner needs to demonstrate that the drug-related activity is a commercial activity, such as selling or manufacturing drugs.[157] Judges find several factors

151 Lloyd Realty Corp. v. Albino, 146 Misc. 2d 841, 843 (N.Y. Civ. Ct. 1990); Marwyte Realty Assoc., Ltd. v. Valcarcel, 150 Misc.2d 1044 (N.Y. App. Term 1991); Howard Ave. Assoc. v. Rojas, N.Y.L.J., Apr. 5, 2002, at 20, col 6; Normandy Realty Inc. v. Boyer, 2 Misc. 3d 407 (N.Y. Civ. Ct. 2003).

152 Rodriguez, 140 Misc. 2d at 471.

153 21 U.S.C. § 881(a)(7).

154 *See* Report of the District Attorney County of New York 2000 – 2009, at 130, www.manhattanda.org/sites/default/files/ANNUAL%20REPORT%202000-2009.pdf (last visited Dec. 5, 2017).

155 Finn, *supra* note 93, at 5.

156 Matthew Desmond, *Eviction and the reproduction of urban poverty*,118 AJS 1 (2012), at 95.

157 1165 Broadway Corp. v. Dayana, 166 Misc. 2d 939, 944 (N.Y. Civ. Ct. 1995); Normandy Realty Inc., 2 Misc. 3d 407, 410, 411; NYC Hous. Auth. ('Lexington Houses') v. Fashaw, 2016 NY Slip Op 51,548 (U), 51,557 (N.Y. Civ. Ct. 2016).

relevant to distinguish between personal use and commercial use. Factors of a case that may prove commercial use of the premises are testimonies, a prior criminal conviction, a prior drug felony, quantity of drugs discovered, attempts to destroy the evidence, the presence of large amounts of cash, customer lists, weapons, packaging and scales.[158] It is not required that drugs are discovered in the housing unit as long as there is other evidence connecting the premises to the alleged drug activity and revealing the operation of a drug business.[159] To prove that the tenant conducted commercial activities in the property, the mere possession or personal use – regardless of the discovered quantity – is usually insufficient evidence.[160] Yet, in one case, the court held that any reasonable person would believe that drugs were used for sale when 193 vials of crack and cocaine were found in the apartment, together with a 9 mm machine gun, a pistol with shells and other guns. This was a sufficient amount to prove that the apartment was used for illegal business.[161] In another case, sixty crack vials, a razor, and empty ziplock bags did not prove that the apartment was used for illegal drug business.[162]

Second, the petitioner needs to prove that the drug-related activity is ongoing and continuous.[163] This implies that an isolated or single incident of illegal drug-sale is insufficient evidence.[164] Similarly, personal use, even if habitual and customary, does not constitute illegal use of the premises in terms of RPL§231or RPAPL 715(1).[165] The available case law shows that it may be difficult to establish such an ongoing, continuous activity. For example, in one case, six drug sales over several months were seen as an ongoing, continuous enterprise.[166] Yet, in another case, two buys in three to four weeks was insufficient to prove such a business.[167]

158 *See, e.g.*, Kings County Dist. Attorney's Office. v. Underwood, 143 Misc. 2d 956, 968 (N.Y. Civ. Ct. 1989); N.Y. County Dist. Attorney's Office v. Geigel, N.Y.L.J., Dec. 27, 1991, at 24, col 6; People v. Daley, 281 A.D. 2d 244 (N.Y. App. Div. 2001); People v. Freeman, 106 A.D. 3d 590 (N.Y. App. Div. 2013); Fashaw, 2016 NY Slip Op 51,548 (U), 51,557.

159 Flores v. ERC, 686 N.Y.S. 2d at 281; Clifton Court, Inc. v. Williams, N.Y.L.J., May 27, 1998, p. 28, col. 6 (App. Term. 2d Dep't 2d & 11th Jud. Dists.); Howard Ave. Assocs. N.Y.L.J., Apr. 5 2002, p. 20, col. 6; Geigel, N.Y.L.J. Dec. 27, 1991, p. 24, col. 6; Finn, *supra* note 93, at 3.

160 1165 Broadway Corp. v. Dayana, 166 Misc. 2d 939, 944 (N.Y. Civ. Ct. 1995); Normandy Realty Inc. v. Boyer, 2 Misc. 3d 407, 410, 411 (N.Y. Civ. Ct. 2003); Fashaw, 2016 NY Slip Op 51,548 (U), 51,557.

161 Underwood, 143 Misc. 2d 965, 968 (N.Y. Civ. Ct. 1989).

162 Clifton Court Inc. v. Williams, N.Y.L.J., May 27, 1998, p. 28, col. 6 (AT 2d Dept.).

163 St. John Hous. Dev. Fund Corp. v. Hernandez, 154 Misc. 2d 141, 145 (N.Y. Civ. Ct. 1992); Normandy Realty Inc. v. Boyer, 2 Misc. 3d 407, 412 (N.Y. Civ. Ct. 2003); Fashaw, 2016 NY Slip Op 51,548 (U), 51,551.

164 Lituchy v. Lathers, 232 N.Y.S.2d 627, 627 (N.Y. Sup. Ct. 1962); People v. Ramos, 685 N.Y. S. 2d at 582–83; Boyer, 2 Misc. 3d at 41–2, 410.

165 1165 Broadway Corp. v. Dayana, 166 Misc. 2d 939, 944 (N.Y. Civ. Ct. 1995).

166 People v. Freeman, 106 A.D. 3d 590 (1st Dept 2013).

167 Fashaw, 2016 NY Slip Op 51,548 (U), 51,557.

Lastly, the petitioner needs to demonstrate a nexus between the drug-related activity and the premises.[168] In most cases, the petitioner has to prove that the housing unit is the location of the drug business.[169] Yet, case law shows the term premises is pretty inclusive; its definition depends on the circumstances of a case.[170] For example, in one case, the front of the building was a sufficient nexus between the drug business and the apartment.[171] In another case, drug sales throughout the building justified nexus between the illegal conduct and all apartments on the three floors of the building.[172]

The second main issue revealed by case law is proving that the tenant 'knew or should have known' about the drug business.[173] The petitioner must demonstrate that the tenant participated in, knew, or at least acquiesced in the alleged drug activities.[174] For situations in which there is no proof of actual knowledge, case law developed various factors to determine whether a tenant should have known. These are the presence of drugs, whether the drugs and/or related items were in plain view, the size of the premises, the drug-arrest history of the person who committed the drug activity, heavy flow foot traffic in and out of the apartment, and the connection between the person who committed the drug activity and the subject premises.[175] Another factor that plays a role is the time that the drug sale was conducted. If the sale took place at a time most people are asleep, this is evidence that the activity took place outside of the presence and knowledge of the tenant.[176]

This New York's 'knew or should have known' standard is a different standard than the federal 'strict liability' standard that is applicable in the one strike you're out evictions as discussed in the *Rucker* case.[177] In the wake of *Rucker*, the court held in the *Perez* case that the strict liability standard should also be the standard in NEP

168 City of New York v. Omolukum, 177 Misc. 2d 796, 801–02 (N.Y. Civ. Ct. 1998); RRW Realty Corp. v. Flores, N.Y.L.J., Feb. 10, 1999, at 28, col. 3; City of NY v. Rodriguez, 140 Misc. 2d 467, 531; Marwyte Realty Assoc., 150 Misc. 2d 1044.

169 Omolukum, 177 Misc. 2d 796. Lebovits & Seidman, *supra* note 147, at 37.

170 *See* Lebovits & Seidman, *supra* note 147, at 37.

171 Rodriguez, 140 Misc. 2d 467.

172 Kellner, 135 Misc. 2d 759.

173 Omolukum, 177 Misc. 2d 796, at 921; NYC Hous. Auth. v. Lipscomb-Arroyo, 2008 NY Slip Op 51,085(U) [19 Misc 3d 1140(A)].

174 Lloyd Realty Corp. v. Albino, 146 Misc. 2d 841, 843 (N.Y. Civ. Ct. 1990); *Marwyte Realty Assoc.* N.Y.L.J., Nov. 6, 1991; Howard Ave. Assoc., N.Y.L.J., Apr. 5, 2002, at 20, col 6; Normandy Realty Inc., 2 Misc. 3d 407.

175 *See* Lebovits & Seidman, *supra* note 145, at 37–39); Lipscomb-Arroyo, 2008 NY Slip Op 51,085(U).

176 Lloyd Realty Corp., 146 Misc. 2d 841, 844.

177 N.Y.C.H.A. v. Grillasca, 18 Misc. 3d 524 (N.Y. Civ. Ct. 2007); Lipscomb-Arroyo, 2008 NY Slip Op 51,085(U).

cases.[178] However, in *Grillasca* the court set the record straight: the standard of strict liability does not apply to NEP cases.[179]

The NYC Housing Authority (NYCHA), which runs all public housing across the City's five boroughs, can choose to initiate eviction proceedings based on a breach of the lease or based on a violation of the law under the NEP.[180] If NYCHA chooses for the latter course, the lease becomes void per statute (RPL §231(a)) and New York's standard of 'knew or should have known' applies.[181] If the NYCHA chooses for the former course, the *Rucker* standard of strict liability applies. The NYC Housing Authority decides on a case-by-case basis whether to proceed under New York's standard of knew or should have known, without having to terminate the lease, or under the federal standard of strict-liability.

III. Comparative analysis

In this section, we conduct a comparative analysis to juxtapose and identify similarities and differences in the use of eviction to fight drug-related crime in the Netherlands and the US. The main aim of a comparative analysis is 'to explain differences and similarities as they arise from the description of legal systems under consideration'.[182] We hence do not summarize all findings presented throughout the chapter, but mainly focus on exploring and analyzing differences and similarities. These differences and similarities are explored and analyzed on three different levels, each reaching a more comprehensive level of analysis than the one before: an exploratory level (A), legal level (B), and theoretical level (C). The current section is structured accordingly.

The first step in our comparative analysis is at the exploratory level. In this part, we identify and analyze differences and similarities at an empirical and descriptive level. We compare and contrast the housing context, the characteristics of drug-related crime, the use of evictions to address this type of crime and the availability of data in both countries.

The next step is the comparison on a legal level, which assesses similarities and differences at a more comprehensive level than the exploratory level. In this part, we compare and contrast the applicable legal frameworks and the safeguards offered to evictees. This comparative analysis has two different layers. The first

178 ARJS Realty Corp v. Perez, N.Y.L.J., August 27, 2003 at 19 col. 6, 2003 N.Y. Slip Op. 51,220(U), 2003 WL 22,015,784.

179 Grillasca, 18 Misc. 3d 524, 528. For other cases *see, e.g.*, Fashaw, 2016 NY Slip Op 51,548 (U), 51,558; Lipscomb-Arroyo, 2008 NY Slip Op 51,085(U).

180 *See* Escalera v. New York Hous. Auth., 924 F.Supp. 1323 (S.D.N.Y. 1996); Howard Ave. Assoc., N.Y.L.J., Apr. 5, 2002, at 20, col 6; Grillasca, 18 Misc.3d 524, 528; Lipscomb-Arroyo, 2008 NY Slip Op 51,085(U).

181 Grillasca, 18 Misc. 3d 524, 528.

182 *See* Gerhard Danneman, *Comparative Law: Study of Similarities or Differences, in* The Oxford Handbook of Comparative Law (Mathias Reimann & Reinhard Zimmerman ed., 2006).

layer is an internal legal comparison within each country between drug eviction procedures in the different areas of law, such as administrative law and landlord–tenant law. The second layer concerns the external legal comparison, comparing the use of eviction to fight drug-related crime between the Netherlands and the US.

The third and last step is the comparative analysis on a theoretical level, which is the most abstract level. In this part, we provide an explanation for the use of eviction as a tool to fight drug-related crime. We use the third-party policing theory as an explanatory framework to understand and explain the current reliance on eviction in the War on Drugs.

A. Comparison on an exploratory level

In this section we describe and assess the most relevant similarities and differences between both countries on the most basic, factual level. We specifically focus on the first aim of this research: analyzing to what extent eviction is used to combat drug-related crime in the US and the Netherlands. We concentrate on three main issues. The first issue we want to touch upon is differences and similarities with regard to the composition of the housing market in the Netherlands and the US. To truly understand the use of eviction as a tool in the War on Drugs, it is essential to take into account the housing context in both jurisdictions. The findings discussed in the sections above show that the current housing market in the Netherlands and the US are both dominated by owner-occupied housing units. This is not surprising as both governments have promoted home ownership. In fact, promoting home ownership has been the cornerstone of the US and Dutch federal housing policy, leading to active interventions in the real estate sector and the financial sector in both countries.[183] Still, in both countries a substantial minority of the housing stock consists of rental housing units. Roughly 35–45% of all housing units in both countries are rental premises. A big difference, however, can be observed in the amount of public rental housing. Whereas housing associations (semi-public landlords) own the vast majority of the total rental housing stock in the Netherlands (about 70%), public housing in the US accounts for less than 3% of the rental housing stock. The largest share of the rental properties in the US is owned by individual investors (74%). This difference is important to take into account when analyzing and explaining the differences and similarities in the use of eviction in the fight against drug-related crime in both countries.

The second issue concerns the occurrence of drug-related crime problems in residential communities and the attention it receives in both countries. The findings presented above show that both the Netherlands and the US witnessed a rapid increase of drug-related crime problems in the second half of

183 *See* Stephen Dane, *Eliminating the Labyrinth: A Proposal to Simplify Federal Mortgage Lending Discrimination Laws*, 26 U. Mich. J. L. Reform 527 (1993); Vols, *supra* note 77.

the twentieth century. Several scholars and the governments of both countries claimed that, especially, rental housing estates were increasingly used as sites for illegal drug activities. In reaction, public authorities in both countries started to target (semi-)public and private landlords to engage them in the fight against drug-related crime. Looking at the composition of the rental housing stock in the Netherlands, it was the obvious choice for the government to concentrate its efforts on housing associations. Similarly, in the US, the federal government aimed directly at the PHAs to fight the War on Drugs in residential premises. This might not seem the most obvious choice looking at the relatively small percentage of public housing in the US. Yet, according to Congress, especially public housing developments were plagued by drug-related crime.

The findings also show a movement in semi-public and private housing towards eviction in the fight against drug-related crime. Seeking to rid all types of housing units of drug-related crime, local authorities in the Netherlands received the power under administrative law to close any type of housing unit if drug-related activities occurred at or near a housing unit. In the US, private landlords and property owners were dragged into the War on Drugs through the use of civil nuisance abatement laws. One such example is the NYC's Narcotics Eviction Program. Under the NEP, both public and private housing tenants are facing eviction if they engage in drug-related activities. As a result, we maintain that the War on Drugs has pushed authorities to create a shadow system outside the traditional criminal law procedures that relies on eviction and homelessness as sanctions. Using private law and administrative law to fight drug-related crime, local authorities, landlords and property owners received a prominent role in the current War on Drugs.

The third issue concerns the number of drug-related evictions. The findings presented above reveal that drug evictions are evident in both countries. Nevertheless, the size of this shadow system is unknown as the data on the number of drug evictions in the Netherlands and the US are either scarce, outdated or both. As a result, we have no clear overview of how many people are affected by these evictions nor any evidence of the effectiveness of eviction as a tool for crime control. Moreover, as previous studies as well as our own results already indicate, the majority of drug evictions in both the Netherlands and the US are probably informal evictions, which means that they happen 'beyond the purview of the court' and hence do not appear in court records.[184] Nevertheless, for both countries we can draw two main conclusions from the data we presented above. First, we now know that drug evictions are not just provided by the law, but actually applied in practice. In other words, the data provide a small bridge over the gap between the 'law in the books' and the 'law in action'. Second, the data availability and lack thereof shows that drug evictions are poorly documented.

184 *See* Desmond & Valdez, *supra* note 4; Matthew Desmond & Monica Bell, *Housing, Poverty, and the Law*, 11 Annual Rev. L. & Soc. Sci. 15 (2015); Vols, *supra* note 77.

This exploratory analysis provides some insight into the extent evictions are used to abate drug-related crime from housing units in the Netherlands and the US. The following legal analysis yields a more comprehensive examination of drug evictions by comparing the applicable legal frameworks, relevant case law, and role of actors on two levels: *within* both countries and *between* both countries.

B. Comparison on a legal level

In this section we focus on the second aim of the research: showing to what extent the law provides protection against drug-related evictions in both countries. Again, we do not want to repeat all findings presented in the sections above. Instead, we focus on four key issues.

The first issue concerns the creative use of all types of law in the fight against drug-related crime. Comparing the use of eviction to curb drug-related crime in the Netherlands and the US reveals that the solid barriers between the various areas of law have weakened and become blurry as the traditional field of drug control has been extended with other areas of law. The time that criminal law was the main legal discipline that deals with crime seems to be over. The finding presented in the sections above show that administrative law and private law are often mixed, which makes it difficult for most laymen as well as for lawyers to truly understand which legal framework is applicable and what level of legal protection should be offered. What is more, using eviction not only incorporates other areas of law into the business of crime control, but also adds a variety of actors such as landlords and local authorities.

The second issue has to do with the 'legal trigger' to use eviction. With legal trigger we refer to the legal reason or basis that enables a landlord or an administrative authority to apply their eviction powers. In both countries, two triggers can be distinguished: a breach of the lease or a violation of the law. In the Netherlands, drug evictions initiated by local authorities are based on violation of the law (the Opium Act). Anyone selling, delivering, providing or possessing drugs for these purposes, at or near a housing unit violates the law and may be evicted as a result of a closure order issued by a local authority. Similarly, in the US tenants face eviction if they violate nuisance laws. By labelling drug-related activities as public nuisance, nuisance statutes and ordinances can be used to combat drug crimes occurring in residential premises. We specifically focused on drug evictions under the NEP in NYC. Under that program, tenants risk eviction if they use their housing unit for illegal drug business.

Under Dutch law, landlords can carry out drug evictions based on a breach of the lease. Any drug-related activity will generally breach a lease and provide ground for termination of the tenancy. Similarly, PHAs in the US may evict tenants based on a breach of the lease if they or a member of the household, or guest or other person under the tenant's control engaged in a drug-related criminal activity on or off the premises. Every PHA in the US is required to include such a provision in the lease.

The third issue concerns the scope of drug-related activities subject to eviction. For local authorities in the Netherlands as well as landlords in NYC, personal drug use is an insufficient ground for eviction. In the Netherlands, local authorities may only evict after drugs are sold, delivered, provided or present for the purpose to sell, deliver or provide. Similarly, under the NEP, landlords in NYC must prove commercial activity (e.g., selling or manufacturing drugs). Besides that, an isolated or single incident is not sufficient; the commercial drug activity should be continuous and ongoing. To decide whether the found drugs are for personal use, the court in New York often decides that the mere possession is insufficient evidence and requires additional evidence that proves the commercial activity.

The analysis of drug evictions in the Netherlands shows that the scope of local authorities' power to evict increased over the years. As a result, less strict requirements are applicable. Under Dutch administrative law, courts mainly look at the quantity of discovered drugs to decide whether the discovered drugs are for personal use or for sale. Drug possession for personal use in the Netherlands is acceptable up to five grams of soft drugs, five cannabis plants or half a gram of hard drugs. Any amount above this threshold is sufficient evidence to demonstrate that the drugs are used for sale (i.e., drug possession for commercial purposes). Hence, the scope of local authorities' power to evict no longer just covers drug sales, but also possession and cannabis cultivation.

Landlords in the Netherlands can initiate eviction proceedings after drug possession and cannabis cultivation since generally any drug-related activity breaches the lease. Yet, in many cases courts dismiss the landlord's eviction claim if the quantity of discovered drugs is small (e.g., one cannabis plant or eight grams of cocaine). In the US, a more harsh eviction policy exists in public housing. The findings presented above show that PHAs may evict after tenants engaged in the illegal manufacture, sale, distribution, use or possession with intent to manufacture, sell, distribute, or use, a controlled substance, regardless of the quantity of discovered drugs.

The fourth issue concerns the burden of proof for landlords and local authorities and the legal protection against drug evictions. Our findings show that under Dutch law local authorities are allowed to evict a household based on the drug-related activity that occurred in the property. If the local authority can prove sale or possession of drugs or cultivation of cannabis, the household may be evicted, regardless of who engaged in the drug-related activity as long as the activity occurred at or near the housing unit. This bears similarities with the strict liability standard for drug evictions that is applicable in the US public housing sector. The *Rucker* case demonstrates that public housing tenants are responsible for their own activities and the activities of others despite their knowledge of or participation in the alleged activities; the mere drug-related activity is sufficient proof for eviction.

The sections above also reveal a difference in the level of protection of evictees. The right to respect for one's home laid down in both Dutch constitutional as European human right law requires that the violation of the law or breach of the lease (i.e., drug-related activity) should justify the eviction. This means that circumstances surrounding the drug-related activity should be taken into account to decide if a less intrusive measure should be applied. For drug evictions conducted by private landlords in the Netherlands this means that the court should examine the circumstances surrounding the drug-related activity and the possible consequences of eviction for the household if a tenant puts forward a proportionality defense. Yet, as discussed above, a quantitative analysis of case law shows that a proportionality defense mostly functions as a procedural hurdle.[185] Similarly, prior research on Dutch administrative drug evictions, including a quantitative case law analysis, revealed that a proportionality defense is hardly successful in court as well.[186] Courts generally agree that the drug-related activity is in itself a sufficient breach of the lease or violation of the law that justifies the eviction.

The standard of proof for private landlords in NYC is much higher than the standard of proof for drug evictions in the Netherlands and for PHAs under the one strike policy in the US. Under the NEP, the petitioner must prove that the tenant participated, knew, or at least acquiesced to the drug activity. In the wake of *Rucker*, the question was whether the strict liability standard should also be applied in NEP cases. Eventually, several courts ruled that the standard of strict liability does not apply to NEP cases. The statutory burden of proof 'knew or should have known' applies to NEP cases. This means that private landlords in NYC are required to apply a much more contextual approach than PHAs.

Lastly, the findings presented in the sections above show that a claim for a more contextual approach arose in both countries. In the Netherlands, local authorities and lower district courts are called upon by the highest administrative court, while PHAs in the US are encouraged by academics and sometimes even by the federal HUD to apply a more contextual approach. Yet, the significant discretionary power of Dutch local authorities and PHAs in the US may intervene with this trend.

C. Comparison on a theoretical level

In this last section of the comparative analysis, we compare and contrast the practices in the Netherlands and the US on the third and most abstract level. In this theoretical analysis we focus on the last research aim by providing an explanation for the use of eviction to combat drug-related crime. The third-party policing theory is used as an explanatory framework through which we observe, analyze and eventually explain the current reliance on eviction in the War on Drugs. First, we describe the meaning of third-part policing. Next, we apply the framework of third-party policing to drug evictions in the Netherlands and the US.

185 *See* Vols et al., *supra* note 74.
186 *See* Bruijn et al., *supra* note 6.

The theory of third-party policing represents a shift in the field of crime control that started in the second half of the twentieth century, but became known as third-party policing in the 1990s.[187] This theoretical framework has become influential in criminology and sociology, and has been heralded in legal oriented research as well. The main idea of third-party policing is that crime is no longer merely prevented and controlled by criminal law officials; third parties (i.e., non-criminal law officials), such as public housing agencies, property owners and local authorities, are frequently engaged in the business of crime control.[188] Central to third-party policing practices is the use of legal levers to 'motivate' third parties into taking some responsibility for preventing or controlling crime.[189] Legal levers are legal instruments used to co-opt third parties to take on a role in crime control, such as civil forfeiture, orders to control behavior and mandatory reporting.[190]

By bringing a variety of actors into the field of crime control the arm of law becomes longer and reaches beyond the area of criminal law.[191] The once solid barriers between the various areas of law are weakened and become blurry as the traditional field of crime control is extended with other areas of law such as private law and administrative law. Private law for example is no longer just used for resolving private law disputes between individuals; private law procedures and remedies are also used to control and prevent criminal activities.[192]

We hold that third-party policing can be used as the theoretical lens through which the findings presented above can be analyzed to provide an explanation for the use of eviction in the War on Drugs.[193] Looking through this theoretical framework we can identify the different elements of third-party policing in the discussed drug eviction strategies. The third parties engaged in crime control are landlords, PHAs and local authorities. The legal levers, if there are any, may vary from fines to risking lock down of the property. The crime control activity that the third parties should undertake is evicting the tenants and their household who engage in drug-related activities.

Yet, not every third party in our analysis is coerced to use eviction; hence, not every type of drug eviction fits the definition of third-party policing we use. Therefore, we made a distinction between two types of eviction: (1) the third party evicts out of its own initiative, (2) the third party is coerced to use eviction by external forces.

187 *See* Michael Buerger & Lorraine Mazerolle, *Third-party Policing: A Theoretical Analysis of an Emerging Trend*, 15 Just. Q. 301 (1998); Mazerolle & Ransley, *supra* note 6; Desmond & Valdez, *supra* note 4.

188 *See* Buerger & Mazerolle, *supra* note 191, at 301; Mazerolle & Ransley, *supra* note 6, at 2–3, 47.

189 *See* Buerger & Mazerolle, *supra* note 191, at 301; Mazerolle & Ransley, *supra* note 6, at 3, 45, 51.

190 *See* Mazerolle & Ransley, *supra* note 6, at 75.

191 *See* Garland, *supra* note 6, at 170.

192 *See* Mazerolle & Ransley, *supra* note 6, at 67.

193 *See* Creswell, *supra* note 9, at 52, 62.

The first category of drug evictions lacks the central element of third-party policing activities: the legal lever. These particular third parties are PHAs in the US and local authorities in the Netherlands. PHAs have long been encouraged to rid public housing from drug-related crime strictly enforcing the one strike eviction policy. They were even forced to include a specific provision in their lease that allows immediate eviction of tenants engaged in drug activities. Yet, changes in administration and developments under state landlord–tenant law, but even the *Rucker* case, show that PHAs can use discretion in deciding whether to evict a tenant despite the governmental policy. There is no legal lever that coerces PHAs into evicting public housing tenants engaged in drug-related activities. Similarly, in the Netherlands, local authorities' power to close a housing unit and subsequently evict the residents if the housing unit is used for drug-related activities is an autonomous power. No legal lever is forcing them into controlling drug crime by using their closure power.

From a theoretical point of view, these drug evictions lack the central element of third-party policing: the legal lever; both Dutch local authorities and US PHAs are not legally forced to take on a crime control role. However, they may still encounter political pressure through governmental notices and policies.

The second category represents the drug evictions that are the epitome of third-party policing. In both the NEP in NYC, and drug evictions exercised by private landlords in the Netherlands, a government agency – respectively a DA or local authority – coerces crime control activities by drawing on legal levers: civil sanctions or closure of the premises. The onus for drug activities occurring at housing units are, directly or indirectly, placed on landlords and property owners, which gives them little to no choice but to initiate eviction proceedings.

Under the NEP, a landlord will be asked to begin eviction proceedings against tenants and their household who use the premises for illegal drug business. If the landlord refuses or fails, the DA will take over, 'acting as though it were the owner or landlord of the premises' and the landlord becomes the defendant (together with the tenant) instead of the petitioner in the eviction proceedings. Moreover, the landlord risks a fine up to $5,000 and even forfeiture of the property.

The NEP is an example of using nuisance abatement laws to place the responsibility to curb drug-related crime on landlords and property owners. Landlords risk fines, revocation of licenses, closure or forfeiture of the property and even imprisonment if they fail to abate the nuisance. The threat of these remedies is for most property owners and landlords enough incentive to evict the problem tenant.[194]

In the Netherlands, private landlords do not face direct consequences if they fail to curb the drug-related crime such as landlords in NYC, but they do risk severe consequences. Landlords might face closure of their premises if they fail to

194 *See* Barbara Smith et al., *Ridding Neighborhoods of Drug Houses in the Private Sector*, Washington, DC: American Bar Association (1992); Fais, *supra* note 107, at 1194; Desmond & Valdez, *supra* note 4; Werth, *supra* note 108; American Civil Liberties Union, *supra* note 107.

rid the premises of drug-related crime. If a local authority closes a rental housing unit, not only the household will be removed, but the landlord loses the possibility to rent the place to someone else for the remaining time of the closure period.[195] In fact, even if the landlord is the one to report the drug activities to the police, the landlord might face closure of the rental premises and hence loss of income.[196] As such, landlords are (indirectly) forced to assume some responsibility for the drug-related activities of others and hence for correcting it.

Concluding thoughts

This chapter has shown that the use of eviction as a tool for crime control has spread throughout the US and the Netherlands. Crime control is becoming more decentralized and a variety of actors other than criminal justice officials have been allocated to curb misconduct. In many Western jurisdictions, such as the Netherlands and the US, local authorities and civil society are incorporated into the field of crime control, especially within the War on Drugs. Yet research on this topic stayed behind. Taking evictions to fight drug-related crime as an example of this form of crime control, we reached three main conclusions.

First, eviction has become a common strategy to curb drug-related crime from housing units in both countries. Second, the analyses of applicable legal frameworks and case law in both the Netherlands and the US reveal that the judiciary aligns with the 'tough on drugs' approach. The third conclusion concerns an explanation for the first two: landlords and local authorities are pressured and coerced to evict entire households if a resident is engaged in drug-related activities. This approach is identified by the term third-party policing. Landlords are held responsible for drug activities occurring at their premises and are coerced to abate these activities or else they risk severe consequences such as fines or closure of the housing unit. Financial and political pressure is used to encourage local authorities in the Netherlands and PHAs in the US to evict households engaged in drug-related crime.

However, a consequence of these third-party policing activities in the War on Drugs is that not only landlords and local authorities become responsible for the drug-related criminal activities of others, but also citizens. We hold that the onus is placed on the law-abiding members of the household and the legal lever to engage them in the fight against drug activities is eviction. A resident who takes no part in drug activities can be forced to remove from the housing unit if another member of the household (in some cases even a guest) engaged in drug activities. Future in-depth research is needed on the exact consequences of third-party policing in the War on Drugs.

195 *See* Michel Vols & L. Michelle Bruijn, *Case note: ECLI:NL:RVS:2015:1447: JG, 15.0045, No. ECLI:NL:RVS:2015:1447, 3 p., May 06, 2015*, Jurisprudentie voor Gemeenten 4, 2015.

196 ABRvS May 6, 2015 (ECLI:NL:RVS:2015:1447).

Over the years, various scholars criticized these drug eviction practices.[197] Yet, our intention was never to conduct normative research. The aim of this chapter was to show that eviction is one of the most powerful instruments used at the disposal of third parties in the Netherlands and the US to control drug-related crime. As such, we provided an overview of how the drug eviction laws in the Netherlands and the US read and work and explained these findings to deepen our understanding of how drug-related crimes at or near residential properties are combatted. With this chapter, we contribute to the growing body of scholarly literature on eviction, the war on drugs and third-party policing.

197 *See, e.g.*, Weil, *supra note 94*; Levy, *supra* note 111; Langley, *supra* note 106; Michelle Ewert, *One Strike and You're Out of Public Housing: How the Intersection of the War on Drugs and Federal Housing Policy Violates Due Process and Fair Housing Principles*, 32 HARV. J. ON RACIAL & ETHNIC JUST. 57 (2016).

5 Urban citizens and water

Johannesburg and Dublin's experience with the human right to water

Scott McKenzie

Introduction

Urban governance impacts how residents experience the human right to water. International and state laws are more frequently discussed around human rights, but they are far from the only regulations that impact this issue.[1] This adds a layer of particular complexity when discussing the human right to water, which exists in many forms: a key substantive socio-economic and environmental human right, a normative framework, an activist rallying point, and as a diverse set of policies implemented in cities across the world. This suggests that comparative and legal pluralism approaches may be useful in understanding how the human right to water is implemented and experienced in different contexts. This chapter uses Johannesburg, South Africa, and Dublin, Ireland, as examples because their approaches to the right to water mirror broader hegemonic trends in water governance and are illustrative for cities around the world.

The human right to water has increasingly come to the forefront of international policy and academic debates; particularly, grappling with how best to realize the right in contexts of water scarcity and harsh economic conditions. Two major anchors for the human right were the recognition of the substantive right by the United Nations General Assembly through Resolution 64/292 (2010) and the normative framework proposed by the United Nations Committee on Economic, Social and Cultural Rights (CESCR) in General Comment 15 (2003).[2] Substantive right focuses on the firm establishment of the right while the normative framework focuses on measures used to define expected actions. Despite this, there is there is still debate around certain measures such as the economic cost of water – as suggested by the Dublin Principles. While it is fair to say the right exists, the specifics are still much in debate.

Urban water governance is rarely a mirror reflection of international law, with some cities following a substantive (judiciable) right to water, while others implement elements that create a normative framework. Johannesburg and Dublin show a

1 Peter Rogers & Alan W. Hall, *Effective Water Governance*, Global Water Partnership (2003).

2 D. Misiedjan & S. McKenzie, *Human Right to Water, in* Encyclopedia of Human Rights and the Environment: Indivisibility, Dignity and Legality? J. May & E. Daly, eds. (forthcoming 2019).

number of environmental, historical, and socio-economic differences, but they are clear and contemporary examples of the substantive and normative framework routes for urban water rights. In South Africa, the 1996 constitution has been a lonestar for the right to water. After a long history of socio-economic disparity with roots in apartheid, the new constitution included progressive social protections for all citizens, including a right to water. In the court case of *Mazibuko v. City of Johannesburg*, the town argued to establish quantities below international standards. Dublin presents a different perspective. Ireland has no constitutional protection. Nevertheless, citizens had completely free domestic water. Quantity was of little concern. While recent reforms have changed this policy, new guidelines are still aimed at helping citizens access water on par with international guidelines, regardless of an ability to pay.

The first section of this chapter uses a legal pluralism framework to explore the connection between different parts of water governance; international human right to water, state protections, and local implementation. The second section considers the right to water in two respective contexts. The discussion of Johannesburg focuses on the judgment of the Phiri court case, whereas Dublin considers the history and recent changes to the domestic "free water" policy. The final section uses these experiences to provide a nuanced view of how the human right to water and urban water governance reflects international human rights, constitutional and national laws, and the implementation of normative frameworks. This chapter concludes that urban water governance benefits from both substantive constitutional protection and a robust normative framework to protect and shape the right.

The right to water in the urban context is important to study because it rests at the confluence of three streams of public policy; the first is a strong discourse of rights from international treaties and declarations, the second is state constitutions, which the majority of the world's citizens hope protects their basic rights, and the third are steps taken for local implementation where citizens are most impacted.[3] Understanding any one in isolation provides a limited view.

I. The human right to water – practice and law

Despite general agreement that access to water is important for human health, and a diverse history of state or local scale implementation, the international legal and governance community has only recently adopted a human right to water.[4]

3 *See* Dinah Shelton, *Human Rights, Environmental Rights, and the Right to Environment*, 28 STAN. J. INT'L L. 103 (1991).

4 Lee-Yee Huang, *Not Just Another Drop in the Human Rights Bucket: The Legal Significance of a Codified Human Right to Water*, 20 FLA. J. INT'L L. 353, 354, 363 (2008); *see also* RICHARD PIERRE CLAUDE & BURNS H. WESTON, HUMAN RIGHTS IN THE WORLD COMMUNITY: ISSUES AND ACTION 21 (2006); World Conference on Human Rights, *Vienna Declaration and Programme of Action*, art. 1 § 5, U.N. Doc. A/CONF.157/23 (1993). Because the right to water seems to fit into a single category of human rights, it is instructive to think of the right to water in the paradigm proposed by the Vienna Declaration on Human Rights, which describes all human rights as "universal, indivisible and interdependent and interrelated."

In part because of the realization of the Millennium Development Goals (and more recent Sustainable Development Goals), 2.6 billion people have achieved access to drinking water. However, a Pacific Institute report found that dirty water was still responsible for 3.7 percent of all deaths.[5] Citizens and researchers have highlighted that there is a significant gulf between international instruments on water provision and actual water service, including reflection on a number of specific issues including quality or affordability considerations.[6]

A. A foundation of pluralism

Legal pluralism has been defined as "a situation in which two or more legal systems coexist in the same social field."[7] This recognizes that there are multiple types of law (including examples, such as religious for example, that exist outside of the state). These legal systems each come from different sources and with their own "foundations of legitimacy, validity, power and authority."[8] A great deal of social science and legal scholarship has focused on the concept of legal pluralism from a customary law perspective, looking at grassroots and informal sources of law at the local and community level, but it can be applied in a number of other contexts.[9] Here, legal pluralism can also be applied to a discussion of the interaction between international law and urban regulation of water governance. The "human right to water" for urban citizens is a concept rife with plural meanings. This phrase can be used to invoke either the substantive or normative right, can be drawing on the legitimacy of international law, and also state or local regulation (or even customary or religious law).

B. A multifaceted human right

Historians have pointed out that water was not included in the United Nations Universal Declaration of Human Rights because framers considered it too obvious, and thought that water was as essential as air.[10] The formulation of the concept

5 *World Water Quality Facts & Statistics*, PACIFIC INSTITUTE (Mar. 22, 2010), http://pacinst.org/wp-content/uploads/2013/02/water_quality_facts_and_stats3.pdf.
6 Rhett Larson, *The New Right in Water*, 70 WASH. & LEE L. REV. 2181–2267, 2188 (2013).
7 Sally Engle Merry, *Legal Pluralism*, 22 LAW AND SOCIETY REVIEW 869, 870 (1988).
8 Franz von Benda-Beckmann & Keebet von Benda-Beckmann, *Places That Come and Go: A Legal Anthropological Perspective on the Temporalities of Space in Plural Legal Orders, in* THE EXPANDING SPACES OF LAW: A TIMELY LEGAL GEOGRAPHY 30 (Irus Braverman et al. eds., 2014).
9 *See* DIK ROTH, RUTGERD BOELENS & MARGREET ZWARTEVEEN, LIQUID RELATIONS: CONTESTED WATER RIGHTS AND LEGAL COMPLEXITY (2005); *see also* June Prill-Brett, *Indigenous Land Rights and Legal Pluralism Among Philippine Highlanders*, 28 LAW & SOCIETY REVIEW 687 (1994); *and see* ALISON DUNDES RENTELN, FOLK LAW: ESSAYS IN THE THEORY AND PRACTICE OF LEX NON SCRIPTA (1995).
10 Peter H. Gleick, *The Human Right to Water*, 1 WATER POL'Y 487, 491 (1998).

"human right to water" at the international level is often traced by appearances in international declarations that have pushed the issue forward, providing salient points for the progression of broad governance themes.[11] One of the first points was the United Nations Water Conference held in Mar del Plata, Argentina in 1977.[12] The 1992 Dublin Statement on Water and Sustainable Development highlighted the economic aspects of water in addition to its central role in human life.[13] This emphasis on financial issues, including cost recovery, has proven controversial, as many activists have rejected language and policy that commodifies water.[14] More recently, in July 2010, the United Nations General Assembly passed non-binding resolution A/64, which "declares the right to safe and clean drinking water and sanitation as a human right that is essential for the full enjoyment of life and all human rights."[15] This statement has been taken as the definitive step in establishing the substantive human right at the international level.

This substantive element of the human right to water has been formulated in two ways. First, the right was "derived" because it was fundamental for the existence of other rights that were already codified, such as a right to health or to a particular standard of living.[16] This formulation has been used to justify water rights for Indigenous people in Paraguay and Botswana, among others.[17] Second, as seen in a number of international legal instruments, the right has been made explicit. This formulation has been used in reference to protected groups such as in the Convention on the Elimination of All Forms of Discrimination Against Women, which states that rural women should have adequate sanitation and

11 Christine Chinkin, *The Challenge of Soft Law: Development and Change in International Law*, 38 INT'L & COMP. L. Q. 850, 851 (1989).

12 Arun K. Biswas, *From Mar del Plata to Kyoto: An Analysis of Global Water Policy Dialogue*, 14 GLOBAL ENVTL. CHANGE 81, 492 (2004).

13 Muhammad M. Rahaman & Olli Varis, *Integrated Water Resources Management: Evolution, Prospects and Future Challenges*, 1 SUSTAINABILITY: SCI., PRAC. & POL'Y 15, 15 (2005).

14 Sharmila L. Murthy, *The Human Right(s) to Water and Sanitation: History, Meaning, and the Controversy Over-Privatization*, 31 BERKELEY J. INT'L L. 89, 93 (2013).

15 UN General Assembly, *The Human Right to Water and Sanitation*, G.A. Res. 64/292/Rev.1 (July 26, 2010), www.un.org/en/ga/search/view_doc.asp?symbol=A/RES/64/292.

16 For examples of water as a derived right *see e.g.*, Universal Declaration of Human Rights, art.¶ 25 (health and food), G.A. Res. 217A (III), U.N. Doc. A/810 at 71 (1948); International Covenant on Economic, Social and Cultural Rights, arts. 11 (adequate standard of living) – 12 (health), Dec. 16, 1966, S. Treaty Doc. No. 95-19, 6 I.L.M. 360 (1967), 993 U.N.T.S. 3; International Covenant on Civil and Political Rights, art. 6 (right to life) Dec. 16, 1966, S. Treaty Doc. No. 95-20, 6 I.L.M. 368 (1967), 999 U.N.T.S. 171. More recently this formulation has been used to argue that there is right to water for productive purposes as well, such as when needed by subsistence farmers for agricultural reasons. Ralph Hall et al., *The Human Right to Water: The Importance of Domestic and Productive Water Rights.*, 20 SCI. ENG. ETHICS 849 (2014).

17 *See Yakye Axa v. Paraguay: Upholding and Framing the Human Right to Water, in* THE INTER-AMERICAN COURT OF HUMAN RIGHTS: THEORY AND PRACTICE, PRESENT AND FUTURE (Yves Haeck et al. eds., 2015); *see also* Cynthia Morinville & Lucy Rodina, *Rethinking the Human Right to Water: Water Access and Dispossession in Botswana's Central Kalahari*, 49 GEOFORUM 150 (2013).

water supply.[18] This form was also used in the United Nations resolution and has become the norm when discussing the right.

Separate from the substantive element of the human right, a normative framework explains how the right should be implemented so that it is realized by everyone. This content was most thoroughly explained by the Committee on Economic, Social and Cultural Rights (CESCR) in General Comment 15 (GC15). Comments such as the GC15 provides guidance for how human rights should be implemented, but are not considered legally binding. While covering a range of issues related to the human right to water, four aspects of the right can be considered to illuminate this analysis. The first three deal with how residents experience water and deal with adequacy, access, affordability, and the last focuses on the state's role in water provision.[19]

First, these guidelines state that water must be made available "in quantities and of a quality necessary" to meet citizens' basic needs.[20] Adequacy is a difficult amount to define, with experts noting between 7.5 liters and 50 liters as a sufficient amount – depending on the standard they are applying. The lower amount covers only basic human hydration, while the higher estimates include enough water for hygiene, food-preparation, and sanitation.[21] Today, most experts gravitate towards a target amount near the higher end of this range, with 50L being perhaps the most common and frequent number mentioned. GC15 also says that all people should have the right to accessible water.[22] This suggests water should be no more than 1 kilometer from the home and without a wait of more than 30 minutes. Key here, is that while the right involves domestic water, there is no requirement for indoor plumbing or a faucet. However, access to water should be safe and residents should not be placed in dangerous situations. This is a key concern for some communities, for example, where shared toilets have become a target for theft and crime.

Next, people are entitled to affordable water. But, the right does not require water to be free, only priced so that it does not trade-off with other protected rights such as the ability to afford food. Although the percent is not fixed in the GC15, conservative estimates suggest not more than 3 percent of a household's income.[23] The economic valuation of water has become one of the main

18 *See* Convention on the Elimination of All Forms of Discrimination Against Women, art. 14, Dec. 18, 1979, 1249 U.N.T.S. 13; *see also* Convention on the Rights of the Child, art. 24(c), Nov. 20, 1989, 1577 U.N.T.S. 3. This treaty follows language found in the CESCR and creates an obligation on states to combat disease and malnutrition through "the provision of . . . clean drinking-water." *Id.*

19 This is not to shortchange the other aspects of the normative framework for the right to water.

20 United Nations (UN) Committee on Economic, Social and Cultural Rights (CESCR), General Comment No. 15: The Right To Water, UN Doc. E/C.12/2002/11 (2002).

21 Huang, *supra* note 4, at 358.

22 General Comment 15, *supra* note 20.

23 *International Decade for Action "Water for Life" 2005–2015*, UNDESA, www.un.org/waterforlifedecade/human_right_to_water.shtml (last visited Dec. 12, 2017).

lightning rods for protection and criticism in changes to water governance, particularly in the subject of private investment in urban water utilities.

Finally, the human right to water often hinges on state involvement. This calls on each state to progressively (meaning forward movement, not in a political sense) help citizens realize the human right, "expeditiously and effectively." In such a progressive framework, state attainment is not measured by looking at actual realization of the right for citizens.[24] States must take steps that are deliberate, concrete, and targeted towards the full realization of the right to water, however not in any certain speed nor with a dedication of a certain level of the budget.

This section has focused on the broad pieces of the human right to water that have come together under international human rights law, but that is only one element of a legal pluralist view. While much focus of pluralism analysis has focused on customary law, the international scale will be an increasingly important area, particularly for subjects such as human rights.

II. The human right to water in Johannesburg and Dublin

The earlier section covered international law, which applies to everyone. However, international law itself is not the law that most citizens can turn to nor does it create the entirety of their experience with water. But, a legal pluralism analysis of the human right to water shows the international level is only one place to find its legitimacy; for many urban residents, state and local law and regulation is the critical link to realizing these rights. However, as this section shows, there is great diversity in how citizens experience water governance – from the substantive right (Johannesburg) to water policies that closely fit the normative framework (Dublin).

A. Johannesburg – constitutional protections fall short

This section explores the substantive aspect of the human right to water for the residents of Johannesburg. As the now well discussed case of *Mazibuko v. City of Johannesburg* (Phiri) demonstrates, the substantive right can be subject to a variety of local regulations and judicial interpretations which many may feel fall short of the goals of the human right to water.[25] While it is certainly important to locate how and where on the ground implementation diverges from the normative framework, it is also important to note the protections the right does provide.

After decades of minority rule by the white population, the African National Congress took power in the mid 1990s and promised social sector reforms

24 Jeanne Luh et al., *Equity in Water and Sanitation: Developing an Index to Measure Progressive Realization of the Human Right*, 216 INT'L J. HYGIENE & ENVTL. HEALTH 662 (2013).

25 Louis J. Kotzé, *Phiri, the Plight of the Poor and the Perils of Climate Change: Time to Rethink Environmental and Socio-economic Rights in South Africa?*, 1 J. HUM. RTS. & ENV'T 135 (2010).

including expanding the right to water for all citizens.[26] Discussions early in the South African constitutional process reiterated that water was a common resource for all South African citizens and the state had a responsibility to protect these resources for present and future generations. As a result, South Africa was one of the first states to formally protect the human right to water in its constitution and has been noted as one of the more progressive in the world.[27] Section 27 of the South African constitution states that "Everyone has the right to have access to ... sufficient food and water ... [and] ... the state must take reasonable legislative and other measures, within its available resources, to achieve the progressive realization of each of these rights."[28] In addition to the constitution protection, governance was largely implemented through the National Water Act, whose goal is to answer past racial and gender inequalities, connect water management with economic development, and ensure that all citizens receive a "minimum basic quantity of potable water."[29]

South Africa's drinking water supply policy situates responsibility for water delivery to local municipalities (following global governance trends in the decentralization and subsidiarity), and each city adopted a water policy that was intended to meet national guidelines and satisfy the constitutional protection.[30] Johannesburg's initial policy was not economically sustainable because of poorly maintained and wasteful infrastructure, households with unauthorized water connections, and a backlog of unpaid water bills.[31] Thus, free water delivery was limited only to households that were unable to pay, and was limited to 6 kiloliters (kL) per household per month (the goal was 25 L per person per day) in an attempt to reduce how much money they spend on water delivery by minimizing waste and improving revenue sources. For amounts over this allotment, the city installed a special type of meter that required pre-payment. However, there were numerous criticisms of this policy: 1) there is no guarantee of enough water to realize the

26 In addition to the right to water, the South African constitution is notably progressive on a range of socio-economic rights including healthcare and food. Andrew L. Magaziner, *The Trickle Down Effect: The Phiri Water Rights Application and Evaluating, Understanding, and Enforcing The South African Constitutional Right to Water*, 33 N.C. J. Int'l L. & Com. Reg. 510, 530 (2008). In contrast to the use of the word progressive to describe the implementation of the human right, in this sense, progressive is used to mean socially forward thinking. John Cantius Mubangizi, *The Constitutional Protection of Socio-Economic Rights in Selected African Countries: A Comparative Evaluation*, 2 Afr. J. Leg. Stud. 1, 2 (2006).

27 Magaziner, *supra* note 26 at 514–520.

28 Constitution of the Republic of South Africa (1996) § 27.

29 *National Water Policy for South Africa: White Paper*, G.A. South Africa (1997), www.dwaf.gov.za/Documents/Policies/nwpwp.pdf.

30 *See* Jackie Dugard, *Civic Action and Legal Mobilisation: The Phiri Water Meters Case in* Mobilising Social justice in South Africa: Perspectives from Researchers and Practitioners 73 (Jeff Handmaker & Remko Berkhout eds., 2010); *see also* Larson, *supra* note 6, at 2211; *and see* Rose Francis, *Water Justice in South Africa: Natural Resources Policy at the Intersection of Human Rights, Economics, and Political Power*, 18 Geo. Int'l Envtl. L. R. 149 (2005).

31 Larson, *supra* note 6, at 2211.

human right; 2) the policy allocated water by households and not per person, which was relevant because the average household size in Phiri was larger than the South African standard; 3) the policy could be expensive or dangerous for citizens whose water use went above the free allocation.[32] The pre-paid meters particularly caused considerable hardship for the residents; in one case residents were unable to put out a fire because the water available was insufficient.

This context frames challenges and shortcomings to Johannesburg's water governance. The plaintiffs in *Mazibuko* came from Phiri, a township in Soweto. This area suffered from significant overcrowding and a lack of basic public utilities, including water, but also, this area has long played a critical role in social organizing for equality. The applicants in the *Mazibuko* case sought the resolution of two issues related to the human right to water in their community; first, they asked that the state be required to provide 50 free liters of water per person per day, and second, they asked that the use of pre-paid meters be ruled unconstitutional.

The trial court found for the applicants and ruled that Johannesburg's policy violated the constitution. The court found that the policy of 6 kiloliters per household and the installation of prepaid meters were not congruent with the human right to water in the constitution. The court ordered the minimum provision be set at 50 liters per person per day. The appellate court lowered the requirement to 42 liters per person per day. Instead of relying on international experts to estimate the amount of water needed to fulfill the human right, the court heard expert testimony from a local engineer who was more familiar with the township and its environment. It came as a shock when the Constitutional Court overturned the lower court decisions. This ruling permitted the use of the prepaid water meters, and set the amount of water that should be provided based on a standard for the reasonableness. The Constitutional Court ruled that the substantive right needed to be read as a progressive right, and could not be enforced against the state without reference to economic realities.[33]

B. *Dublin – a free water future*

Dublin has a different approach to its citizen's right to water – focusing on the spirit but neglecting the letter of the law. Unlike Johannesburg and South Africa

32 Francis, *supra* note 30; Magaziner, *supra* note 26.

33 Larson, *supra* note 6 at 2212; Karin Lehmann, *In Defense of the Constitutional Court: Litigating Socio-Economic Rights and the Myth of the Minimum Core*, 22 AM. U. INT'L L. REV. 163, 164 (2006). These shortcomings were seen initially in the case *Soobramoney v. Minister of Health, KwaZulu-Natal* 1998 (1) SA 765 (CC) (S. Afr.) which denied the critically ill applicant priority access to dialysis on the basis that he was not requiring emergency medical treatment. A later case, *Government of the Republic of South Africa v. Grootbroom* 2001 (1) SA 46 (CC) (S.Afr.) upheld the applications demand for adequate temporary housing on the basis that the housing program was unreasonable. In *Minister of Health v. Treatment Action Campaign*, 2002 (5) (SA) 721 (CC), the court ruled for the applicants in a case that argued that the government's limited distribution of an important AIDS fighting drug was unreasonable.

more broadly, there is no constitutional protection for water, or any environmental human rights. While Dublin and Ireland have a vastly different economic and environmental situation than Johannesburg, the city has been subject to many of the same broad global trends in international law and water governance – including questions of human right and the financial ability to provide water for citizens. Significant policy changes after the 2008 recession tested the balance of power between the state and local scales but also gave citizens a chance to consider new water policies.

For more than 25 years Ireland had an unusual free water policy.[34] The policy was designed for simplicity: Section 105 (1) of the National Water Services Act 2007 banned charging for water. The free water policy was first implemented between 1977 and 1983, and a second iteration of the program had its genesis in 1996 during parliamentary elections for the Dáil Éireann.[35] At that time, water charges were unpopular because they were too confusing for consumers. There were wide discrepancies between the amount of water used by the consumers and the amount billed. Compounding the problem, infrequent billing made it difficult for homeowners to budget, compounding that social services to help those in need were disorganized. The policy resulted in even higher than expected costs to provide water, and Ireland's water use increased to the highest amount per capita in Europe because of negative consumption patterns. For example, people were no longer as incentivized to buy appliances with a lower water use.[36] Because water use was no longer constrained by the economics of supply and demand, the Irish public became less concerned about water's economic value.

As in Johannesburg, in Ireland the local government was responsible for the supply and payment for the majority of domestic water, accounting for approximately 80 percent of the water used.[37] But, Ireland's free water policy did not support local water governance, and infrastructure was rarely improved or addressed. This wasted significant amounts of treated water and reduced resident services.

This was not an environmentally or economically sustainable policy. Ireland was hit hard by the 2008 worldwide economic crisis, which caused significant internal and external pressure for reform. At the prompting of international creditors, the government of Ireland adopted a raft of austerity measures known as the Irish National Recovery Plan to cut expenses and increase revenue, and

34 Yaqian Zhao & Dara Crosbie, *Water Pricing in Ireland: A Techno-economic and Political Assessment*, 69 INT'L J. ENVTL. STUD. 427 (2012).

35 Susan Scott, *Abolition of Domestic Water Charges in Ireland*, THE WORLD BANK GROUP AGRICULTURE AND RURAL DEVELOPMENT (2003); Zhao and Crosbie, *supra* note 34.

36 Scott, *supra* note 35.

37 Liam McCumiskey & P. F. Toner, *Water Resources and Management in the Republic of Ireland*, 6 WATER & ENVT. J. 89, 98 (1992).

singled out the free water policy in particular. In the words of one expert "the case for water charging has never been stronger."[38]

The new policy proposals raised significant public concerns, particularly related to the effective supply of water to all citizens. There have been numerous public protests and the suggestion of boycotts.[39] An initial draft of the new policy moved responsibility from Dublin itself to a new national body known as Irish Water. This policy initially allowed a free allowance of 58 liters per day per child (21,000 per year).[40] Above this amount, households pay either a set fee per year or per cubic meter, depending on whether or not they have had a new post-pay meter installed. These meters proved no more popular in Dublin than Johannesburg.[41]

In the wake of significant public protest the government relented. Ireland passed the Water Services (Amendment) Act 2016 and Water Services Act 2017 which suspended, and then repealed the collection of water tariffs. These new policies focus on preventing wasteful water use. However, they siloed water governance at the national level, leaving the city relatively less options and flexibility.

38 *Ireland Timeline*, BBC NEWS (Feb. 2, 2011), http://news.bbc.co.uk/2/hi/europe/country_profiles/1038669.stm. *See also* Liz Alderman, *Ireland Unveils Austerity Plan to Help Secure Bailout*, N.Y. TIMES (Nov. 24, 2010), www.nytimes.com/2010/11/25/world/europe/25ireland.html; *and see Austerity Puts an End to Free Water in Ireland*, 12 GLOBAL WATER INTELLIGENCE (2010), www.globalwaterintel.com/archive/11/12/general/austerity-puts-end-free-water-ireland.htm; *and see* Government of Ireland, *The National Recovery Plan 2011–2014*, www.budget.gov.ie/The%20National%20Recovery%20Plan%202011-2014.pdf (last visited Dec. 12, 2017).

39 Gavan Reilly, Irish Government "Fears Boycott of New Water Charges," THEJOURNAL.IE (Jan. 12, 2013), www.thejournal.ie/euroleaks-delay-in-water-charges-749689-Jan2013/; Water Services Bill 2013 [Seanad] www.oireachtas.ie/viewdoc.asp?DocID=22592&&CatID=59 (last visited Mar. 26, 2014). The government of Ireland has noted that there are no plans to privatize the water sector, but public doubt remains. Shane Darcy, *The Right to Water and Privatisation in Ireland*, HUM. RTS. IN IRELAND (May 6, 2013), http://humanrights.ie/civil-liberties/the-right-to-water-and-privatisation-in-ireland/; Carroll, *supra* note 39.

40 Global Water Intelligence, *supra* note 38; Government of Ireland, *supra* note 38, at 12; Steven Carroll, *Earlier Date Set for Water Charges*, IRISH TIMES (Dec. 2, 2010), www.irishtimes.com/newspaper/ireland/2010/1202/1224284574022.html; *see also* Zhao and Crosbie, *supra* note 34, at 1. For more information, *see* Daniel McConnell, *Revealed: What Your Family Will Have to Pay in Water Charges*, INDEPENDENT.IE (Jan. 11, 2014), www.independent.ie/irish-news/revealed-what-your-family-will-have-to-pay-in-water-charges-29906616.html; Arthur Beesley, *Households Will Not Learn Extent of Water Charges Until August*, IRISH TIMES (Feb. 11, 2014), www.irishtimes.com/news/politics/households-will-not-learn-extent-of-water-charges-until-august-1.1688045; Christian Ritter, *Digital Dublin: the Water Protests and Social Media in Ireland*, AOIR SELECTED PAPERS OF INTERNET RESEARCH (2017), http://spir.aoir.org/index.php/spir/article/view/1354; Martin Quinn et al., *Domestic Water Charges in Ireland – Issues and Challenges Conveyed Through Social Media*, WATER RESOURCE MGMT. (2016), http://link.springer.com/article/10.1007/s11269-016-1374-y; Jennifer Brady & Nicholas F. Gray, *Reform of the Irish Water Sector: Opportunities and Challenges*, 170 PROCEEDINGS INST. CIV. ENGINEERS – WATER MGMT. 165 (2016).

41 *See generally* New Domestic Water Charges, www.water.ie/.

III. Understanding the human right to water in light of state practice and local implementation

These two urban examples highlight the interaction of many sources and scales for water governance. They provide counterpoints by which to understand the influence and interaction of international, state, and local law. Johannesburg provides an example of substantive aspects of the human right, yet with key failures to implement a normative framework, which is critical to achieving the goals of the human right. By contrast, Dublin, has few legal protections and less local flexibility, but comes closer to adopting a policy that would provide adequate water for all.

It is, of course, important to acknowledge certain factors where these two areas differ. Environmentally, they have different geographical considerations. South Africa noted while drafting the new constitution that its climate and terrain are dryer than those of Europe, while Ireland's renewable water resources are approximately four times that of a relatively water rich country such as France.[42] Economically, while suffering negative effects of the global economic crisis, Dublin has more economic resources to put towards the realization of all human rights. Finally, the historic arc for each country is dramatically different, with South Africa's recent struggle against apartheid most prominent. However, questions of human rights are factors that should not be taken to diminish the applicability of these findings, particularly in light of the international nature of the human right to water.

The first element to discuss in more depth is the relationship between the substantive right and urban law. This is a contentious issue, with many asserting that the right to water has not been efficient in securing access to water. Johannesburg perfectly illustrates this criticism. The right alone was not sufficient to require the courts to rule that water policy needed to fit the normative framework because the law itself contained no reference to these standards, leaving the court free to make its own interpretations. Although there are relatively high rates of water connections, the policy in place did not achieve the goals of the human right to water through adequacy and access. However, there are many reasons that substantive protections are valuable at the local law level. First, the substantive right gives a basis for which applicants can bring claims, making the right judiciable. This opens a route through the judicial system to let citizens demand services, rather than indirectly influencing change at the political level through elections or lobbying for increased water services. The right endows all citizens with the ability to access at least some services, and provides a series of obligations for governments to fulfill (even if these fall short of full realization).[43] Certainly, other parts of law might provide a hook on which to hang similar claims, but a substantive protection may provide entry

42 *See* G.A. South Africa, *supra* note 29; Zhao and Crosbie, *supra* note 34.
43 *See* Zhao and Crosbie, *supra* note 34.

to certain courts which may not be available when a claim is brought under another law or provision. Some believe the mere existence of the human right to water has been instrumental in promoting the provision of water for citizens, rather than cases where it is obviously used as a legal tactic.[44] It is through these city and national water policies that most peoples would seek to have their human right realized.[45] Second, substantive human rights often act as a winning argument, resolving issues of conflicting laws and policies. While this alone did not overcome economic concerns in Johannesburg, Dublin showed evidence of a strong push against charges for water. Third, substantive human rights are more difficult to alter. While water governance may change depending on the election cycle, constitutional changes are far more difficult to carry out than under the normal legislative process. Dublin shows that while free water programs have come and gone and returned again, the addition of specific rights is more difficult. Fourth, the promotion of the right to water also advances other normative goals, such as equality. As the human right is intended to be applied without discrimination, it can be used as a tool to address historical wrongs.

By contrast, Dublin's citizens experience comes far closer to the human right to water's normative framework, but does not recognize the existence of the human right, provide these essential protections, or provide further options for the city. As the recent policy shifts show, governance changes can come rapidly. There are a number of reasons why a more open policy based normative framework is helpful for promoting human rights. The first is it provides a flexibility both in initial implementation and over time. As was noted by the courts in South Africa, there is probably not a fixed amount of water that fits all populations around the world. 50L is given as a standard, but the actual conditions where people live is probably more helpful in making a final decision. Similarly, while Dublin has set an unlimited amount of water for now, it is possible that in the future, economics and politics could combine to change policy again. A normative framework based approach can provide more chances to change policy in the future. Finally, a normative framework approach can be necessary when constitutional reform is difficult or impossible, a lesson particularly useful for cities in the United States.

This underscores the importance of understanding urban law and governance in the context of other laws at different scales. As Johannesburg and Dublin illustrate, while rights and normative frameworks exist or can be implemented at various levels, often responsibility and resources are awkwardly fit to the urban context. As both cities show, despite the best attempts by local government, being responsible for water management is difficult and can strain financial

44 Erik B. Bluemel, *Implications of Formulating a Human Right to Water*, 31 Ecology LQ 957, 977 (2004).

45 *See* Chad Staddon et al., *A Right to Water – A Geographico-Legal Perspective, in* The Right to Water: Politics, Governance and Social Struggles (1st ed. 2011).

resources. However, the answer may not be to keep all responsibility at the national level, as Dublin shows. Local law has a place in maintaining the flexibility of national laws and in implementing international rights.

From a more broad theoretical level, a legal pluralism comparison between international law, state law, and local governance can be useful for at least three reasons. First, it provides a way by which to judge international laws based on their on-the-ground implementation. Human rights law, perhaps more than other parts of international law, is focused on protecting individuals. Second, legal pluralism comparisons provide a means to find improvement for state law and local implementation. International law, human rights law specifically, is in a period of rapid expansion, but local laws are still the source for what directly impacts citizens' daily lives, including water access. Third, human rights law has shown a greater degree of variety than other types of international law (such as investment), whereas state law directly mirrors the international plane. Recognizing how legal pluralism plays a role in the formation of different types of governance can improve the normative content and application of these laws.

Conclusion

The human right to water exists, but for urban areas, unpacking the details and contours of the right has been an ongoing process. Unlike many simple positive or negative rights, such as freedom of religion or protection from torture, the complex evolution and implementation of the right has been the source of debate for scholars, jurists, activists, and those hoping to improve their own water governance. These instruments are the culmination of hard work by activists and human rights lawyers alike to raise awareness about the importance of clean water and to more clearly define key issues that underlie the right, such as: quality, quantity, access, and affordability. However, the emergence of the human right to water has also caused numerous detractors, which suggests that this international law lacks effective enforcement mechanisms, and is at best hortatory, and at worst, masking critical racial, ethnic, or gendered differences in water access.

This chapter used a legal pluralism approach to compare the substantive right and the normative framework in two distinctly different urban centers: Johannesburg and Dublin. These cities provide a context for how the right to water and potentially other environmental rights can be viewed.

Johannesburg, through the South African constitution, was an early adopter of the substantive right to water. However, as shown though the *Phiri* case, the city does not have broader regulations as part of its governance to implement the substantive right. The court's ruling left in place a policy that can fail residents. However, there are still numerous reasons to be positive about the substantive right, as it provides a specific and significant means for litigants to bring their case to court. By contrast, Dublin is in a state of flux, but its systems more closely mirror the normative framework contained in the human right to water, including both academically and popularly contentious issues such as charging for water. As the case studies of Johannesburg and Dublin show, there are still significant questions pertaining to the human right to water in the urban law context, emanating in different fashions from different sources, but all particularly, asking how to provide sufficient amounts of this essential service to all people.

6 Who owns the sidewalk?

Analysing spatial reorganization amidst regulation and hierarchies in the Pondy Bazaar Street Market, Chennai, India

Padmapriya Vidhya-Govindarajan

Introduction

Soundarapandian Angadi, popularly known as Pondy Bazaar, used to be a large sprawling street market located in a prominent retail-store based area in the city of Chennai, Tamil Nadu, India. It was home to a variety of street vendors who peddled their wares in a plethora of ways, relying on visibility to booster sales among the large milieu of pedestrians, both locals and tourists, who plied the area. Often described as a space of bustling activity where one could find trinkets of every sort, for decades it was an important identifying marker in the Thyagaraya Nagar ward of the city. This chapter, in its project to examine the policy implications of legal change and in its implementation, examines the case of Pondy Bazaar and the impact of change in regulations upon its working dynamics.

On November 5, 2013, 629 vendors and pushcart settlements across the sidewalk-pavements of Pondy Bazaar and its neighbour, Usman Road (Gateway to Ranganathan Street, a retail hub of Chennai) sidewalk-pavement were moved into a single complex consisting of four storeys and four subdivided blocks within each. This move took place after a month's notice and over twenty years of attempts at regulating the area in a way that ensured that street vendors, their wares and their pushcarts did not spill into the street.[1] This chapter looks at the changes that this previously informally governed space has undergone after decades of being an important part of Chennai's street landscape, and the impact of regulation on its stakeholders. This is done through studies at two points in time – first, exactly one year after this move occurred; second, on the precipice of two years from the move.

While primarily capturing the stories of the most visible stakeholders, the street vendors of Pondy Bazaar, it also documents the views of the street vendors on Usman Road and the flower sellers of Pondy Bazaar and its neighbouring streets. In her article "Slumdog Cities: Rethinking Subaltern Urbanism" Ananya Roy rethinks intervention in urbanism through examinations of the ways in which

1 Interview with street vendors at Pondy Bazaar area at Usman Road, (Aug. 2015) (on file with author).

informality operates within urban governance of subaltern groups.[2] This chapter uses Roy's framework, reading Pondy Bazaar as the "scuffle of multiple informalities."

The first part of this chapter argues that the forms of regulation attempted are in themselves a form of informality from above – the convenient alternation of regulation and deregulation of Pondy Bazaar by the Chennai Municipal Corporation (henceforth, CMC) places its economy within, as Roy theorizes, a "grey space" that constantly flirts with illegality.[3] Simultaneously however, the path to legalizing their ownership of the space on the streets is unavailable to the vendors of Pondy Bazaar, thus denying them the ability to break this pattern. The chapter then proceeds to look at the emergent forms of spatial violence, such as the vertical alignment of a sprawling horizontal market, which has resulted in the need for once relatively harmonious street vendors to rework sales strategies as well as negotiate with each other for space.

In this context, the latter half of the chapter argues that within these informal structures there are different contestants for the sidewalk. The scramble for space created by these markets' complexes forces the sellers of different goods to form networks that push their interests forward, creating "peripheries" that are relegated to a position where they are forced to barter with other members of their own neighbourhood for extra space that they have gleaned from strategic partnerships.

Through the narratives from Pondy Bazaar and Usman road, placed against newschapter archives that cover this two-year period, the chapter attempts to map the conflicts that have emerged between the stakeholders of this ecosystem and the way the altered arrangements have created spatial hierarchies in this mini economy.

I. Overview of the Pondy Bazaar study

Conducted in two stages, the study that culminated in this chapter attempted to understand the transformation of the Pondy Bazaar Street Market in Chennai in response to the eviction of street vendors from the Pondy Bazaar–Usman Road area. The first stage was conducted a year after the move occurred. The first visit was conducted mid-August 2014 and involved no study-based verbal interaction with any of the respondents from the region.

Subsequently in November 2014, the area was revisited. Key interviews were conducted on the anniversary of the move of the vendors to the new complex (which coincided with the day of Muharram). This date is of particular importance for multiple reasons. First, the Muharram holiday, like every other national or religious holiday, is a day when most residents of Thyagaraya Nagar, as well as

2 Ananya Roy, *Slumdog Cities: Rethinking Subaltern Urbanism*, 35 Int'l J. of Urb. & Regional Res. 223–38 (2011).

3 *Id.*

other parts of Chennai, may be found in large numbers at Pondy Bazaar and Usman Road indulging in street shopping. The crowds are typically ubiquitous and street traffic soars post 5:30 pm. Secondly, a significant percentage of the street vendor population follows the religion of Islam and may have opted to choose to close shop in order to observe the cultural rituals associated with the festival. In past years, this had typically not deterred any of the shops from being open to absorb the evening influx of customers. Thirdly, the incidence of the field visit with the eve of the anniversary of the move to the complex meant that the leaders of seven *Sangams* were all present at the place and had also met to air and compile grievances and discuss the way forward.

At this point, twelve vendors of items such as toys, jewellery, shoes, clothing and miniature gifts were interviewed about their year in a new complex. Eleven out of the twelve respondents were placed on the upper first, second and third floors and only one was placed on the bottom floor. Each of the twelve respondents had originally put up stalls in the Pondy Bazaar area on the streets. Over February and March of 2015 they were revisited, and three more vendors from the bottom floor were interviewed. Additional focus was placed upon the three bargain-booksellers that continued to operate in the area.

The second stage of the study occurred between August and November 2015 – the focus here was more on the flower sellers of the Pondy Bazaar area and the street vendors who continued to operate on Usman Road, selling items such as clothing, accessories, jewellery, and toys. Twelve vendors were interviewed at this stage. Due to rain-induced flooding in December 2015, however, this stage could not be concluded within the time frame. The final set of interviews could not be conducted as both the areas were washed out, rendering significant damage to the property and stockpiles of all those who operated in the area. The results from the study can therefore only be treated as an initial set of trends and will be placed against the trends of the first stage to better map the impact of the move.

II. Locating Pondy Bazaar – subaltern urbanism on the streets?

"Think of a city and what comes to mind? It's streets. If a city's streets look interesting, the city looks interesting. If they look dull, the city looks dull," wrote Jane Jacobs when describing streets and their sidewalks as both the most important public spaces as well as vital organs of a city.[4] These words echoed in my head as I walked into Pondy Bazaar for the first time since the eviction of the hawkers from the street and their reallocation into a single four storey unit. The most striking change that I observed was the utter lack of vibrance of this once effervescent part of Thyagaraya Nagar. As my eyes grew accustomed to vastly

4 Jane Jacobs, *The Uses of Sidewalks in* SAFETY, THE DEATH AND LIFE OF GREAT AMERICAN CITIES 106–14 (Vintage Book ed. 1961).

expanded space of the road and the flood of light it brought in, I realized that there was one more very obvious absence that I hadn't noted: the absence of crowds.[5]

Pondy Bazaar, for the longest time, has been among the most crowded parts of all of Chennai. Street shopping in this region has arguably been inextricably linked to the cultural history of at least four generations of residents. Lined with small shops, the occasional push-carts, and even simply cotton bed sheets on the pavements, vendors here bore the fabled Chennai heat. Clothing, toys, books, shoes, and trinkets (both unique to the city and shipped in from all over) filled the pores of this street – with some vendors constantly moving, such that one could not find them, without significant effort, while others lined similar wares right next to each other to fight for competitive prices. Some, typically toy sellers, did not even find spots – but merely decked their wares on parked cars to engage pedestrians and retail store customers.

Visibly, Pondy Bazaar could easily be romanticized as an energetic, colourful and incredibly lively street market. However, this crowded bazaar area caused a problem – the pavements could not be easily used by pedestrians, causing issues of walkability and also congestion of traffic as a result. To fix this problem, the CMC constructed a "Hawker Complex," costing an estimated 4.3 crores in Indian rupees, with the intent of relocating the vendors from the streets to the complex.[6] This was an ad-hoc measure. The corporation did not follow the National Policy on Urban Street Vendors[7] which lays guidelines for inclusive planning, nor did they design footpaths with vendors in mind. Met with much opposition from the street vendors, the complex was an unwelcome change in scene for the most frequent sellers in the Pondy Bazaar mini economy, and stayed empty for three whole years. In 2012, the police even forcibly cleared out 100 unauthorized street vendors from the area, citing traffic and congestion as a result of the metro projects. The street vendors were finally evicted and moved into this complex in 2013, following a Madras High Court directive. The lowest floor of the complex was allocated to the sellers of flowers, fruit and other perishable goods. The lots on the floors above were allocated at random to the vendors of all the other non-perishable goods. This complex was not just for the vendors of the Pondy Bazaar stretch but also the Usman Road stretch – covering an estimate of 629 street-vendors in total.

A. Pondy Bazaar analysed through the lens of global urbanism scholarship

The first step towards locating Pondy Bazaar within literature is to see where street markets themselves fall today. Most theory within Subaltern Urbanism

5 Field Notes from Padmapriya Govindarajan (Aug. 2014) (on file with author).

6 The Hindu (2010). www.thehindu.com/news/national/tamil-nadu/Pondy-Bazaar-commercial-complex-to-be-ready-in-April/article16814039.ece.

7 Protection of Livelihood and Regulation of Street Vending Act, No. 7, Acts of Parliament, 2014 (India).

locates squatter settlements, slums or illegal housing settlements as the primary site of exercise.[8] The reason this lens is used to understand Pondy Bazaar here is because, as a review of literature would suggest, there is common ground both in terms of the context and in terms of the shape taken by slum dwellers and street vendors in navigating with informality. In Roy's words, subaltern urbanism, and the theory collective within it, attempts to "confer recognition on spaces of poverty and forms of popular agency that often remain invisible and neglected in the archives and annals of urban theory."[9] She critiques this by drawing on postcolonial theory to instead posit that there is a need for a shift in this meaning through the recognition of four categories within emergent research strategies: peripheries, urban informality, zones of exception and grey spaces.

Peripheries, she argues, are not just spaces generated through policing and control but also spaces that are generative in themselves. Often viewed as sites of degradation, Roy instead identifies them as a "site of metropolitan innovation."[10] Thus, while peripheries are demonstrative spaces of closure, they also possess the ability to transcend location. She sees them as spaces that complicate political agency and, within theory, spaces that expand the notion of subaltern urbanism.

Urban informality here is identified as a "logic through which different spatial value is produced and managed."[11] Rather than restricting it to spaces of poverty, Roy points to a flitting relationship between the formal and the informal – where spaces are arbitrarily relegated to either bases such as state or class power. Zones of exception are identified as "non-contiguous and differently administrated," drawing upon Aihwa Ong.[12] There are zones of superior privileges that coexist with denial. Ong argues that the idea of the exception is invoked against politically excluded classes when using universal ideas of humanity against them.[13] Although affected by the repercussions of these same ideas, the excluded are not allowed to draw upon them in their favour. Finally, grey spaces, Roy argues, are placed somewhere in-between this already arbitrary separation of the formal and the informal. They are spaces conferred with negative denotations, yet tolerated through exercises of sovereign power.

Locating Chennai within this framework, we see that it has had a bad track record of implementing the National Policy on Urban Street Vendors, instituted with the purpose of apportioning street ownership such that competing claims received equal weightage. This policy requires a ward-level unit that allows street vendors to participate and construction of the resultant footpath, post

8 Gautham Bhan, *This is No Longer the City I Once Knew: Evictions, the Urban Poor and the Right to the City in Millennial Delhi*, 21 Env't. & Urbanization 127 (2009).

9 Roy, *supra* note 2.

10 *Id.*

11 *Id.*

12 Aihwa Ong, Flexible Citizenship: The Cultural Logics of Transnationality 215–17 (Duke U. Press 1999).

13 *Id.*

implementation, with spaces for hawkers and street vendors in mind.[14] None of the above have been observed in the case of Pondy Bazaar-Usman Road; rather, evictions or layered constructions that are not actually on the street, like those in Pondy Bazaar, are the result. Moreover, some of these evictions often occur at the behest of residents in the areas, prioritizing these residents above those that rely on the streets for income. Street markets have always been an important feature of the Chennai landscape, however, and they have been resilient even through shifts in Chennai Municipal Development Authority plans and other urban variables in the past. In the subsequent sections, Roy's categories are drawn upon to make sense of the persistence of these markets as a result of their complicated relationship with the state.

The informal, as a category, looms large in this study of Pondy Bazaar. Jeemol Unni argues through empirical evidence that there is a growing informalization of the labour force in South Asian countries.[15] In this context, it is important to widen the concept of the "informal" as envisioned in the 1990s to take stock of the invisibility and related vulnerability of actors within the informal economy.[16] When discussing the informal economy in Accra, Ghana, Bob-Milliar and Obeng-Odoom describe informal traders as "victims of decongestion."[17] This references the fact that their lives can constantly be "on the run" – with them fleeing at the sight of authority. They describe the ways in which these victims survive attacks on the activities – through disobedience, manipulation of official discourse, and mediation through civil society.[18]

Resistance was in no way a universal strategy adopted in Pondy Bazaar but was certainly significant in the creation of spatial hierarchies. None of the vendors of Pondy Bazaar expressed a complete regret over the move. Rather, most spoke of the protection from the elements that such a move gave them. But this was dismissed in the wake of the palpable unfairness that each of them noted – the way the Usman Road vendors continued to ply on the streets. "*They never even moved here*" note some of the vendors.[19] "*Some of them (Usman road vendors) moved in, but then they chose to head right back*" note other vendors in Pondy Bazaar, with some quickly accusing them of bribing the police to turn a blind eye.[20] The vendors on the top floors point to

14 Protection of Livelihood and Regulation of Street Vending Act, No. 7, Acts of Parliament, 2014 (India).

15 Jeemol Unni, *Gender and Informality in the Labour Market in Southeast Asia*, 36 ECON. & POL. WKLY. 2630 (2001).

16 *Id.*

17 George M. Bob-Milliar & Franklin Obeng-Odoom, *The Informal Economy is an Employer, a Nuisance and a Goldmine: Multiple Representations of and Responses to Informality in Accra, Ghana*, 40 URB. ANTHROPOLOGY & STUD. CULTURAL SYS. & WORLD ECON. DEV. 263–84 (2011).

18 *Id.*

19 Interviews with street vendors, in Pondy Bazaar Usman–Road Area (Nov. 2014) (on file with author).

20 *Id.*

shuttered shops that they declare have not been opened in months. These are said to belong to the absentee owners from Usman Road. *"No one questions them. And even if they place a notice, the vendors come here once in a while just to tear down the posters."*[21]

If some of this anxiety is directed at the Usman Road vendors, a significant portion is also directed to the floors below as well.

> Most of the flower sellers decided not to move in. They instead rented out their spaces to people from the upper floors. Whoever could go there, ran there. I did not have the money, so I stayed here. Who will come up, when you can get everything in the floors below?

asks a vendor from the second floor.[22] This is a sentiment echoed by many, who feel like any chance at the competitiveness they enjoyed on the streets was taken away from them. The fact that most are resigned to their fate while a few, with better savings, get ahead, is the final blow for street vendors who did not have the ability to strategically locate themselves within the inconvenient structure of the complex.

Drawing upon Roy's critique of Appadurai's "governmentality from below," Bandhyopadhyay argues that the deep democracy practice that links NGOs to state and world institutions is what generates consent from the poor in favour of massive urban renewals that result in the displacement of the poor.[23] Roy's critique reveals how "this in fact points to potential sites of complicity and practices of compromise effected at the deeper structural changes for the Urban poor."[24]

In the case of Pondy Bazaar, the streets, as a result of the move, are far emptier and far wider than anyone can remember them ever being. The reactions to this emptiness, however, are mixed. Archiving this issue in the news chapters of the 2013–15 period provides a primary indicator of this mixture. Residents of Thyagaraya Nagar, the area these streets are located in, are reported to be much happier at the reduced traffic congestion. Buyers, on the other hand, are reported as nostalgic. The CMC is professed as invested in incorporating more changes that make Thyagaraya Nagar a less traffic-filled area. The street vendors' stances, however, are far from prominent in the media's attention.

B. A closer look at field notes from Pondy Bazaar

The interviews seem to find strong resonances with Roy's critique. *"We moved as soon as they asked us to"* said one vendor, as his friends who are watching the interview nod their heads.

21 *Id.*

22 *Id.*

23 Ritajyoti Bandhyopadhyay, *Politics of Archiving: Hawkers and Pavement Dwellers in Calcutta*, 35 Dialectical Anthropology 295 (2010).

24 Roy, *supra* note 2.

> They gave us one month to ponder over this, but what could we even think about? They call this a Bazaar. A Bazaar should be on the streets. Where we could stop the walkers and peddle our wares. But we moved when they asked us to. We asked them to give us 10-foot by 10-foot plots. Instead, they gave us 4 by 4. Did you know that there were no spaces in between the plots?[25]

The lack of promise fulfilment in the face of their compliance seems to hit several of them quite hard as they proceed to explain how they restructured the plots themselves to ensure more walking space. Almost all of them spoke of the investment in metal scaffolding to better delineate the plot lines. A few interviewees have also said that the Corporation (CMC) inspector who came by soon after these were implemented verbally praised their efforts at working together to convert the space into one more conducive for sales. This was particularly highlighted by the vendors in an attempt to establish their own attempts at complying with and making peace with the move.

The compliance in the move is strategically reiterated as they list the unfulfilled parts of the bargain – the size, the divisions, the provision of ATMs, upgraded generators. These promises were not all made at the time of the move, however, they say. Over subsequent visits within the first three months, they aired their grievances. For the first time, officials were all too willing to listen. As the months drew on, their representative drew up a list of demands to be presented at each meeting. *"The lists grew shorter – but not because they were realized. Only because we hoped that some of the demands would at least be met,"* said one vendor ruefully.[26]

Arvind Rajagopal seems to note this complicated relationship between those typically identified as "encroachers" and the rungs of authority – in the Pondy Bazaar case this would refer to the inspectors from the CMC and the local government authorities of the Thyagaraya Nagar ward.[27] He argues that the very issue of encroachment cannot arise unless sanctioned by the relevant political bosses and ward officers. While it is visibly evident that very few flower sellers have chosen to actually stay at Pondy Bazaar, the crowd at Usman Road, particularly under the bridge, does not betray who has chosen to stay and who has left. While a couple of the interviewed vendors said that they moved from Pondy Bazaar about six months after being relocated, most declare that they have known no spot other than Usman Road for as long as they have been in the trade. *"No one will admit to it"* laughs one respondent.

> They won't tell you even if they have actually moved. It isn't that they fear the police. The police don't care very much – they come by once in a while

25 Interview with street vendors from Pondy Bazaar area at Usman Road (Feb. 2015) (on file with author).

26 *Id.*

27 Arvind Rajagopal, *Violence of Commodity Aesthetics*, 19 ECON. & POL. WKLY. 91–113 (2001).

> and we pack up on those days. We come back as soon as they have gone. They know this. We know this. But still no one will admit to having moved.[28]

Looking at the streets of Mumbai and Kolkata, Rajagopal draws upon ethnography, which seems to place hawkers in the position of the "new class enemy."[29] In Mumbai particularly, the discourse seemed to be surrounding that of hygiene and appearance. Footpaths are viewed as spaces encroached by hawkers, and the plight of pedestrians is pitied, according to some, while others view support for hawkers as "patronization of vermin."[30] In this scenario, the shopkeepers also turn against them, seeing them as people who divert business. But this is not the sole narrative – hawkers are also seen as providing a range of services for drivers, masons, carpenters, security staff, etc. The heterogeneity of hawkers' activity allows them to cater in a manner that sellers in a formal sector cannot. Rajagopal further notes that hawkers have also learnt to use the courts instrumentally. Some appeal for injunctions against demolitions or evictions. If the case is lost they appeal higher, attempting to secure themselves in better economic positions than what the street can directly offer them.

Interestingly, at the Usman Road end of the site of study, a stretch of shops have combined together to launch a case in the court for either a licence to ply on the street or a provision of an independent Usman Road complex, similar to the Pondy Bazaar one. Some express scepticism as well – *"It isn't so much about wanting a space as it is about making sure the authorities don't evict us. For as long as the case is in the court, no one can make us move."*[31]

But whether they see it as an elevation in status, a compulsion to comply with the law, a loss-inducing inconvenience, a possibility of permanent stockpiling, or one of many other possibilities, it is important to note that within even the seemingly homogenous category of Street Vendors, multiple opinions and ways of navigating these laws persist. In this context, it is important to see how these navigations can be understood, all the while placed against the larger context of spatial transformation.

III. Informality from above: understanding the eviction and the incidence of costs

Most street vendors that peddle in Pondy Bazaar trace the origins of their jobs to the generations of at least their grandfathers, but only a handful can proudly

28 Interview with street vendors from Pondy Bazaar area at Usman Road (Oct. 2015) (on file with author).

29 Rajagopal, *supra* note 27.

30 Rajagopal, *supra* note 27.

31 Interview with street vendors at the Pondy Bazaar area at Usman Road (Oct. 2015) (on file with author).

display a laminated copy of their official licence. The reason for this is the scrapping of licence distribution since 1993, when the government realized that single licences issued were used to set up multiple shops.[32] However, no official legislation followed to order the eviction of illegal encroachments or stoppage of new ones until 1996.[33] Despite the presence of legal resolutions, nearly six terms of State Governments and Municipal Corporations have continued to informally allow the strictly extra-legal commercial transactions in Pondy Bazaar.[34] The nature of the informality of this economy is derived from the purposeful dereg ulation of this entire stretch of commercial activity.

Drawing upon Roy's definition, deregulation is indicated as calculated informality, involving purposeful action and planning, where the seeming withdrawal of regulatory power creates a logic of resource allocation, accumulation and authority.[35] For over two decades, no legal systems of regulation intervened with the peddling and hawking, licences were not demanded, and security and traffic management were both handled by the corporation. Despite the occasional resurgence of dialogue about the "illegality" of these settlements in mainstream media, no action towards investigating the legality of the hawkers' claims or permanent eviction of any hawkers was contemplated. The hawkers in return, have particularly strong political leanings.

With the passage of the Street Vendors Bill, however, pressure was placed on state governments to rework the provision of space in roads and rights to street vendors. The Bill demanded that roads be spatially restructured to accommodate the vendors.[36]

In Chennai, action was put off for nearly two whole years before the ultimate eviction of hawkers. Spatial reorganization of these roads would involve taking action upon two categories of stakeholders: shop owners and street vendors. While most visibly the encroachment upon the road occurs because of street vendors, over half the footpath is seized by shop owners who extend their display to attract customers. These, however, continued to be designated as formal settlement by the State and the move was directed only at street vendors, who were given a month to evict, as the only way the corporation could comply with the demands of the Bill was to allocate a separate space for street vendors.[37] Here again, the logic of the exception is evoked in the scrabble for the footpath. The Bill, cited as the larger criterion for the move, is evoked against vendors on the street. As "grey spaces," they were allowed an avenue to articulate claims, but

32 Interview on *Street Vendors Field Work*, Transparent Chennai: Blog (June 20, 2012) www.transparentchennai.com/street-vendors-field-work/.

33 *Id.*

34 *Id.*

35 Roy, *supra* note 2.

36 Protection of Livelihood and Regulation of Street Vending Act, No. 7, Acts of Parliament 2014 (India).

37 Interviews with street vendors, in Pondy Bazaar Usman-Road Area (Nov. 2014) (on file with author).

due to the arbitrary ability of the corporation to confer and revoke their status of legality and illegality, the demands were eventually sidelined. This valorization of comparatively more elite informality and criminalization of the subaltern informality produced an uneven distribution of value. In Roy's terms, this can be said to create an urban geography of not just spatial value, but also of economic value.[38]

To begin with, the move took a few informal forms in itself. Rather than make room for legality through encouraging the application of hawking licences now, the regulation of street vendors continued to happen through informal systems. The most direct impact of this was seen once the last street vendors agreed to move. The demand of 10ft by 10ft spaces had not been adhered to and the allocations for each store resembled a 4ft by 5ft area with inadequate spacing allocated between stores. No warehousing was provided and the street vendors had to pay for their own uninsured metal scaffolding and walls as separators. Promises of items such as ATMs and generators to combat power fluctuations, which were made at the meetings held with the authorities prior to the move, did not materialize.[39]

Street vendors, resigned, restructured the space to allow for more movement of customers as well as quick exit routes in case of a fire. Approximately Rs 30,000–50,000 was spent by each store-owner on the construction and decoration of their unit. Meanwhile, some of the actual store owners have more recently begun to rent out the spaces in front of their shops to hawkers, on the fringe roads of the Pondy Bazaar area, which are much less policed.[40]

The returns, however, did not match the investment. Even on Muharram day, the footfall within the complex's ground floor could at best be described as paltry. Several street vendors did not even show up for the evening traffic, choosing to stay home and observe the rituals instead. Street vendors could more often be seen chatting to one another over tea than handling a rush of bargaining customers traditionally associated with Pondy Bazaar, as was typical when on the streets. These trends got worse as one moved up the storeys. The number of customers dwindled leaving behind a ratio of seven or even twelve shopkeepers per customer.[41]

The absence of the advantages of the streets – convenience of movement, space for display, chance for split second purchases, etc. took its toll on profits, according to the street vendors. Most of them estimate that they earn around 20% of what they did in the years before the policing; now, they barely make enough for sustenance. They do not see a clear scope for upward movement either, since the successful foundation of this manner of sales was indeed the street as an entity. These events, through the lens of Roy's definition of

38 Roy, *supra* note 2.

39 Field Notes by Padmapriya Govindarajan, (Nov. 2014) (on file with author).

40 Interview with street vendors at the Pondy Bazaar area at Usman Road (Oct. 2015) (on file with author).

41 Field Notes by Padmapriya Govindarajan, (Nov. 2014) (on file with author).

informality, portray a relationship that is both arbitrary and fickle and yet is the site of considerable state power and violence.[42] The very impermanence that sustained the commercial economy of Pondy Bazaar was used as an instrument to break down the system and an excuse to avoid compensation.

IV. Auto constructed peripheries and geographically differentiated power relations: understanding the profit distribution

Most street vendors do not entirely hate the new situations that they have been thrust into. They see the permanence of their new settlement as a promotion up the ladder. They see the infrastructural expenditure as an investment. They recognize that there are advantages – like that of protecting their goods from monsoon conditions and extreme summers and also the stability to having a shop with a roof overhead. However, as one walks up the storeys the number of closed shops increase in the same proportion as the number of customers dwindles. If those that stay see enough of a reason to not move back into the streets and risk trysts with the law, why did the others leave?

The reasons for this are a little more complex. All the street vendors who are part of this study seem to suggest that on one hand they saw this as a move up the social ladder with the gain of a permanent unit, but on the other hand, they are unhappy with the way the distribution occurred in the first place. Allotments in the complex were made through the selection of lots for the first, second, third and fourth storeys to the hawkers of Usman Road and Pondy Bazaar, but were allotted as a block in the ground floor alone. This was because the entire ground floor was allocated to the vendors of perishable goods – the flower and fruit vendors.[43] The aim of this policy was to ensure that their wares were not affected by too much movement and similarly so that the liberal usage of water by the flower vendors would not affect the others. The way it played out was different.

The politically charged megastores on Usman Road have allowed street vendors to rent the spaces of sidewalk in front of them. Most of the street vendors native to the region chose to seize this opportunity rather than risk losses. The rest took advantage of the lax attitude of policemen in the region to risk once more setting up their wares on the street. They continue to enjoy the patronage of their old customers and the incidental shopping crowd while having their risks offset by the patronage of well-connected megastores. Rent seems to be a small price to pay.

The absence of Usman Road street vendors ensured that the upper storeys of Pondy Bazaar grew more vacant and thus attracted fewer customers. This was worsened by the policy adopted by the vendors of perishable goods. They chose to rent out the entire ground floor to street vendors that wanted it and either

42 *Id.*

43 Field Notes by Padmapriya Govindarajan, (Nov. 2014) (on file with author).

made nearly double their previous earnings off rent alone or supplemented the same by moving to the complex's sidewalk intermittently to avoid detection by authorities, and sometimes even plying other parts of Chennai.

The advantages of a ground floor shop were self-evident: some commonly cited advantages are that people of all ages would find the wares they needed on one floor, no one was required to traverse stairs or enter the elevator which had a habit of getting stuck due to power fluctuations. Those in the ground floor were eager to make good of permanent shops by supplementing the same with profits garnered by strategically locating themselves on the most accessible floor. Thus they effectively solely attracted the customers who would have in the past had a chance to walk by all 629 stores on the street, and split them amidst their 120 alone by virtue of their location on the most accessible part of the complex.

While the number of customers these 120 vendors attracted still did not match the ones they saw in the street even during peak festive seasons despite being on the most accessible floor, their ability to arrest the customers in one floor made them the new core of the street vendors system. As in Holston's analysis, these forms of settlements constructed peripheries within the once openly and evenly competitive commercial zone.[44] The geographical distinction and its spatial advantages delineated the customer base in a manner that gave the Ground Floor hawkers more legitimacy than all the upper storeys. Despite the unintentional nature of this delineation, even within the informal structure, a periphery and core are created with differential power relations that manifest as profits.

Conclusions

This study provides an understanding of the vendors' perception of authority, legality, threat and change. The market vendors' relationship with the authorities across sites seems to be very complicated. The respondents from Thyagaraya Nagar are very aware of the fact that the policemen, for instance, have the ability to evict them. But this realization of power and precariousness doesn't translate into fear. In fact, the constant possibility of eviction is discussed in a very matter of fact manner. The monthly visits by policemen and the need to completely shut down business on these days are viewed as routine rather than actual tussles with the authority, as the media portrays it. Most respondents passed this off – talking about their tea-time sessions with police officers, or laughing at the monthly raid incidents without batting an eyelid.[45] Neighbouring stores narrated radically opposite experiences regarding these run-ins, but at the same time, there were no references made towards fear or deference in terms of these relationships. Rather they seem to just be another part of the informal fabric this economy operated in and was governed by.

44 Roy, *supra* note 2.

45 Interview with street vendors at Pondy Bazaar area at Usman Road, (Aug. 2015) (on file with author).

Easily identifying routines in their lives, the street vendors spoken to did not take very easily to terms such as risk or threat. There are no advantages or disadvantages, and it is unfair to draw vending into this binary. Rather, the routines change and revert back depending on changing circumstances. Authority, legality and economic uncertainties all fall within the mechanisms of street vending. For something to be a threat, the vendors needed to perceive it as external. While several people identified aspects of street sales as discomfiting and uncomfortable, the identification of a threat from street vending by nature as an occupation only arose if prompted. More easily, it was just another aspect they had to contend with – it came with the job.

Legality was not something anyone particularly shied away from talking about. Several vendors were free to discuss the absence of rent requirements and even the necessity to bribe. Legality was referred to as simply something they did not have. "Care of platform" was a term heard often when describing their circumstances, and nonchalant references to the associated uncertainties came with this.[46] This lack of legality was connected back to their vulnerability to unannounced eviction – but it also did not really feature as an aspiration. In vague terms, references were made to being legal as upward mobility – but at the same time no decision was expressed at the lack of a particular avenue. It seems that legality is more than just a concept, rather than an abject positive or negative position to attain. Without drawing on its language, ownership of the streets, the spaces and membership of the economy was freely discussed. Ownership, to these street vendors, came from presence and persistence – the notion of illegality could only interrupt it, never break it.

Change features hugely in the experiences discussed. Some vendors dealing in items such as unbranded but fancy footwear and personalized keychains find that developments around them, such as increasing influxes of tourists or outward expansion of the city, are welcome. They believe that urban development changes the perception of the place and makes it more "happening," brings in more tourists and thereby customers, and also brings in relocation of famous people, which give them respect for being in a certain workspace.[47] Vendors dealing in utility, for example plastics such as buckets and mugs, find it more difficult to cope with urban development because chain stores that sell cheap but quality goods are popping up, and they are unable to compete with these stores. Some vendors simply perceive it as good or bad, without according actual positive or negative value to the terms, since more than anything else, it is a feeling that they relate to business, but aren't sure about what exactly the relationship is in descriptive terms.

In sum, however, it appears that it was not change that really bothers street vendors, but stasis. It is particularly important for policy makers to note that while change was accepted as part of the parcel, it often came with an avenue for

46 Field Notes by Padmapriya Govindarajan, (Nov. 2014) (on file with author).

47 Field Notes by Padmapriya Govindarajan, (Feb. 2015) (on file with author).

mobility in some direction. Change involved renegotiation – never just uncritical acceptance of all that came with it. It was the stasis that immediately followed change that seemed to bother – the inability to effect change, rather than inability to cope with it.

The information gained from the case study is particularly indicative given how recent the move is. Even within these early trends, two things are clear. The nexus of informality that characterizes the relationship between the shopkeepers and the State can be used as a tool for negotiating and making spaces by street vendors. However, power play within this nexus still tilts on the side of the government as the same tools have the ability to water down the necessary conditions under which the informal economy thrives. Moreover, even in this climate of informality, all stakeholders do not negotiate in the same manner. Roy's analysis outlines the possibility of the emergence of a periphery within the periphery of informal settlements like slum developments. In the case of the former Pondy Bazaar-Usman Road street market, the negotiations that spatially favour some street vendors result in the creation of a core-periphery environment with the removal of the street as an equalizer, with the upper floors being relegated to the status of this periphery within.

7 'Better city, better life?'
Urban transformation and conflict management in the global south

Malcolm MacLaren

Introduction

This chapter constitutes the conceptual basis for a multi-stage research project that addresses an acute concern of contemporary politics internationally, namely urban areas in the Global South, as settings for group conflict, and as sites for governance efforts and experiments.

The project studies the dynamics of violent conflict, peace-making, and state-building in an urban context. It aims from a public law perspective to identify strategies to meet challenges of urban transformation and to develop policy initiatives to manage (potential and real) conflict. Which strategies and initiatives are conceivable, plausible, and advisable in such settings?

Two political principles will be focused on (in general terms and in specific cases), namely subsidiarity and democracy. Can and if so, how far can, the competences from national and/or constituent unit 'levels' to the city 'level' or the democratization of local government systems (including via direct democracy) be transferred to the sought-for 'Better City, Better Life'?[1] According to their impact on conflict management amid urban transformation, the principles of subsidiarity and democracy might serve as guidelines in government design.[2]

1 The 2010 Shanghai World Expo's slogan was 'Better City, Better Life', the Expo's aim being to stimulate discussion of 'urban maladies'. The Expo highlighted the importance of the issue of urbanization and urbanism today, especially in relation to Asia. *See* Shanghai World Expo: Living the Dream, Economist (Apr. 29, 2010), www.economist.com/node/16009079. The city of Shanghai is itself an example of a growing and diversifying urban population. *Id.*

2 The phenomena of urbanization and urbanism are multifaceted and complex. To an extent they are also country-/city-specific. As such, my analysis benefitted considerably from the international, comparative, and interdisciplinary perspectives at the Second Annual International and Comparative Urban Law Conference in Paris, France, June 29, 2015.

I. An overview of global urbanization

My starting point is that the contemporary worldwide trend to urbanize is both irresistible and potentially destabilizing politically.[3] Cities[4] are spaces in which great numbers of people and differences come in contact, as well as places where interpersonal tensions are particularly palpable. Indeed, urbanization may itself spur consciousness and valorization of group/individual identity; it may encourage social differentiation where differences were not previously perceived. Tensions such as these can give rise to public disgruntlement, complaints, protest, and *in extremis* open violence. Tensions may relate (singly or together) to: immigration from in- or outside of the state, but in either case, new movements of people threatening old arrangements (who, what, and where is to be 'the community' now?); to plurality of languages, religions, races, etc., and attempts, official and unofficial, at integration, accommodation, segregation, or assimilation; distribution of wealth (class-based affiliation), access to services/resources (such as potable water, clear air, adequate shelter), as well as provision of infrastructure (hard and soft); and cultural differences, urban areas being traditionally more tolerant and cosmopolitan than rural areas, as well as being settings of ideational strife and even revolt against illiberal and authoritarian states.

Saskia Sassen rightly calls 'the large complex city, especially if global … a new frontier zone. Actors from different worlds meet there'. These actors make competing, and sometimes contradictory, claims to the city '[B]ut', the US doyenne of urban sociology observes, 'there are no clear rules of engagement'.[5] The city is, in other words, a new, authentic reference point for many millions around the world, and governance must be matched to their actual horizons. Since issues of urban transformation can exceed existing political competences, legal provisions, and financial means, a redefinition of sovereignties – individual, local, regional, and national – seems called for.

Decision-makers, citizens, and academics have responded to this phenomenon by proposing various reforms of political-administrative structures. Foremost among proposals are more power, money, and respect for cities (nationally and internationally); novel orderings in- and outside state structures;[6] wider opportunities to

3 More than half of humanity lives in cities today, and more than one million people in the developing world move from the countryside to a city every five days. City dwellers' proportion of the world's population could reach 75% in 2050. *See* Schumpeter, *Mayors and Mammon*, ECONOMIST (July 13, 2013), www.economist.com/news/business/21581695-city-leaders-are-increasingly-adopting-business-methods-and-promoting-business-mayors-and-mammon.

4 'City' is understood here as the general term for all types of conurbation, while 'urbanization' refers to the growth of cities and 'urbanism' to life in cities. *See generally* Boris Graizbord, *Governance of Megacities in Federal Orders, in* FORUM OF FEDERATIONS (ED.), 4TH INTERNATIONAL CONFERENCE ON FEDERALISM: CONFERENCE READER 468–70 (2007).

5 Saskia Sassen, *The City: Today's Frontier Zone*, GLOCALISM: J. CULTURE, POL. & INNOVATION 3, 3 (2014), www.glocalismjournal.net/issues/global-cities/articles/the-city-todays-frontier-zone.kl.

6 *E.g.*, partnerships between local authorities, between local and other governments, and/or between local authorities and private agencies.

participate in political processes; and a larger say in local developments.[7] The ideals of political decentralization and popular participation have been emphasized thereby as fundamental norms.[8] Indeed, in many places, 'bits of territory, authority and rights, once ensconced in *national institutional* frames' have already been re-mixed and local democracy partly allowed.[9]

II. (Re-)assessing governance

In my research project, I argue that leadership and regulation of cities must be (re-)assessed in keeping with contemporary urban transformation. I presume thereby that law and ordering here are not predefined or natural, but are constantly invented, developed, and appropriated by actors in society. I also presume that the 'business' of governments in urban areas includes managing conflict as well as creating conditions for economic growth, planning new subdivisions, and like conventional tasks.[10] Further, I presume that public politics (as practised by a city's leadership, administration, and inhabitants) can either escalate conflict or play a significant role in its de-escalation, thereby bettering life in cities. The success or failure of different approaches in turn depends on the degree that 'bottom-up' governance is pursued in cities.[11]

If these presumptions are correct, what is the most promising governance approach to meeting inhabitants' demands (qua needs, values, and interests) and to fulfilling universally desired ends (i.e. a stable environment of human security, social cohesion, and economic prosperity) amid urban transformation? In principle, there is a wide spectrum of alternatives, at one extreme 'authoritarian, supra-community reformation' and at the other 'democratic, territorial polycentrism'. What does analysis (theoretical and empirical) recommend as to the political

7 Sociologists observe a greater appreciation of smaller political units and an increased support for co-determination in Western society over the last decades. Voters have tended to resist limitations being placed on local governments and municipalities being consolidated. *See, e.g.*, Silke Marzluff, *Boom der Bürgerbeteiligung*, DER SONNTAG, Feb. 10, 2013, www.zze-freiburg.de/assets/pdf/2013-02-10Boom-der-Brgerbeteiligung-Interview-m-Silke-Marzluff.pdf.

8 *See* United Cities and Local Governments, *Decentralization and Local Democracy in the World: First Global Report*, 302 (2008).

9 Saskia Sassen, *When the Center No Longer Holds: Cities as Frontier Zones*, CITIES, 4, May 7, 2012, www.saskiasassen.com/PDFs/publications/when-the-center-no-longer-holds.pdf (emphasis added).

10 Indeed, fulfilling these tasks (e.g., deciding where housing should be built to provide for population growth, or deciding what the desired social and economic activities of government locally are) may destabilize group relations in the city according to related hopes and fears, advantages and disadvantages.

11 According to some commentators, sustainable development could contribute to the solution of conflict in the Global South, regardless of origin (economic, political, religious, or cultural). *See, e.g.*, DOUG SAUNDERS, ARRIVAL CITY: THE FINAL MIGRATION AND OUR NEXT WORLD 294 (2010) (citing the mayor of Amsterdam).

discretion, administrative authority, fiscal autonomy, constitutional status, and like structures that local governments[12] should possess in future?

It is to be noted that the possibilities for, and potential of, particular public programmes for conflict prevention and resolution are acknowledged but not considered here.[13] Likewise, civil society's role in conflict – how unofficial forms of governance (such as interest groups, citizens' committees, community organizations, and ethnic leaders) encourage order in cities – is not examined here. These can, of course, work for (or against) coexistence and comprehension in a heterogeneous population. Joan Clos speaks of building 'community institutions and mechanisms capable of circumventing the disagreements, misunderstandings and local conflicts that get in the way of the kind of urbanisation that generates prosperity'.[14] Instead, the present chapter focuses on how – i.e. the structures and the processes by which – government is to cope with the consequences of urban transformation.

III. A bottom-up approach?

Many commentators have identified cities as a favourable arena for collective decision-making in view of the proximity between inhabitants and government.[15] In keeping with proposals commonly made, a 'bottom-up' approach to urban governance will be hypothesized here as ideal in the context of protean surroundings and pressing urges. Subsidiarity (as a determinant for the distribution of competences)[16] and democracy (as a basis for public legitimacy) can – should – serve as guidelines for governance locally.

How then are these fundamental norms, subsidiarity and democracy, understood here? For its part, subsidiarity is a principle to guide division and interaction between levels of public authority. On the prevailing understanding, the smaller political community is to take care of its own matters of concern (be that through deliberation, decision-making, or implementation); only those matters

12 'Local government' is defined here as 'a legally-prescribed government structure directly interacting with its constituent population without any other order of government in between'. Nico Steytler, *Comparative Conclusions, in* Id, Local Government and Metropolitan Regions in Federal Systems 396 (2009).

13 These might include government attempts to promote human rights and harmonious relationships in the city through multicultural dialogue, youth exchange, school materials, or press and communication strategies of local government. *See* First World Conference on City Diplomacy, *Hague Agenda on City Diplomacy, Article III* (June 13, 2008), www.uclg.org/sites/default/files/EN_474_fin_eng_the_hague_agenda_on_city_diplomacy_0.pdf.

14 Joan Clos, *Towards a New Urban Agenda*, LSE Cities (last visited Nov. 13, 2017), https://lsecities.net/media/objects/articles/towards-a-new-urban-agenda/en-gb.

15 Philipp Rode & Priya Shankar, *Governing Cities, Steering Futures*, LSE Cities (last visited Nov. 13, 2017), https://lsecities.net/media/objects/articles/governing-cities-steering-futures/en-gb.

16 Following, for example, the UN Habitat 'Guidelines on Decentralization and the Strengthening of Local Authorities' (2005), for which the principle of subsidiarity provides the rationale.

that exceed its specific interests and regulatory ability should be left to a larger political community. The principle's consequent application means that local authorities (executive, legislative, and administrative) should be assigned public tasks as much as possible through decentralization, empowerment, and related capacity-building.[17]

Augmenting the power of this level of government is alleged to have the following advantages. Local government, being nearest to the inhabitants, is most likely to be aware of their needs, to be a source of innovative solutions, as well as to react adequately and quickly.[18] The principle's application is also said to improve administrative clarity, transparency, and expertise.[19] Policy initiatives of the local government will *ceteris paribus* have a positive impact.[20]

Democracy is here taken to be more than simply holding 'periodic, fair and free elections'. It is broadly understood as the ideal of dialogue among inhabitants and as the opportunity for all to participate equally and effectively in common affairs. An increase in 'democratic intensity' can be achieved through, for example, granting voting rights or establishing direct democratic institutions.

As such, democracy embodies inherent values (above all, recognition of human dignity and self-determination as distinct individuals). Democracy is also – in this context, more importantly – an instrument by which the collective may control, qua direct and discipline, political power generally and government policies in particular. Ideally, having the right to vote enables citizens to choose the public services, and more broadly, to realize the society, that they prefer.

In short, the application of these two principles is to stimulate government's proximity to citizens, for the closer and more representative government is vis-à-vis the people, the better it works. The *locus classicus* is the autonomous municipality offering citizens extensive political rights common in Switzerland.

IV. Prospects for positive change

My analysis indicates that the application of the subsidiarity principle and the realization of its vaunted benefits are elusive. In practice, tasks and competences do not allow themselves to be distributed neatly and consequently among government levels – let alone to the lowest possible level according to prevailing notions of subsidiarity. 'Gargantua' (e.g. one big unit through amalgamation)

17 *See generally* Walter Haller et al., Allgemeines Staatsrecht 166–67 (5th ed. 2013).

18 *See* Posting of Shachi Sanghvi, Centre for Urb. Equity, to H-Announce Academic Announcements (Sept. 30, 2015), https://networks.h-net.org/node/73374/announcements/80135/international-conference-urban-planning-governance-and-design.

19 *See generally* Jean Blondel, Comparative Government: An Introduction 229–33 (2nd ed. 1995).

20 Centralization's own advantages should also be taken into account: *ceteris paribus* centralization improves task fulfilment by promoting 'economies of scale, efficiency of service delivery, better strategic planning, and management of spillover effects'. Steytler, *supra* note 12, at 401.

may not be the ideal model for the government of a city, as the principle's advocates argue,[21] but 'grassroots' (e.g. many small units through fragmentation) is not either. An expert on urban law puts it bluntly: '[r]omanticising local-decision-making is not a good idea'.[22]

A few examples that directly concern conflict management in local government systems should explain this finding. First, arguments in favour of subsidiarity presume that a local government has been already constituted and is willing and able to act. That presumes too much in cases of 'divided cities'.[23] Local government will not play the mediating role among groups foreseen if the city in question is segregated politically as well as socially, i.e. if actors will not serve their neighbours and the general good but pursue their own interests.[24] Integrating groups at a 'higher level' or putting the issue in a larger context may militate against conflict. These strategies could promote new common values and enlarge the space for balancing interests,[25] thereby preventing and resolving tense standoffs.[26] In addition, it is generally recognized that for the sake of conflict management socio-economic disparities in urban areas (in services such as education and security) should be reduced. Where political systems are dispersed and divided, local governments may not have the finances, know-how, or personnel (relative at least to regional or national government) needed to affect such policies. In fact, local governments in the Global South typically lack the capacity to diminish disparities.[27] Finally, many cities in the developing world suffer from destabilizing population flows that must be urgently dealt with. Such problems are, however, difficult to solve, because they are 'generated by systems of power and wealth [that cities] neither originate nor control'.[28] Insofar as states originate

21 Put concretely, '[t]he total political community in a city of three million population may not be an appropriate decision-making mechanism in planning a local playground'. Vincent Ostrom et al., *The Organization of Government in Metropolitan Areas: A Theoretical Inquiry*, 55 Am. Pol. Sci. Rev. 836 (1961).

22 Gerald Frug, *Who Decides Who Decides*, LSE Cities (last visited Nov. 13, 2017), https://lsecities.net/media/objects/articles/who-decides-who-decides/en-gb.

23 *See generally* Scott A. Bollens, City and Soul in Divided Societies (2011).

24 A corollary is that local officials will be all-the-less able to draw on 'resources of consent, goodwill, Good Samaritan values, community spirit, compliance, and collective public action' in governing the city. Anwar Shah & Sana Shah, *The New Vision of Local Governance and the Evolving Roles of Local Governments*, in Anwar Shah, Local Governance in Developing Countries 16 (2006).

25 *See* Leila Tania, *Strategic Variants: How the Conflict Between Georgia and Abkhazia Can Be Settled*, CA&CC Press (last visited Nov. 13, 2017), www.ca-c.org/journal/2003/journal_eng/cac-05/05.taneng.shtml.

26 Local conflicts may, of course, be an extension of national conflicts, which reignite, exacerbate, or intensify them. Without national reconciliation, local reconciliation is unlikely.

27 *See generally* Arnold Koller et al., Principles of Federalism: Guidelines for Good Federal Practices – A Swiss Contribution 48–51 (2012).

28 *Democracy in Crisis: An Interview with Dr. Benjamin Barber*, 11 Democracy & Soc'y 22 (2014).

or can control these, cooperation with the national government is imperative for effective governance locally.

Put otherwise, urban transformation in the Global South, if not also in the Global North,[29] poses novel challenges vis-à-vis the principle of subsidiarity and raises questions about the appropriateness of regulating state organization accordingly in the present context. Foremost are 'scale' problems. (Governments may be 'too big for the small problems in life but too small for the big problems', as the saying goes.) These and other problems subvert subsidiarity's relevance and content as a political guideline. Coping with urban transformation in practice does not simply require a distribution of powers among different governments, with powers being allocated by default to local government based on notions of 'freedom', 'own responsibility', and 'self-initiative'. A 'full transfer' of competences to a local government that is 'fully independent of the devolving authority and that has clear geographic and legally recognised [...] boundaries within which to exercise its authority and perform its public functions'[30] proves illusory as regards conflict management and contemporary urban transformation.

Given the problematic nature of subsidiarity as a guideline, the challenges of urban transformation call for a *holistic* governance approach. Ours is an age of 'fuzzy' and 'fluid' boundaries – here notably in terms of demography (as demonstrated in the newer movements of people worldwide) and geography (in globalization's transcending of borders).[31] It should also be politically and legally. Public authority is to be allocated to multiple centres, and it is to be exercised according to a certain ethos of coexistence, namely respect, mutual support, and loyalty.[32] Perhaps this change in approach is best captured by regarding 'levels' of government non-hierarchically as 'orders', the orders as equal 'parts' of a larger 'whole' (i.e. necessary but not sufficient), and the whole as a *continuum*, extending from the neighbourly to the universal. At all events, governments must cooperate productively on issues of urbanization and urbanism: 'relationships are more important than structures per se'.[33] Initiatives run

29 In many developed countries, 'the increasingly dispersed, fragmented, and divided nature' of urban areas poses new problems for effective intergovernmental and political representation. *See* United Cities and Local Governments, *supra* note 8, at 273.

30 United Cities and Local Governments, *Decentralisation Processes at a Crossroads: State of Affairs and Perspectives* 2 (2010), www.uclg-decentralisation.org/sites/default/files/concept_paper_cglu_comision_descentralizacion_EN.pdf.

31 'Not only is urbanization increasingly reaching everywhere, everywhere is increasingly reaching into the city'. P.D. Smith, *Big Smokes*, Times Literary Supplement 10 (Feb. 4, 2011) (quoting Edward Soja).

32 Ideally, cooperation between orders will be directed at generating common advantages and not compensating for respective disadvantages. *See* Wolf Linder, Schweizerische Demokratie: Institutionen, Prozesse, Perspektiven 192–95 (2nd ed. 2005).

33 Steytler, *supra* note 12, at 435. Notably, this alternative approach increases the need for mechanisms that ensure that interactions between the different orders are managed peacefully and productively. These mechanisms should include recourse to conflict settlement, as conflict between the orders is likely to ensue.

the risk otherwise of being piecemeal and incomplete as well as uncoordinated and even at cross-purposes.[34]

The situation of cities undergoing transformation is also – inevitably and irreducibly – complex and should be reflected in government systems. Rather than propose a single institutional model for all urban areas, 'tailor-made' solutions should be sought in response to management challenges in specific cities. Competences cannot be expected to be coterminous, either as between government branches as regards an urban challenge or symmetrical as regards all, the same for each and every case of urban transformation, or for that matter, exclusive to particular governments.[35]

Diachronically, it must be acknowledged in the re-formation of government systems that cities undergoing transformation are very dynamic and that the patterns of social interaction, and with them the challenges of conflict management, will change. Government designs should therefore provide no more than a rough guideline; flexibility in arrangements and operation must be maintained so as to adapt to continually changing circumstances and conditions.[36]

For its part, the policy prescription of augmenting local democracy (not local government) for the sake of conflict management also proves problematic upon closer analysis. Many dilemmas present themselves in practice. The more sensible strategy, in the Global South at least, may be to pursue an objective alternative to augmenting local democracy. Specifically, is enhancing the effectiveness and efficiency of governance efforts preferable scientifically as well as preferred popularly?

Allow me to elaborate on this unconventional finding. First, if the principle of subsidiarity is applied, 'subsidiary' should not be thought synonymous with 'bottom-up'.[37] The principle does not require a simultaneous pursuit of democracy in conflict management. When applied in the context of the growing size, complexity, and territorial connectedness of cities, it suggests instead a trade-off between 'scale' and 'voice' in government. Government on a larger scale is recommended by subsidiarity, but the larger that is, the harder it is for the voice of local units, neighbourhoods, civil society organizations, and individual citizens to be heard. Lastly, democratic traditions and ideals (such as inclusive political participation, popular control of the legislative and executive branches, or transparent and accountable administration) may be limited – and democratization

34 *See* Anwar Shah & Theresa Thompson, *Implementing Decentralized Local Governance: A Treacherous Road with Potholes, Detours and Road Closures*, World Bank Policy Research Working Paper 3353, 21 (2004), http://elibrary.worldbank.org/doi/abs/10.1596/1813-9450-3353.

35 On actual reforms made along these lines from around the world. *See* United Cities and Local Governments, *supra* note 8, at 2666–67, 273–74.

36 Often, institutional arrangements are made 'obsolete soon after they are promulgated'. *Id.* at 298.

37 *Cf.* argument that decentralisation in and of itself brings increased democracy. *See* United Cities and Local Governments, *supra* note 30, at 6.

not expected – in the country concerned. This undoubtedly holds true for the Global South.[38] Populations there may also long for the prevention and resolution of conflict, as their governments have been generally unable to keep pace politically with related societal developments and demands.

The question – and related policy option – presents itself: could it be that urban inhabitants in developing countries are prepared, at least in early stages of development, to sacrifice some 'input legitimacy' (achieved through enhancing popular political participation) for the sake of 'output legitimacy' (public outcomes)?[39] Is local governance capability popularly deemed to be the most important consideration in such countries? If so, this trade-off[40] in favour of alleviating the underlying problems of urban poverty, polarization, exclusion, etc. would not be unreasonable from the following perspectives.

In principle: while aspects of democracy and good governance may correlate in terms of accountability, transparency, and participation, good governance resulting in poverty reduction, better services, and like improvements is not necessarily related to a particular political system.[41] Taken on its own terms, it would contradict democratic principles to ignore inhabitants' judgement and will in order to impose democratic government on the city. (Polls in developing countries suggest in fact a public preference for 'policy' over 'politics'.[42]) Considered more broadly: upping input legitimacy need not mean Western-style democratization (as generally equated in the literature). The possibility of traditional forms or customs of participation and representation being developed on[43]

38 The European Charter of Local Self-Government (1985) commits parties to applying basic rules guaranteeing political, administrative, and financial independence of local authorities. While all 47 member states of the Council of Europe are parties to it, only 13 states have ratified its additional protocol on the right to participate in the affairs of a local authority.

39 *See generally* Martijn Klem & Georg Frerks, *How Local Governments Contribute to Peace-building*, in ARNE MUSCH ET AL., CITY DIPLOMACY 54 (2008).

40 *Cf.* Caroline Andrew et al., *Theme 4: Local Government in Federal Systems, in* FORUM OF FEDERATIONS (ED.), INTERNATIONAL CONFERENCE ON FEDERALISM, *supra* note 4, at 390. ('For nations to realize full potential ... equal participation of vulnerable segments of population in society must be ensured'.)

41 *See Towards a Set of Urban Governance Indicators*, GDRC PROGRAMME ON URBAN GOVERNANCE (last visited Nov. 13, 2017), www.gdrc.org/u-gov/indicators.html.

42 *See generally* PARTHA CHATTERJEE, THE POLITICS OF THE GOVERNED: REFLECTIONS ON POPULAR POLITICS IN MOST OF THE WORLD (2004). *Cf.* A study finds that most poor people value democracy, which they equate with the freedom to vote, think, speak, move, protest, and work. *See* DEEPA NARAYAN ET AL., MOVING OUT OF POVERTY: SUCCESS FROM THE BOTTOM UP (2009). *See also* Andrew, *supra* note 40, at 388 ('[d]istance from decision making and a sense of being devalued [manifest themselves] as apathy, anger and a weakening of the civic culture').

43 *See, e.g.*, NELSON MANDELA, LONG WALK TO FREEDOM 24 (1994).

> I watched and learned much from the tribal meetings that were regularly held at the Great Place. ... It was democracy in its purest form. There may have been a hierarchy of importance among the speakers, but everyone was heard ... [t]he foundation of self-government was that all men were free to voice their opinions and were equal in their value as citizens.

should not be overlooked. Further, the trade-off would not be unreasonable given that the multi-level participation model is performing weakly as a democratic institution, as evidenced by the declining political and electoral participation in many developed countries, and that there may be government structures 'beyond that can provide real empowerment to make participation meaningful [...] from neighbourhoods to metropolitan councils'.[44] Finally, it would not be unreasonable due to the risk of greater conflict through 'premature' democratization (alone consider the possibility of a local tyranny of the majority or a capture of democratic institutions by elites and special interests[45]).

In short, it is arguable from a scientific and popular perspective that in devising government strategies for cities in the Global South, international actors involved should give lower priority to increasing popular political participation and higher priority to establishing basic state functions, especially those that are matters of life and death. (If local democracy is nonetheless preferred in policy-making, whether or not to extend voting rights to non-citizens, non-property holders, homeless, and unregistered persons must be carefully considered and pragmatically answered for the sake of conflict management.)

The relevant questions become i) who should be the policy- and decision-makers concerned with establishing basic services (such as scientific experts, civil servants, political appointees, and/or group leaders[46]), and ii) if not through democracy, how can it be ensured that local government is 'benevolent', i.e. centred on the community, representative of the entire population, and geared toward development?

A corollary of the preceding is that if democratization qua introducing voting rights in non-democratic countries of the Global South proves problematic, then providing for greater popular participation in government through direct democratic institutions is all the more so. In democracies, such institutions can have a complementary function: they are mostly referred to when it is no longer possible to reach agreement on a given issue. In non-democratic countries, an educated citizenry, responsible politicians, proper public debate, and thereafter, an accepted result are sorely lacking. Creating additional 'space for civic dialogue' in the form of recourse to referendum, popular initiative, or recall would not contribute to conflict prevention or resolution and improved social outcomes – rather the opposite.

44 Steytler, *supra* note 12, at 276 (e.g. structures that enable public participation in governmental planning and budgeting).

45 *See* Malcolm MacLaren, *'Sequentialism' or 'Gradualism'? On the Transition to Democracy and the Rule of Law*, NCCR WORKING PAPER 38 (2009), www.nccr-democracy.uzh.ch/publications/workingpaper/pdf/wp38.pdf (regarding democratization of autocracies).

46 For example, a council manager form of executive could be adopted. Political functions are separated from the complex day-to-day operations of running a large modern city, which are entrusted to a manager with certified, professional skills.

Conclusion

In this chapter, I have analysed conflict and governance debates in the urban context in general and in particular instances. The focus has been on the ways in which the political architecture of cities in the Global South is mediated, sized, and negotiated. For as these cities grow and diversify rapidly, they create a need for 'Konfliktbereinigung, Interessenregelung und Zielbestimmung' within the state[47] for social peace to be vouchsafed.

In the earlier sections, I reviewed existing theory and knowledge, and have developed my own conceptual framework and hypotheses, about processes of urban transformation and conflict management. I conclude tentatively that i) amid urban transformation, politically destabilizing claims are made, in particular by socially, ethnically, and economically marginalized groups; ii) official responses can lead to or trigger civic unrest on one hand, or they can prevent or terminate it on the other; iii) of late, urbanization and urbanism have been characterized more by conflict than by consensus, especially in the Global South; iv) government forms in these urban areas should be carefully studied, their adequacy should be evaluated, and where found lacking, alternative approaches should be considered;[48] v) though often recommended, the pursuit of subsidiarity and democracy in the design of a city's political system does not necessarily result in good governance practice; vi) indeed, these principles seem more suited to countries and cities with no present or past experience of internal conflict; and vii) a differentiated and controlled approach to subsidiarity and democracy may be, depending on circumstances, more likely to better city-dwellers' lives.

Notably, I am not hereby putting into question the principles of subsidiarity and democracy, just the sense behind applying them dogmatically in cases of contemporary urban transformation. No *a priori* judgement should be made in their favour when designing local government systems to manage conflict arising from urbanization and urbanism. Observers' expecting the principles' application is not *per se* wrong-headed, but it only takes into account half of the relevant context. Considered empirically, application may not always bring the added functional value sought after.

Whether my conclusions are convincing or not, it may be agreed that a fundamental clarification of the role, competences, and formation of different political systems is urgently needed – and then, if a comprehensive public strategy is to be formulated, of the relation of one system to another.[49] Urban issues will only loom larger in states worldwide, and scientists can help to document

47 Or 'conflict resolution, interest regulation, and goal determination'. *See* REINHOLD ZIPPELIUS, ALLGEMEINE STAATSLEHRE 21, 233–35 (13TH ED. 1998).

48 The Urban Governance Survey, https://urbangovernance.net/en/ (last visited Nov. 13, 2017). This survey offers a database on how cities around the world are governed that looks promising for government performance research.

49 *See* United Cities and Local Governments, *supra* note 8, at 283 ('only a handful of nations have framed a comprehensive policy on decentralization, blending political reform (power-sharing),

changes, interpret their significance, and facilitate positive transformation through new research and new ideas.[50]

As mentioned at the outset, this chapter constitutes the conceptual basis for a multi-stage research project. The intent is to identify the possibilities and potential of government, qua political-administrative structures, to bring about positive urbanization and urbanism.

In the project's next stage, a comparative perspective on the design and operation of urban government will be adopted. Society and politics are not the same in time or space; the situation of specific cities may not be captured by the historical experience or a given perspective from elsewhere; and conflict management strategies that have been common in one region (above all in the Global North) should not be adopted *tout court* elsewhere.[51] (For '[w]ithin [...] broad commonalities, urban regions in the developed North and those in the developing South have distinctive characteristics and face markedly different challenges'.[52]) Case studies of the governance of rapidly changing cities in Asia will be therefore carried out to complement the preceding theoretical discussion. These are primary settings for conflict, conflicts that can be politically threatening, endangering variously the stability of governments, the longevity of regimes, the functioning of states, and even the existence of countries. In other words, I will test the arguments made above through (extensive and detailed secondary) research of different political constructions of place and space (namely in Mumbai, Singapore, and Hong Kong).

In the concluding stage of the project, I will discuss how conflict-charged demographic shifts and group relations in cities should be – from a pragmatic perspective – handled. (Do the three case-studied cities, for example, suggest themselves as centres of innovation and of good or bad practice?) The dependent variable in the success or failure of different strategies of conflict management focused on will remain the degree to which cities pursue a 'bottom-up' approach. In particular, arguments in favour of augmenting local democratic self-government will be assessed and related initiatives recommended – or not, as the case may be.

economic development, and democratic choice-making with capacity-strengthening and financing in order to produce a long term solution').

50 *See generally* First World Conference on City Diplomacy, *supra* note 13.

51 *See* observations that '[r]eforms from around the world are boosting municipal authorities' with references to Canada, the European Union, and the United States; and that voters in developed countries tend to resist limitations on local governments and the consolidation of municipalities. *Federation of Canadian Municipalities*, COMMUNITIES IN AN URBAN CENTURY 8 2002; *see* Steytler, *supra* note 12, at 430.

52 United Cities and Local Governments, *supra* note 8, at 261.

Part II

Innovation and urban governance in legal perspective

8 Financing local governments in times of recession

Financial and legal innovation in the face of the 2008 crisis

Daniel B. Rodriguez and Nadav Shoked[1]

Introduction

This year marks the ten-year anniversary of the economic collapse, since christened the "Great Recession"—the 2008 breakdown of the American financial system that generated painful reverberations throughout the globe. In the intervening years, policymakers and scholars working in different economic and legal systems have spent much time and effort discussing and debating the crisis's causes and effects. Following these conversations, a plethora of reform measures were adopted worldwide. Still others were, and are, proposed. From the outset the commentary—and the ensuing push for reform—has, and for good reason, focused on the industry whose troubles bred the recession: the global financial system. Accordingly, the focal point for policy discussion has been the national level governmental institutions that manage that system. The administrative bodies overseeing banking establishments (mostly central banks and industry-specific regulators) and the political bodies (mostly, treasury departments) that, alongside the administrative bodies, infuse liquidity and credit into the market, have been the governmental institutions whose role and challenges have been the subject of most of the discourse. Other, non-national level governments were at best located at the periphery of the policy discussion of the 2008 crisis's aftermath.

This relative neglect is regrettable. While national institutions create the overall legal and policy infrastructure within which individuals live and firms operate, local institutions play an important role in designing the social and economic environment just as well. They are key actors in the market and thus we cannot solve the problems generated by the recent recession—or any other—without attending to local institutions and their performance.

Here we turn to these institutions and discuss those governments' reaction to, and adjustments fostered by, that crisis: we review the challenges faced by local

1 We are very grateful to Nestor Davidson for organizing the Annual International and Comparative Urban Law Conference and for, alongside the other participants, helping us develop the ideas incorporated in this Chapter. For exceptionally helpful research assistance we are thankful to Joshua Yim (Northwestern J.D. 2019).

governments in a global age of economic contraction. True, local governments were not the source of the crisis in the U.S. or elsewhere. They do not, accordingly, hold the keys for averting such calamities in the future. Yet local governments, and more specifically, their financial standing and activities, should form at least part of the academic and policy picture.

To begin with, individuals and associations are by definition subject to local governance, since they are located somewhere. A bank failure, a foreclosure, the laying off of employees—all these events, by definition, happen somewhere, and that place will be within the sphere of some local government. Local governments will thus, inevitably, be impacted by a serious financial crisis. No matter their size—small hamlets or large central cities; their nature—rural, suburban, urban; or their legal status and title—city, county, township, prefecture, local governments are invariably the place where a financial collapse occurs and where economic pain is endured. Accordingly, at the most prosaic of levels, local governments feel economic distress alongside the actual individuals and groups that are its direct victims.

Moreover, as entities distinct in their legal architecture and standing from, on the one hand, private corporations, and, on the other hand, national governments, local governments will experience those economic impacts in a distinct fashion. Consequently, the 2008 crisis had special effects on local governments—different in quantity, and often quality, from those effects experienced by other, national-level, governments. Necessarily, therefore, local governments were also forced to react in peculiar ways.

In the U.S., the dramatic, and unfortunate, effects of the downturn on cities and other local governments (i.e., counties, school districts, and special districts) have been painfully pronounced. The largest municipal bankruptcy in American history took place as Detroit, once the proud symbol of American industrial dominance, entered bankruptcy. Many other cities and counties throughout the land similarly found themselves entering such proceedings. The nation's third largest city—Chicago—endured the indignity of witnessing its debt downgraded to junk bond rank by the major rating agencies; the following year, the city's school district predicted an inability to open the schools due to lack of resources. Most recently, a whole federal territory—the Commonwealth of Puerto Rico—proclaimed its incapacity to repay debts and was, soon thereafter, placed under the supervision of a federal financial oversight board.

In reaction to these and similar events, the American legal literature about local governments has, in the past decade, turned, as never before, its critical eye to the problems of local finances. American jurists and policymakers now enjoy a much richer understanding of issues such as municipal financial distress, local bankruptcy, local debt, and novel means of municipal funding.[2]

2 *See*, for example, Michelle Wilde Anderson, *The New Minimal Cities*, 123 Yale L.J. 1118 (2014); Clayton P. Gillette, *Dictatorships for Democracy: Takeovers of Financially Failed Cities*, 114 Colum. L. Rev. 1373 (2014); Clayton P. Gillette, *Fiscal Federalism, Political Will, and*

Yet these topics and phenomena the literature now richly discusses are not inherently American. The financial trends and problems they pertain to are, or can be, characteristic of any legal system. Similarly, the local government coping mechanisms the writers describe or propose are, or can be, universal in their relevance. Luckily, at the same time that the American legal literature about local financial distress was, as just described, burgeoning, so was the literature in the emerging field of global and comparative urban law, as exemplified by the other chapters in this book as well as by the contributors' previous writings.[3]

Following the call of such works, in this Chapter we bring the two bodies of literature—the literature on the law of local government finances and the literature on comparative local government law—together. We review the effects of the crisis of 2008 on local governments worldwide and the reaction of those governments to the crisis. We focus on the commonalities that can be detected among the circumstances faced by, and the actions of, cities operating in different legal systems. Such a comparative endeavor holds the promise of providing a fresh perspective to scholars in distinct systems, aiding them in appreciating that which is possible—and also, that which is impossible—for their own cities. It should enable local commentators, and policymakers, to consider potential courses of action, drawing on the experience of other cities.

The usefulness of such a comparative discussion of local finance law extends beyond its contemporary relevance for policymakers still facing the repercussions of the recent crisis of 2008. The spike in interest in local finances following the crisis—a spike of which this Chapter is a symptom—affords legal scholars an opportunity to devote more attention to the key issue of local finances. The latter is always, irrespective of the economic environment, a vital and unescapable concern of local governments, wherever they might be. A local government can provide no services—it cannot even exist itself—unless it has means for paying off its expenses. Yet, largely, legal scholars tend to concentrate their attention elsewhere, leaving the field to public finance economists and political scientists. The result is unfortunate since public finance challenges and solutions are to a great extent impacted, if not fully designed, by legal constraints. We thus hope that this Chapter's tentative insights will not only provide ideas to those contending with contemporary policy challenges, but also aid in the drawing of a more complete picture of global local government law by adding the often missing component of local finance laws.

Strategic Use of Municipal Bankruptcy, 79 U. Chi. L. Rev. 281 (2012); Clayton P. Gillette & David A. Skeel, Jr., *Governance Reform and the Judicial Role in Municipal Bankruptcy*, 125 Yale L.J. 1150 (2016); David A. Skeel, Jr., *When Should Bankruptcy be an Option (For People, Places, or Things)?*, 55 Wm. & Mary L. Rev. 2217 (2014); Richard C. Schragger, *Democracy and Debt*, 121 Yale L.J. 860 (2012); Richard Briffault, *The Most Popular Tool: Tax Increment Financing and the Political Economy of Local Government*, 77 U. Chi. L. Rev. 65 (2010).

3 *See also* Nestor Davidson & Nisha Mistry, Law Between Buildings: Emergent Global Perspectives On Urban Law (2017).

Our aspiration is thus that this Chapter will be helpful to both scholars and lawmakers. We are also, however, very much aware of the modest ambition of our effort here. Our pretenses at originality are limited: we hardly claim to be the first to note the financial travails cities have been experiencing or the novel responses they have adopted. We report, aggregate, and categorize more than we uncover. Even more important, though we draw much of our prescriptions for legal reform from the U.S. experience—with which we are naturally most acquainted—we by no means intend to imply that in this, or any other, element of its legal system the American framework should serve as a model to others. Indeed, as the stark examples of municipal hardship listed earlier already establish, the American story of local finances is far from a success story. We still draw on it heavily, and believe that writers and legislators in other legal systems could benefit from observing it, simply because U.S. cities have a long modern history—dating back to the Revolution and before—of relatively independent financial agency. As cities elsewhere, partially in reaction to the imperatives of this new era of national-level austerity, become more economically autonomous and active in financial markets, they can look at the triumphs and failures of American cities for inspiration respecting desirable avenues of action and reform—and those avenues that are to be avoided.

To explicate these avenues, desirable and undesirable, the Chapter proceeds as follows. Part I explores the effects of an economic downturn on cities. To do so, it explores the different degrees of financial autonomy cities may enjoy in distinct legal systems, and the attendant different ways in which cities worldwide fund themselves. It then analyzes the extent to which each of these funding mechanisms are impacted by economic downturns, highlighting the special predicament generated by the crisis of 2008. The decades of legal, political, and ideological realignment that preceded that crisis assured that its effects on local governments would be unprecedented. Following that conclusion, Part II turns to identify the novel common mechanisms cities worldwide were forced to develop to cope with the new economic realities wrought by the recent economic downturn. We point at four such tools meriting attention: issuance of debt, the sale of municipal assets, investment in sophisticated financial vehicles, and public–private partnerships particularly in the form of development impact fees. Part III highlights the problems each of these new, market-oriented tools generates for cities, and sketches the legal scheme that should be created in order to address those problems and effectively accommodate each of the new tools.

I. Financing local governments in a recession

The global crisis of 2008 sent shockwaves worldwide, and thus almost all cities were, to one degree or another, affected by it. Still, while the shockwaves were largely identical in source and nature, the legal environments they hit were not. Different cities affected by the same economic force experienced a different effect—at least in terms of degree—in correspondence to their jurisdiction's system for financing local governments. In this Part, we will explore the pertinent alternatives, stressing the different mechanisms through which a downturn can wreak havoc in municipal finances. Special attention will be paid to unique effects of the most recent downturn—and the austerity regime that followed it.

A. *Local fiscal powers and sources*

Local governments are responsible for the provision of some of the most vital public services on which citizens rely. In systems that place the greatest emphasis on localism, even policing and education are among such services. Systems that refrain from going quite that far in prioritizing local powers, tend to entrust local governments with the provision of services such as sanitation, transport and transit, certain welfare benefits, the maintenance of streets and public spaces, the regulation of land uses and development, and more. To fund these services, local governments must have some sources of revenue. These sources will be identified by the national legal system.

In defining the sources available to their local governments, national legal systems determine the level of autonomy local governments enjoy from the higher level (national or province/state level), government. Financial independence is an essential, if not dispositive, element in political independence. Accordingly, there are two opposing legal poles molding the spectrum along which local governments can be located: full fiscal dependence and complete fiscal independence.

One extreme is full dependence on higher level government. In this model, the local government raises no funds on its own. It is fully funded by another government. It is, in essence, a branch or subdivision of that government. An administrative agency of the government—say, the Department of Motor Vehicles—does not raise its own funds or set its own budget, and neither does the city. Very much like the DMV, the city, in this model, is merely a vessel through which the central government provides services to a defined geographical sub-area. That central government thus decides how much funds to allocate to the city, its vessel.[4]

The other extreme model establishes the city as the opposite image of the feeble instrument of the central government just described. In this rival model, the city is a full-blown independent government. Like state and national governments, it funds itself in whichever way it pleases. That is, the city determines both the amount of monies it will raise for its uses, and the manner of raising those monies.

These two extreme poles—utter dependence and complete independence—are ideal archetypes. In their pure form, neither probably exists. Complete independence is hardly imaginable as it institutes the city as a separate city-state, and utter

4 Even in such a model some local agency is imaginable: for example, the city, as an agency, may, as part of the budgeting process, suggest to the central government the size of the allocation it requires.

dependence, albeit perhaps imaginable, is highly unlikely given the inevitable discretion "street-level" agents and agencies will exercise. Hence, rather than placing their local governments at one of the two poles, legal systems place them on the spectrum that runs between these two poles; no system establishes local governments as fully independent financially, but some accord their local governments more financial independence than others.

The degree of this independence—of closeness to the notional pole of full fiscal autonomy—is determined by two related factors: the local government's recourse to grants and its freedom in setting autonomous revenue sources.

One factor is the extent of the local government's dependence on grants from higher levels of government. The more a local government's budget draws on allocations of funds from the national/federal or province/state government, the less it controls the amount of money available to it.

Studies show that most metro areas in the world are strongly dependent on such central transfers. With the exception of China, this is particularly true in developing countries (Mexico City relies on grants for 70 percent of its budget), but not only there: Berlin and London receive 80 percent of financing from intergovernmental transfers.[5] Central governments appear reluctant to devolve taxing powers to local governments for fear of having to compete over the same tax bases and for a desire to maintain control over social policy. Consequently, worldwide, intergovernmental transfers are the preferred solution for financing local governments.[6]

From a financial independence perspective, not all grants are created equal, and thus even two systems in which local governments rely on grants to pay for the exact same portion of their budgets will in actuality offer their respective localities a varied level of autonomy. Some grants allow for local discretion—in applying for the grants, in determining their use, etc.[7] Such variation may have major effects on the possibilities open to a local government and should be borne in mind: these effects came into play in the aftermath of the 2008 crisis, as will be seen later.

Even if to varying degrees in accordance with the grants' terms, reliance on grants, as is common among the globe's local governments, implies much

5 Only Busan, Cape Town, Copenhagen, Helsinki, Melbourne, Mumbai, Pune, Seoul, and Tokyo stand out as largely self-financed metro areas. Anwar M. Shah, *Grant Financing of Metropolitan Areas, in* FINANCING METROPOLITAN GOVERNMENTS IN DEVELOPING COUNTRIES 213, 239 (Roy W. Bahl et al. eds., 2013).

6 *See* Jorge Martinez-Vasquez, *Mobilizing Financial Resources for Public Service Delivery and Urban Development, in* THE CHALLENGE OF LOCAL GOVERNMENT FINANCING IN DEVELOPING COUNTRIES 15 (UN-Habitat ed., 2015).

7 One scheme of categorization lists conditional grants (awarded for specific purposes and after the local government commits to meeting certain requirements), capital grants (awarded for specific infrastructure projects), equalization grants (awarded to local governments of limited means in relation to other local governments), and general grants. The latter two are the least autonomy restricting.

financial dependence. If, and when, it is not relying on higher level grants, the local government endures less such dependence. Yet even then, its financial freedom might be constrained. For there is a second factor setting a local government system's location on the spectrum running from the full independence pole to the utter dependence pole: the local government's power to designate its own sources of income. A local government could operate in a system that leaves it to rely on its own, independent fund-raising devices (rather than grants), but if those devices are defined by the higher-level government, the locality's legal independence is constrained.

Legal systems, even when assigning the local government independent fiscal powers, routinely limit local governments to specific types of taxes, and proceed to cap, if not specifically set, those taxes' bases and rates. Throughout the world, local governments' legal ability to introduce business taxes is practically non-existent.[8] Local income taxes are likewise rare, outside of a few major U.S. cities.[9] Similarly, local sales (or value added) taxes are virtually unknown outside the U.S.[10] Since they cannot tax corporations, income or sales, many local governments worldwide are legally limited to reliance on property taxes (aside from the charging of service fees).[11] The share of the property tax in total local taxes is 100 percent in Australia,

8 In Colombia, for example, the industry and commerce tax has often been the major source of revenue for Bogotá, Cali, and Medellín. Richard Bird, *Fiscal Decentralization in Colombia: A Work (Still) in Progress, in* FISCAL FEDERALISM IN LATIN AMERICA 9, tbl.3 (Bahl & Seeti eds., 2012). There and elsewhere where present, these taxes tend to be crude and archaic, such as the Indian octroy—a levy on goods entering the city. For more on the Indian system *see* M. Govinda Rao & Nirvikar Singh, THE POLITICAL ECONOMY OF FEDERALISM IN INDIA (1st ed. 2005). A more coherent system of local taxation of businesses, in the form of a value added tax, was introduced in 1998 in Italy, 2004 in Japan, and 2010 in France. Massimo Bordignon et al., *Reforming Business Taxation Lessons from Italy?* 8 INT'L TAX & PUB, FIN.191 (2001). Japanese local governments also rely in a consistent fashion on versions of enterprise taxation. The most recent data is provided by the MINISTRY OF INTERNAL AFF. & COMM., *White Paper on Local Public Finance Japan, 2017*, www.soumu.go.jp/iken/zaisei/29data/chihouzaisei_2017_en.pdf (last visited Mar. 17, 2018).

9 The most commonly used form of subnational income taxation internationally is an "at-rate" income tax which functions as a surtax or piggyback tax on the base of the central government individual income tax. This type of tax is almost always collected by the central government and the revenues allocated to subnational governments on a derivation basis. *See* Martinez-Vazques, *supra* note 6, at 21.

10 Only three countries experimented with a subnational value added tax (VAT)—though always on the state not local level: Brazil, Canada, and India. A few other countries have a scheme for sharing their VAT revenues with such subnational governments. Jorge Martinez-Vazquez, *Revenue Assignments in the Practice of Fiscal Federalism, in* FISCAL FEDERALISM AND POLITICAL DECENTRALIZATION 27, 46 (Nuria Bosh & Jose M. Duran eds., 2008).

11 General sales taxes are seldom levied by local governments outside a number of U.S. states, except in the highly undesirable form of a gross receipts tax (e.g., the industry and commerce tax in Colombia and China's local business tax). In Brazil, however, the major source of municipal taxation is the service tax (imposto sobre servicos, ISS), imposed on all services other than communications and interstate and intercity public transportation. Richard Bird & Enid Slack, *Metropolitan Public Finance: An Overview, in* FINANCING METROPOLITAN GOVERNMENTS IN DEVELOPING COUNTRIES 135, 144 (Roy Bahl et al. eds., 2007).

Ireland, and the United Kingdom, and 90 percent or above in Canada, Israel, and New Zealand.[12] In the U.S., despite the relative varied types of taxes available to local governments, it stands at more than 70 percent. Systems not belonging to the English tradition tend to rely on property taxation for local finances much less—extreme examples are Switzerland and Sweden, where the tax forms 1 and 2 percent, respectively, of local tax revenue[13]—but to the very limited extent they allow local governments to autonomously finance themselves, developing countries also often rely heavily on the property tax.[14]

Further limiting local governments' power over their own fiscal resources in many legal systems, even those in which the local government can introduce a tax of any type—property or otherwise—is state level control over the amount of revenue derived from that tax. In the U.S., tax rates are often capped by the state.[15] Elsewhere, property tax rates are not just capped, but fixed by the central government.[16] In China, for example, local governments cannot set tax rates, change the bases of collection, or introduce new taxes.[17] In India, state governments at times exempted almost all properties from the local tax, or even abolished it altogether without even consulting the local government.[18]

Local government law systems, therefore, create distinct fiscal environments for their local governments, defining their freedom through two key elements: dependence on higher-level grants and autonomy in designing local taxes. These variations may exist not only between legal systems, but also within them. Many legal systems accord more financial independence to some cities—normally large and affluent ones—than to others.[19] Thus major cities in the state would, for

12 John Norregaard, *Taxing Immovable Property: Revenue Potential and Implementation Challenges* (Int'l Monetary Fund, Working Paper No. 13/129, 2013), www.imf.org/external/pubs/ft/wp/2013/wp13129.pdf.

13 On average the tax forms 37.7 percent of local taxation in high income countries, and slightly less (35.5 percent) in middle income countries. *Id.*

14 Roy Bahl, *Property Tax Reform in Developing and Transition Countries* 4, USAID, (2009).

15 Roy Bahl & Jorge Martinez-Vazquez, *The Determinants of Revenue Performance, in* Making the Property Tax Work: Experiences in Developing and Transitional Countries (Roy Bahl et al. eds., 2008). The national control over the local tax collections has other facets. For example, as of the time of writing, local governments that have the power to tax sales, do not hold the power to collect sales taxes over internet purchases. The Supreme Court is currently hearing a case that might change this rule.

16 William J. McCluskey & C.D. Franzsen, *Property Taxes in Metropolitan Cities, in* Roy Bahl et al., Financing Metropolitan Governments in Developing Countries 159, 166 (mentioning Cairo, Jakarta, Kigali, and Yaoundé as lacking the power, and Manila, Kuala Lumpur, Dar es Salaam, Kampala, and Lagos as enjoying only limited, and hardly used, discretion). The same is true when a version of local income taxation is allowed. Martinez-Vasquez, *supra* note 6, at 21.

17 *See* Bird & Slack, *supra* note 11, at 152.

18 *See* M. Govinda Rao & Richard M. Bird, *Urban Governance and Finance in India* (Rotman Sch. Mgmt., Working Paper No. 1,568,858, 2010) (discussing examples from India).

19 Toronto, for example, is allowed to impose a number of taxes that other municipalities in the province (Ontario) cannot, such as a vehicle registration fee, a land transfer tax, and a billboard tax. Bird & Slack, *supra* note 11, at 138. In the U.S., New York laws specifically empower New York

example, enjoy powers of taxation that other local governments in that state do not, while the latter would, normally, rely more heavily on grants from the higher-level government.[20] The resulting legally enabled difference between cities operating within the same system illustrates a key point. Throughout the discussion, we have been referring to "local financial independence." But which of the two cities: the one with the greater freedom to design a taxation system or the one receiving greater grants from the central government—is more financially independent? The former has the legal authority to set its own revenue structure, but the latter might have more resources made available to it—at the very least, it is asked to exhort less effort to subsidize its activities.

The term financial, or fiscal, independence, as is useful for legal analysis—and as we use it here—refers to the first option. Financial independence means formal self-dependence on the locality's part, even if self-dependence entails in practice a curtailed freedom to spend funds (as those funds are not granted to the locality from the outside). Legal fiscal autonomy implies a negative form of freedom: immunity from higher-level intervention in local fundraising, but also, and often as an accompaniment, the lack of active financial support from the higher-level government. Thus, while the more financially independent local government might be less dependent on other governments, it is more dependent on the market; or, perhaps more accurately, as shall be seen next, *more directly* dependent on the market.

B. *The effect of the downturn on local financial capacities*

The impacts of market trends on a municipality's finances are a function of the municipality's financial independence, as defined in the preceding subsection. The more reliant the local government is on autonomous sources (as opposed to transfers from the higher-level government) the more exposed it is to the market. The more the municipality lacks the legal power to design those autonomous sources, the less it can adjust to counter the stresses of the market. Market trends have different effects on different government funding mechanisms. Some mechanisms trend in tandem with the market: as the business cycle turns downwards the amount of funds the government raises from these mechanisms decreases. These mechanisms that positively correlate with the overall state of

City to levy an income tax, and Pennsylvania grants that power to Philadelphia as part of its broad home rule powers. Israeli laws allow "financially sound municipalities" to adjust certain taxes without the national-level approvals other municipalities must attain.

20 The relationship of dependence on intergovernmental transfers and size of metropolitan area is mixed (in some places the large areas are awarded more generous grants, in others the reverse is true. *Id.* at 139. In the U.S., state funding formulas are often criticized for distributing aid to less populated areas, whereas money directed to large metropolitan areas might have a greater impact. Richard H. Mattoon et al., *Improving the Impact of Federal Aid to the States*, 34 ECON. PERSP. 77 (2010).

the economy are thus procyclical. To the extent a local government relies on, or can shift to, countercyclical or noncyclical fiscal tools, the better it can weather a recession.

In theory, local governments—unlike their national level counterparts—should not be particularly vulnerable to market crashes. The funding sources they rely on, as just reviewed, are mostly those that economists tend to associate with not too pronounced cyclical features. Indeed, a clear pattern is at play: the more common a funding mechanism is among local governments, the less procyclical it is. The taxes that are subject to direct and immediate market effects are not the taxes on which local governments normally rely. The most procyclical of a government's potential revenue streams—corporate taxes levied on business profits—are, as noted, almost wholly unavailable to local governments. Income taxes, that adjust to an individual's market income from employment and investments, and hence readily react to market trends, are also at most a minor source of local government revenue.

The sales tax, slightly more prevalent—though by no means dominant—among local government funding schemes, is somewhat less procyclical. As a tax on consumption, it is inevitably affected by a downturn: the less income individuals derive from their employment and investments, the less money they have to spend. Yet certain products that are subject to the sales tax will be consumed—and thus taxed—even in difficult economic times. Services and basic goods such as food will be acquired by individuals even if the individuals' financial standing declines, and thus sales tax revenues, unlike income (let alone business) tax revenues, do not perfectly track economic trends.

Local governments' most popular taxation instrument—the property tax—tracks those trends even less perfectly. Unlike income or consumption, the value of real estate is assessed for taxation purposes only periodically, and thus, by definition, the revenue a government draws from its taxation will not immediately decrease even when property values decline.[21] Furthermore, since real estate is not as liquid as other investment holdings, property values will not necessarily decline in tandem and to the same extent as the financial market declines. Even if their incomes decline, individuals would try hard to preserve their homes; businesses will lay off employees before engaging in the much more complicated task of offloading physical facilities. Increases in property tax revenues relative to income tax revenues are thus common during and slightly after economic slowdowns.[22]

The historical trend and the theoretical prediction were borne out by the most recent crisis. Although the 2008 recession was a crisis engendered to a

21 *See, e.g.*, Donald Boyd, *Recession, Recovery, and State and Local Finances* 11–12 (Lincoln Inst. Land Pol'y, Working Paper No. 11DB1, 2011), www.lincolninst.edu/sites/default/files/pubfiles/1959_1280_boyd_final.pdf.

22 *See* David H. Bradley, *Property Taxes in Perspective*, CTR. BUDGET & POL'Y PRIORITIES (Mar. 17, 2005), www.cbpp.org/sites/default/files/atoms/files/3-17-05sfp.pdf.

great degree by the real estate market, data now shows that its effects on local governments' income from property taxes was, in relative terms, limited.[23] Property tax revenues did decrease: in 90 of the U.S.'s largest cities, by more than 12 percent between 2009 and 2014.[24] That decline was much smaller though than the decline in actual property values, and one recent study found that on average a 10 percent decrease in housing prices was associated with only a 1.7 percent decrease in local property tax revenues.[25] Partially accounting for the gap may have been revenues from the taxation of commercial properties, trends in whose valuations do not perfectly correlate to those associated with residential properties. Thus, the fall in government revenue from other taxes tended to be steeper, and of all tax revenue streams, property tax revenues proved themselves the most reliable during the crisis—as theory predicts.[26]

Unfortunately for local governments, however, this most recent of financial collapses upended other key theoretical predictions respecting local governments' revenue in times of market crisis. Two theoretical assumptions were put to the test: the nature of higher-level government grants, and a local government's legal ability to shift its own tax sources in reaction to financing challenges.

As reviewed earlier, in addition to its autonomous revenue sources—the varied forms of local taxation—a local government relies for revenue purposes on grants from higher levels of government. As also noted, for many local governments worldwide, whose own fiscal powers are tightly constrained, this source is, by a fairly wide margin, the most important one. Ever since the post-War acceptance of the tenets of the theory of Keynesian economics, the assumption has been that these grants are not only noncyclical, but countercyclical. An allegedly central

23 State and local tax revenues in the U.S. fell by almost 5.5 percent in 2009, an almost unprecedented decline. However, the fall was driven by sharp declines in receipts from the personal income tax and the sales tax (of 17 percent and 7.5 percent, respectively) while, in sharp contrast, property tax revenues held up by growing more than 5 percent in both 2008 and 2009. Byron Lutz et al., *The Housing Crisis and State and Local Government Tax Revenue: Five Channels* (Fed. Res. Board, Working Paper No. 2010–49, 2010).

24 Howard Chernick et al., *The Effect of the Housing Crisis on the Finances of Central Cities*, LINCOLN INST. LAND POL'Y, 15 (2017), www.urban.org/sites/default/files/the_effect_of_the_housing_crisis_on_the_finances_of_central_cities.pdf.

25 *Id.* at 11.

26 *See* Donald Boyd, *Levying the Land*, ECONOMIST (June 29, 2013); *and see* Donald Boyd, *supra* note 21, at 11; *see also* Yolanda K. Kodrzycki, *Smoothing Tax Revenues over the Business Cycle: Gauging Fiscal Needs and Opportunities* 13 (Fed. Res. Bank of Boston, Working Paper No. 14–11, 2014), www.bostonfed.org/publications/research-department-working-paper/2014/smoothing-state-tax-revenues-over-the-business-cycle-gauging-fiscal-needs-and-opportunities.aspx (describing greater volatility of sales tax revenues than income tax revenues during the 2000s); *and* Jesse Edgerton, Andrew F. Haughwout, & Rae Rosen, *Institutions, Tax Structure and State-local Fiscal Stress*, 57 NAT'L TAX J. 147, 152–53 (2004) (describing greater volatility of New York City's income tax base than its property tax base).

lesson of the Great Depression of the 1920s and 1930s was that at times of deep economic crisis, it is the role of government to infuse funds into the economic system so as to facilitate a recovery. The government can do so through a combination of monetary and fiscal tools.[27] As a matter of monetary policy, the government should lower interest rates—thereby rendering money cheaper for private consumers and investors. As a matter of fiscal policy, the government should invest its own funds in the market, by, for example, buying private bonds, lowering taxes or otherwise funneling money to citizens, and investing in public works. Another such fiscal option for the national government is to transfer money to lower level governments so that they can invest in infrastructure or make more funds available to residents.[28] Inter-governmental grants are thus imagined as countercyclical: they should aid local governments in filling deficits generated by declines in their own tax revenues and increases in their expenses generated by a growing demand for social services at times of economic pain.[29]

That, at least, was the traditional economic theory. The reality in 2008 was quite different. The crisis of 2008 followed almost four decades of an intellectual and policy retreat from these principles of Keynesian economics. In the U.S., the stagflation of the early 1970s removed the luster of the theory.[30] In the U.K. the ascent of Margaret Thatcher's brand of conservativism undercut its political appeal. Worldwide, the academic dominance of economists defining themselves in opposition to Keynesianism—and branded under labels such as Chicago School Economics or neo-liberalism—had for decades effectively battled the influence of the theory on policymakers.[31] International organizations preached—and in places imposed—the new dogma. One of the core elements of this dogma was that government simply cannot alleviate market conditions in bad times—its interferences merely unsettle markets and generate worse results. Governments should refrain from activist macroeconomic policies and instead allow the market's own machinations to contend with the pressures of the business cycle.

The denial of the principles that had guided national and international economic thinking and policymaking since the 1940s, was, at least arguably, a major cause for the 2008 crisis; inarguably, it colored governments' reactions to it. In many places national governments responded to the downturn not by aggressively entering the market—as is the Keynesian prescription—but rather by cutting their expenses. Countries were reluctant to incur large deficits to prop

27 For a literature review on cyclical fiscal and monetary policy *see, e.g.*, Martine Guerguil et al., *Flexible Fiscal Rules and Countercyclical Fiscal Policy*, 52 J. Macroeconomics 189 (2017).

28 *See* N. Gregory Mankiw, Principles Of Economics 814–15 (6th ed. 2012) (discussing traditional fiscal responses).

29 Countercyclical fiscal policy is the prescription typically made by economists. *See*, for example, Christiano Lawrence et al., *When is the Government Spending Multiplier Large?*, 119 J. Pol. Econ. 78 (2011).

30 Daniel T. Rodgers, Age of Fracture 41–56, 63–76 (2011).

31 Melvin W. Reder, *Chicago Economics: Permanence and Change*, 20 J. Econ. Lit. 1 (1982).

up demand for goods and services.[32] Developing countries have always reacted to recessions with procyclical fiscal policy—i.e., by contracting their spending.[33] Following this recession, and in contrast to their prior practice, many countries in the industrialized world have followed developing countries' lead, becoming de facto procyclical by drastically reducing government spending as the recession hit.[34] In the U.K. and many Eurozone nations, austerity became the order of the day. Even when and where Keynesian recommendations made an intellectual and policy comeback, grants to local governments were not in vogue. Both in Europe and in the U.S., much of government's work of infusing money into the market was accomplished through monetary tools—i.e., central banks' interest rates and quantitative easing policies—rather than through fiscal tools—i.e., government investment. In the U.S., where some such investment was made in prominent federal acts such as the "stimulus package" (formally, the American Recovery and Reinvestment Act of 2009), funds were provided in the form of tax cuts or grants for specific infrastructure projects or market activities, rather than as intergovernmental transfers.[35] Faced with the tension between stabilizing the performance of the state and local government sector and providing stimulus to the national economy through infrastructure and capital projects, Congress opted for the latter.[36] In this respect the stimulus package was dramatically different from federal reactions to earlier recessions, where the emphasis was squarely placed on fiscally stabilizing state and local governments.[37] Complicating matters further in the U.S., the 2008 crisis's economic and political strife produced budgetary

32 Robert Pollin, *US Government Deficits and Debt Amid the Great Recession: What the Evidence Shows*, 36 CAMBRIDGE J. ECON. 161, 162 (2012).

33 *See* Jeffrey Frankel, *Fiscal Policy in Developing Countries: Escape from Procyclicality*, 100 J. DEV. ECON. 32.

34 *See* Guillermo Vuletin & Carlos Vegh, *Tax-Policy Procyclicality*, BROOKINGS (Oct. 1, 2013), www.brookings.edu/opinions/tax-policy-procyclicality/.

35 The American Recovery and Reinvestment Act of 2009 targeted three areas. The first was economic stimulus through $288 billion in tax cuts for individuals and businesses. The second was fiscal stabilization through targeted state programs of $224 billion for education, health care, and unemployment insurance. The third component was infrastructure spending targeted to job creation and investment in the form of $275 billion of federal contracts, grants, and loans. The fiscal stabilization portion of the aid package required states to demonstrate a maintenance of effort in health care and education programs to be eligible for the aid; and the infrastructure funding was geared to "shovel ready" projects past the planning stage and ready for construction.

36 *See* Mattoon et al., *supra* note 20, at 66.

37 For example, in response to the recession of 1973–75, Congress enacted the Antirecession Fiscal Assistance (ARFA) program, which was combined with general revenue sharing grants and the Local Public Works (LPW) program to provide unrestricted grants and infrastructure funding to the states. In addition, Congress passed the Comprehensive Employment and Training Act (CETA) in 1973. The package thus consisted of three components: public works, anti-recession general assistance, and public employment and work force training. In all, $14.5 billion was allocated to the states from November 1975 to March 1978. Aid from the three programs was divided as follows: $5.7 billion for local public works, $2.5 billion for anti-recession fiscal assistance, and $6.3 billion for employment and training.

stalemates in many state legislatures, imperiling state fund transfers to local governments.[38] The result was that the U.S. largely followed the new global pattern whereby inter-governmental grants, local governments' main source of funding—and supposedly a countercyclical source of funding—disappeared in the crisis's aftermath. Everywhere local governments were left to fend for themselves.

Not quite left alone, though. In their supposedly autonomous struggle to shore up their finances at these times of economic need, local governments were handicapped by national laws delimiting their options. Faced with an economic downturn breeding a decrease in tax revenues, a rational government, if it is to retain its preexisting levels of funding, should ratchet up the rates of taxes as the value of the tax base to which those rates are applied declines.[39] In addition, it should shift from procyclical revenue sources—that are drying up—to noncyclical ones, that are not as badly affected by the downturn.Local governments are thus urged by economists to place, in such times, more emphasis on property taxes (and sales taxes imposed on necessities) while increasing the property tax's rates (to offset any decline in real properties' assessed values).[40]

These prescriptions experts make could help alleviate the plight of local governments; but the law—and specifically, local governments' limited financial independence—largely prevents local governments from following these recommendations. As noted above, even when drawing on their own tax resources—as a supposedly autonomous economic entity—state or national laws define, and harshly rein in, local government's ability to draft and experiment with those taxes. Laws curtail a locality's ability to switch tax bases and also cap the rates it can charge. The predicament of smaller communities might be worse, since often their autonomous fiscal powers are further decreased.[41] These legal constraints further compound the difficulty generated by practical constraints. Businesses and corporate headquarters are located in specific, mostly large, cities. And even those cities' freedom to devise

38 The decline in state aid began earlier; 55 percent of responding cities reported that changes in state aid had a negative impact on their fiscal 2004 budgets. Michael A. Pagano, *City Fiscal Conditions in 2004*, NAT'L LEAGUE CITIES (2004). From fiscal year 2003 to fiscal year 2004, 24 states reported reductions in aid to cities, amounting to a $2.3 billion decline (9.2 percent) in state aid. Christopher W. Hoene & Michael A. Pagano, *Fiscal Crisis Trickles Down as States Cut Aid to Cities*, NAT'L LEAGUE CITIES (2003).

39 Data indicates that American states have largely done exactly that in the aftermath of the recession, thus maintaining their income, business, and sales tax revenue. Nicholas Johnson et al., *State Tax Changes in Response to the Recession*, CTR. ON BUDGET & POL'Y PRIORITIES (2010), at 4.

40 Leslie McGranahan & Richard Matton, *State Tax Revenues Over the Business Cycle: Patterns and Policy Responses* (Chicago Fed. Letter No. 299, June 2012) (suggesting this course of action for states); David Gamage, *Managing California's Fiscal Roller Coaster*, 49 ST. TAX NOTES 659, 661 (2008) (describing advantageous stability of property taxes). On the desirability of relying on the property tax, *see* James Alm, *A Convenient Truth: Property Taxes and Revenue Stability*, CITYSCAPE 243 (2013).

41 It is also important to note that the tax collection systems are much more developed in larger cities, enabling more flexibility. William F. Fox, *Structuring Service Delivery in Small Urban Areas*, UN GLOBAL EXPERT MEETING (2014), at 77.

novel, extended, tax mechanisms is restrained because those businesses and headquarters can relocate to avoid any threatened new imposts.

Local governments simply cannot effectively react and counter a cyclical decline in their revenue. The desirable move to, or intensification of, the property tax is particularly fraught politically and legally.[42] State level approval might be required. Much of these rate caps and strict regulation of taxation policy was the product of the same post-1970s economic and political trends that encouraged national governments to embrace austerity. On average, income tax rate policy across states has transitioned since 2000 from being countercyclical (i.e., raising tax rates when economic times are bad and lowering rates when times are good) to being largely independent of the business cycle.[43] Until the 1990s, at times when the economy soured, tax rates would increase. Since, rates have been unchanged in the face of economic fluctuations—presumably due to political constraints. Property taxes—the somewhat countercyclical tax base to which local governments should turn during recessions according to economists—are the most loathed politically. Following the tax revolts of the 1970s and 1980s in the U.S. and elsewhere, any potential turn to property taxation is most severely restrained.[44]

The crisis of 2008 was the first major crisis to afflict the world economy in the era of the intellectual and political dominance of the Chicago School, or neoliberalism. As such it hit local governments harder than previous crises. The result is an unprecedented financial predicament, manifested through headline grabbing fiscal disasters. This predicament necessitates novel coping techniques—techniques that must draw on the new political and intellectual imperatives of the era. We turn to those now.

II. Local governments' new funding tools

The inevitable outcome of the fiscal conditions just described—the disappearance of state-level grants and the erosion in cities' ability to adjust their own tax policies to recessionary conditions—is a huge funding gap. Available empirical literature strongly indicates that subnational revenue generation, more often than not nowadays, falls way short of needs and expectations.[45] Cities can, and do,

42 Paul Smoke, *Enhancing Urban Government Revenues: Political Economy Challenges and Opportunities*, UN Habitat (2015), at 43.

43 *See* McGranahan & Matton, *supra* note 41.

44 For a recent study identifying the reasons rendering the property tax exceptionally politically toxic, *see* Marika Cabral & Caroline Hoxby, *The Hated Property Tax: Salience, Tax Rates, and Tax Revolts* (NBER Working Paper No. 18,514, 2012). The problem is not specifically American. One cause for the 2013 electoral downfall of the post-Recession Italian technocratic prime minister was his decision to increase the property tax. Z.M.B., *An Unexploited Resource*, Economist (June 27, 2013).

45 *See, e.g.*, Roy Bahl & Richard Bird, *Subnational Taxes in Developing Countries: The Way Forward*, 28 Pub. Budgeting & Fin. 1 (2008); Paul Smoke, *Why Theory and Practice are Different: The Gap Between Principles and Reality in Subnational Revenue Systems*, *in* Taxation and development: The weakest Link (Richard Bird & Jorge Martinez-Vazquez eds.,

react by simply cutting their services, to try and bring expenditures into line with dwindling revenues.[46] That course of action is often unappealing: the services that are cut might be important to residents, and contracting spending at times of a market downturn is bad for the overall economy, as already noted.[47] Such local practices may deepen the recession.[48] Aside from the social and economic undesirability of spending cuts, such cuts are often legally impossible. Unfunded mandates—edicts from the higher-level government that the local government provide certain services without granting the local government funds for that purpose—have grown into a staple of American federal and state law.[49] The same has been occurring in China, where local governments are deemed responsible for many social expenses:[50] they receive 50 percent of taxes collected but must cover 80 percent of expenses.[51] Surveys find that this trend is expanding throughout the globe.[52]

Limited in their ability to make cuts on the spending side and faced with a decline in traditional fundraising sources on the revenue side, local governments have thus been forced to devise new funding models. Many local governments have proved rather agile in accommodating difficulties through financial innovation. In adopting these novel funding schemes, cities have also adapted to the shift, originating in the 1970s and described in Part I, in intellectual and political winds. Cities worldwide have, in different ways, turned to the private market in their search for funds. Many of the new models adhered to can be perceived as representing different forms of privatization—as advocated, if not ordered, by the academic and political adherents of the Chicago School or neo-liberalism. We focus in this Part on four particularly salient strategies among these.

2014); Bahl et al., *supra* note 16; Richard Bird, *Subnational Taxation in Developing Countries: A Review of the Literature*, 2 J. INT'L COMM., ECON. & POL'Y 139 (2011); United Cities and Local Governments, *Second Global Report on Decentralization and Local Democracy* 306, 315, 329 (2010).

46 Bucking prior history, state and local government spending in the U.S. *declined* by 4% from the Great Recession until 2012. Johnson et al., *supra* note 39, at 4.

47 For a discussion of the extent and effects of decreased employment by U.S. governments as a reaction to the recession, *see* for example Lucy Dadayan, *The Depth and Length of Cuts in State-Local Government Employment Is Unprecedented*, The Nelson A. Rockefeller Institute of Government (Jan. 9, 2013), www.rockinst.org/pdf/government_finance/2013-01-09-State-Local_Government_Employment.pdf.

48 *See* Johnson et al., *supra* note 39.

49 *See* Iris J. Lav & Andrew Brecher, *Passing Down the Deficit: Federal Policies Contribute to the Severity of the State Fiscal Crisis*, CTR. BUDGET & POL'Y PRIORITIES (2004).

50 *See* Bird & Slack, *supra* note 11, at 152.

51 Sara Hsu, *Fears Over China's Local Government Debt Are Growing—Again*, FORBES (Jan. 2, 2018).

52 United Cities, *supra* note 46. *See also* Andras Vigvari, *Is the Conflict Container Full? Problems of Fiscal Sustainability at the Local Government Level in Hungary*, 60 ACTA OECONOMICA 49 (2010).

A. Municipal borrowing

Perhaps most obviously, when faced with a widening gap between their existing revenue streams and their spending needs, local governments can turn to the same tool individuals and corporations routinely resort to in such circumstances: they can borrow to round off the shortfall. Local government borrowing is justified not only in these terms of the need to address temporary financial exigencies. It also draws on solid permanent normative grounds. Funding governmental spending through borrowing is justified—in economic and equity terms—given public expenditures' special nature. Governments often spend funds on capital projects—say constructing a park, school, or sewage system—that will benefit not only existing taxpayers but also future ones. Therefore, such projects' costs should be split among different generations of taxpayers. The borrowing of money to be paid back piecemeal by taxpayers equitably spreads those costs over time.[53]

Practical necessity combined with such temporal justice considerations lead, and have historically led, all national governments, everywhere, to borrow.[54] Recently also local, as opposed to national or state, governments have increased their own participation in the government credit market. In the U.S. the practice dates to the earliest years of the republic, as the power to issue debt was recognized as one of the inherent powers of a municipal corporation.[55] In accordance, the American municipal bond market is huge: the 2012 U.S. Census found local governments liable for close to 1.8 trillion dollars in outstanding debt,[56] and in 2017 alone, American local governments issued debt to the tune of 448 billion dollars.[57] While still leading the pack, the U.S. is no longer a sole outlier. In Canada, after two decades of decline,[58] the net financial debt of local governments has shot up over the past ten years,[59] and in 2015, for the first time ever, the subnational debt there surpassed the national debt in size.[60] In India, borrowing to cover budget deficits has become widespread, and

53 *See* Richard Briffault & laurie Reynolds, cases and materials on state and local government law 792 (8th ed. 2016).

54 *See The World Factbook*, Cent. Intelligence Agency, www.cia.gov/library/publications/the-world-factbook/rankorder/2186rank.html (last visited Sept. 22. 2016).

55 *See* Eric H. Monkkonen, The Local State 21 (1995).

56 *Id.* at 9.

57 Data provided in *US Municipal Insurance*, SIFMA, www.sifma.org/resources/research/us-municipal-issuance/.

58 *See* Statistics Canada, CANSIM Table 385–0014. *See also* Richard Bird & Almos Tassonyi, *Constraints on Provincial and Municipal Borrowing in Canada: Markets, Rules, and Norms*, 44 Canadian Pub. Admin. 84 (2001).

59 *See* Kyle Hanniman, *Why Municipal Borrowing is no Crisis in Waiting*, Globe & Mail (May 17, 2015).

60 *See* Daniel Tencer, *Canadian Provincial, Municipal Debt Hits an Ugly Milestone*, Huffington Post Canada (Oct. 8, 2015) www.huffingtonpost.ca/2015/10/08/provincial-municipal-debt-canada-td_n_8264278.html.

such borrowing has now reached close to 15 percent of the GDP.[61] In Japan the proportion is higher still: it represents one third of the GDP; following a liberalizing legislative reform in the early 2000s, almost all local capital spending in Japan is funded through debt.[62] Even nations in Central and Eastern Europe, where local debt was unheard of before the fall of Communism and where general wariness toward borrowing still reigns, have found the trend impossible to resist. Since the dawn of the new century local governments in the Czech Republic, Poland, Hungary, and Estonia have made increasing use of debt instruments for financing public investments.[63]

Perhaps most dramatic of all, though, has been the entrance of Chinese municipalities into the local debt market.[64] Chinese law has mostly prohibited local borrowing but over recent years local governments devised ways around the statutory restriction. They have created independent, wholly owned companies whose activities are "extra budgetary." These companies provide funding for development projects and as companies, rather than governments, are permitted to borrow on the capital market. The loans these companies issue are backed by assets transferred to them by the municipality creating them.[65] Although, since it is carried out through extra-budgetary entities, such local "shadow banking" escapes national regulation,[66] Beijing estimates total local government debt at $2.2 trillion.[67] And Chinese cities are not the only contemporary cities effectively disregarding a legal prohibition on debt issuance. In Chile too, local governments have circumvented a restriction on borrowing by reverting to leasing and accumulating arrears.[68] These efforts to overcome clear statutory bans indicate

61 *See* Bland D. Lewis, *Asia-Pacific, in* United Cities and Local Governments, *Second Global Report on Decentralization and Local Democracy* 67 (2010).

62 Nobuki Mochida, Fiscal Decentralization and Local Public Finance in Japan (2008).

63 *See* Bernard Dafflon & Krizstina Beer-Tóth, *Managing Local Public Debt in Transition Countries: An Issue of Self-Control*, 25 Fin. Accountability & Mgmt 305 (2009).

64 Indonesia is another developing country whose municipalities have recently turned to borrowing, after laws were amended in 1999 to allow them to do so. Paul Smoke, *Local Revenues Under Fiscal Decentralization in Developing Countries: Linking Policy Reform, Governance and Capacity, in* Fiscal Decentralization and Land Policies (Gregory K. Ingram & Yu-Hung Hong eds., 2008). *See also* Paul Smoke & Rubino Sugana, *Subnational Own Source Revenues and Shared Taxes in Indonesia: Taking Stock and Looking Forward*, International Conference: Alternative Visions for Decentralization in Indonesia (Mar. 12, 2012).

65 *See* Christine Wong & Richard Bird, *China's Fiscal System: A Work in Progress, in* China's great transformation: Origins, mechanism, and consequences of the post-reform economic boom (Loren Brandt & Thomas Rawski eds., 2008).

66 David Barboza, *Auditor Warns of Risk from Local Debt in China*, N.Y. Times (June 28, 2011), www.nytimes.com/2011/06/28/business/global/28iht-yuan28.html.

67 *See* David Barboza, *Building Boom in China Sirs Fears of Debt Overload*, N.Y. Times (July 7, 2011), www.nytimes.com/2011/07/07/business/global/building-binge-by-chinas-cities-threatens-countrys-economic-boom.html.

68 *See* Leonardo E. Letelier S., *Theory and Evidence of Municipal Borrowing in Chile*, 146 Pub. Choice 395 (2011).

nicely the wide increase in the popularity of debt financing as means for localities worldwide to contend with their fiscal predicament.

B. The sale of municipal assets

Borrowing is one way to attain money from the private market; another is to sell assets on that market. Individuals and private entities whose revenues no longer measure up to their spending needs can, and often must, unload goods they own on the market. Cities, faced, as highlighted in Part I, by that same predicament, have also increasingly turned to this practice. The sale of public municipal assets to private entities can serve two goals. One, it can be done in order to promote efficiency in the management of the asset and in the provision of public services through it. A city might sell its waterworks to a private corporation since that corporation is assumed to better manage the provision of water. Two, the sale can simply be a measure to raise money. The city will sell its waterworks to a private corporation—which may or may not be assumed to be able to better manage the provision of water—because the corporation is offering the city money in exchange for the waterworks.

Originally, sales of local assets were probably geared more towards the first of these two goals. Conceived as a part of the Thatcher era privatization drive, such sales were supposed to promote the better provision of public services in the U.K. The model spread to Europe and Australia.[69] Later in the process, and especially after 2008, the focus in municipal assets sales has shifted from the first goal—improved efficiency through privatization—to the second—plugging budgetary holes. In the last few years, American cities have offered their waterworks,[70] airports,[71] bridges,[72] and even municipal buildings for sale or lease.[73] Like the new American administration,[74] Brazil's incoming federal government has also signaled strong support for such sales of assets to overcome crippling debts on

69 *See* Emilia Istrate & Robert Puentes, *Moving Forward on Public Private Partnerships: U.S. and International Experience with PPP Units 8*, Brookings-Rockefeller Project on State & Metro. Innovation (2011), at 11.

70 *See* Danielle Ivory et al., *In American Towns, Private Profits from Public Works*, N.Y. Times (Dec. 24, 2016), www.nytimes.com/2016/12/24/business/dealbook/private-equity-water.html.

71 *See* Rachel Y. Tang, Cong. Research Serv. R43545, Airport Privatization: Issues and Options for Congress 1 (2016).

72 *See* Katie Benner, *Wall Street to Cities: Wanna Sell that Bridge?*, Fortune (June 11, 2010), http://archive.fortune.com/2010/06/11/news/economy/privatization_public_infrastructure.fortune/index.htm.

73 Michelle Conlin, *The Great Government Fire Sale is on*, San Diego Union-Trib. (May 13, 2011), www.sandiegouniontribune.com/sdut-the-great-government-fire-sale-is-on-2011may13-story.html.

74 Patrick Sisson, *The Art of the New Deal: Will Donald Trump Stamp his Name on the Project of a Lifetime, a Plan to Upgrade America's Crumbling Infrastructure?*, Curbed (Jan. 19, 2017), www.curbed.com/2017/1/19/14268628/trump-infrastructure-plan-new-deal.

the local and national levels.[75] Taiwan's central government has lately urged its local governments to explore new revenue sources, including "activating public assets" with private funding.[76] In China, state-owned local (or district) enterprises sometimes set up companies that are "contracted" out to private hands.[77] To fund a freeze in transit fares, London's mayor has endeavored to sell the city's transit authority's technologies (for bike shares, for example) to other cities. Finally, in both Italy and Latvia, entire towns were put on the market.[78] Although these last examples should not be taken as more than somewhat amusing and rather unrepresentative anecdotes, a trend does appear to be afoot. Cities are distinctly more likely, as compared to their behavior in earlier years, to sell assets—and often, for the sole goal of obtaining an immediate pecuniary return at a time of fiscal crisis.

C. *Investment of municipal funds*

Private actors, when they seek to contend with a funding bind, can borrow money; they can sell an asset they own and get money in return; they can also try and generate more money from the money they do have, by investing that existing money. In their own time of need, and in an era when turning to the market is all the rave, local governments worldwide have been doing the same: they have tried to invest their funds so as to enlarge their holdings. The idea is simple: rather than have funds—representing tax revenues, savings for pension payments, or deposits in a rainy-day fund—sit idly, they ought to be used in a manner that should, if all goes well, multiply those funds.

This course of action is appealing in good times and bad: irrespective of the current fiscal climate, existing funds can be used to increase local fiscal capacity and thereby to gird against fiscal crises. Investments in the marketplace and, in particular, investments in growth funds and vehicles which have the capacity to help insure against general financial predicaments are important devices helping local governments attenuate risk. To reap better returns, and to, supposedly, better adjust their investments to their risks and needs, local governments have

75 Andy Robinson, *Brazil for Sale: How a Legal Coup Set the Stage for Privatization*, Nation (July 27, 2016), www.thenation.com/article/brazil-for-sale-how-a-legal-coup-set-the-stage-for-privatization/.

76 Hsin-Fang Tsai, *Municipal Financial Strategy Responses to Fiscal Austerity: The Case of Taiwan, in* Value for Money: Budget and Financial Management Reform in the People's Republic of China, Taiwan and Australia (Andrew Podger et al. eds., 2018).

77 T. Zhang, *Innovation in Chinese Urban Governance: The Shanghai Experience*, in Cities in a Global Era: Urban Innovation, Competition and Democratic Reform (R. Hambleton & J. S. Gross eds., 2007); Fulong Wu, *China's Changing Urban Governance in the Transition Towards a More Market-oriented Economy*, 39 Urb. Stud. 1071 (2002).

78 *See* Romans Koksarovs & Gary Peach, *Latvian Ghost Town Auctioned off for $3.1 Million*, San Diego Union-Trib. (Feb. 5, 2010), www.sandiegouniontribune.com/sdut-latvian-ghost-town-auctioned-off-for-31-million-2010feb05-story.html.

accordingly switched to ever more exotic investment vehicles. Derivatives of all kinds, swaps, and other investments have become targets for local investment.

Financial tools have been a conspicuous part of the municipal fiscal landscape in the U.S. for decades. American local governments have traditionally invested their pension funds, but also their tax funds—and even, at times, money they have borrowed—in all kinds of securities. Since the 1990s, this practice has been taking hold in other regions. Chinese governments have been eager investors,[79] and in 2009, the Bank of Italy found that during the previous year local municipalities there had derivatives exposures with a face value of €24 to 33 billion.[80] French and German cities were assuming similar positions at around the same time.[81]

D. *Impact fees*

In addition to adopting practices that are almost purely private, or market-oriented, in nature, such as borrowing, selling assets, and investing funds, cities try to combat fiscal deficits by leveraging—even monetizing—their public, governmental, powers. This feat can be achieved through strategic public–private partnerships. Such partnerships have long been ubiquitous. But one of the more creative such mechanisms, garnering much recent attention, involves shifting the costs of constructing and maintaining local infrastructure to private firms. The technique can be crucial for avoiding a meltdown in services and infrastructure provision when the local government's own revenues dry up—as has happened in the aftermath of the recession.

Local governments, as noted at Part I's outset, are responsible for the delivery of some of the most important public services: roads, water, sewage, parks, schools, etc. They thus are tasked with funding said services. They can, however, provide those same services while avoiding funding them if they induce private actors to foot the bill on the government's behalf. The inducement governments can provide for this purpose is the permission to develop land in a more intensive manner. When a developer asks for a permit to build on or develop land, a fee will be charged during the approval process, calculated based on the proportional share of the capital costs of providing major local facilities. These fees go by different names in different systems, such as impact fees or betterment levies, and they have seen a recent surge in popularity.[82]

79 *See, e.g.*, Michelle Chen & Polly Yam, *China Lets More Government Firms Trade Commodities Derivatives Overseas*, Reuters (May 6, 2015).

80 Bankitalia, *Debito delle Amministrazioni Locali*, Bank of Italy (2009), www.bancaditalia.it/pubblicazioni/debito-amministrazioni/. For the most recent, and following legal reforms, reduced, numbers see the data for 2017, www.bancaditalia.it/pubblicazioni/debito-amministrazioni/2018-debito-amministrazioni/en_statistiche_FPR_20180228.pdf?language_id=1.

81 R. Dodd, *Municipal Bombs*, 47 Fin. & Dev. 33 (2010).

82 *See* G.S. Burge, *The Effects of Development Impact Fees on Local Fiscal Conditions*, *in* Municipal Revenues and Land Policies (Gregory K. Ingram & Yu-Hung Hong eds., 2010).

The fees are exacted from property owners in places such as Canada, Poland, Colombia, Argentina, and Mexico, and from developers in Canada, Australia, and Mexico.[83] They are widely used in North American jurisdictions (and in other developed locales, such as Santiago, Chile) to pay for all kinds of infrastructure costs (including affordable housing for city residents, roads improvement, school construction, and more). In developing countries, fees are much more often used to pay for infrastructure costs within the specific development project promoted by the paying developer.[84] In essence, the fees are a mechanism for trading in development rights. A particularly striking model, whereby the rights are wholly commodified, is found in São Paulo. There, since 2004, Certificates of Additional Construction Potential (CEPACs) have been auctioned at the São Paulo Stock Market Exchange by the city government. CEPACs give their purchaser the right to build larger floor area ratios and also change the use of the plot.[85]

The Brazilian example embodies—arguably, to the extreme—the logic animating impact fees as a tool facilitating the local government's financial functioning in times of economic distress. These tools allow the government to turn a governmental police power—the power to zone—into a sellable commodity. It generates new revenue from a power that the city already has—but that heretofore was not conceived as a fundraising mechanism.

III. Legal reforms necessary to accommodate local governments' new funding tools

Municipalities' turn to the market—through any of the mechanisms just described or others—is probably, as Part I illustrated, irreversible given current economic, political, and intellectual tides. Scholars and officials can question the turn's normative desirability—indeed, many have—and here we do not engage that important conversation. Rather, we proceed in light of the assumption that these policies are currently on the rise, and that therefore a vital task is to better their design. In this Part we suggest legal reforms that might avert some of the dangers the new funding techniques reviewed in Part II might stir up, without necessarily passing judgment on the normative appeal of any of the techniques.

A. Legal reforms to better municipal borrowing

Borrowing is, as noted in Part II, the most natural—and often, recommended—market reaction to a budget shortfall faced by any entity. Its theoretical appeal to local governments, as seen, is thus obvious. So are, however, its theoretical

83 *See* Bird & Slack, *supra* note 11.

84 *See* George Peterson, Unlocking Land Values to Finance Urban Infrastructure (2009).

85 *See* Paola Sandroni, *A New Financial Instrument of Value Capture in Sao Paulo: Certificates of Additional Construction Potential in* Municipal Revenues *supra* note 83.

pitfalls. Debt is a convenient means to burden future taxpayers with the costs of spending that solely benefits current officeholders and taxpayers (say spending on salaries for service providers as opposed to on long-lasting capital projects). Relatedly, like any private entity that needs funds and proceeds to assume debt, a local government might become overleveraged, default on its loans, and endure one form or another of economic collapse. Prolific borrowing by local governments has, for example, been cited as a cause for several financial crises in South America, such as the Argentinian collapse of the late 1990s.[86] More recently, in 2013 and then again in late 2017, major concern grew that unsustainable Chinese local government debt levels might destabilize that nation's financial markets.[87]

Most legal systems thus realize that local borrowing requires regulation. The most extreme version of such regulation, still prevalent in many systems, particularly in the developing world, is a flat-out legal ban on local borrowing. That course is ill advised, according to much economic literature, since, as already highlighted, local borrowing is efficient and equitable. Moreover, legal experience teaches, unsurprisingly, that cities will devise legal mechanisms to undercut a debt restriction, as highlighted by the Chinese and Chilean examples cited earlier. These mechanisms not only generate administrative costs, but also are highly unlikely to be of sound fiscal design.[88]

Adopting, instead of such a total prohibition on local debt, a cap, or some other restriction on debt issuance, eases many of these concerns. Many systems indeed opt to set a ceiling on the amount of debt an individual municipality may assume. Such caps, if set too low, could still generate the same concern as full bans; alternatively, if set too high, they would do little to negate the dangers of excessive borrowing. Although they are thus highly unlikely to be set at an accurate level, borrowing limits are still necessary if the higher-level government assures the locality's debt: if the state government will bail out a defaulting municipality, that government, naturally, cannot simply leave the municipality to borrow as it pleases. The state government, thus, while not necessarily the best regulator of local borrowing, is often the necessary regulator.

A solution for some systems is to remove the source of this necessity—the prospect of a state bailout—and leave the regulation of borrowing by local governments to the market. Lenders operating in the market are better equipped to assess the borrowing capacity of a municipality than any external actors, such as state legislators. A private lender will not issue credit to a locality in whose fiscal robustness it has no faith. In a well-functioning debt market, debt will thus only be funneled to localities that can carry its costs. Intermediaries—rating agencies—will emerge to aid potential lenders in

86 *See* United Cities, *supra* note 4, at 3606, 315, 205, 322.

87 *IMF and Moody's Sound Alarm Again over Local Debt*, South China Morning Post (Dec. 10, 2017).

88 *See* Nadav Shoked, *Debt Limits' End*, 102 Iowa L. Rev. 1239 (2017).

assessing the credit-worthiness of borrowing local governments. In such a sophisticated market, the risk of contagion—the spread of financial malaise from one entity to another—is curbed, as each locality is assessed on its own merits. This is, for example, the manner in which the municipal bond market in the U.S. normally operates.[89]

To enable an efficient market, however, laws are necessary. The feared implosion of the Chinese local debt market, generated by the opaqueness of local borrowing practices there,[90] exemplifies the risks associated with an unregulated lending market. Legal systems must grant market players the tools to assess the worth of local governments' debt. Transparency in municipal borrowing practices, full reporting of municipal finances, rules for early warning, are all reforms that must be passed by the national or state government. The Chinese government, announcing in early 2018 a series of reforms, appears intent on moving in that direction.[91] A model can be found in Japan's Act on Assurance of Sound Financial Status of Local Governments, passed in 2007,[92] a few years after Japanese localities were freed from the need to obtain national approval for their debt issuance.[93]

To allow the market to effectively rate a city's riskiness, the state must further make a credible assurance that it will not bail out a defaulting municipality. Such an assurance also reduces the state's need to directly regulate the local amount of debt, and permits it to, as suggested here, focus on regulating the procedures of borrowing, rather than on the amounts of borrowing. The latter task should be left to the market. If the state so desires, it can facilitate the formation of a demand for local bonds—and thus of such a market—by providing lenders with tax benefits. In the U.S. and India, for this exact reason, interest income that investors drive from local bonds enjoys a tax exemption.

In their attitude towards local debt, legal systems should focus not so much on prohibitions, but on structuring an efficient private market. They should make the local lending process less opaque, thereby enticing private parties to enter the market. Such reforms could not only help in solving the problem of excessive, and dangerous, debt, but also help address the opposite problem, one that is prevalent in developing countries. There, the challenge local governments face is

89 *Id.*

90 *See* Lingling Wei & Bob Davis, *Debt That Once Boosted its Cities Now Burdens China*, Wall St. J. (Jan. 28, 2015), www.wsj.com/articles/debt-that-once-boosted-its-cities-now-burdens-china-1422415981.

91 Shu Zhang & Engen Tham, *China Tightens Rules on Insurers to Fight Local Govt. Debt Risk*, Reuters (Jan. 18, 2018), www.reuters.com/article/us-china-economy-debt-insurers/china-tightens-rules-on-insurers-to-fight-local-govt-debt-risk-idUSKBN1F70O8.

92 Law No. 94 of 2007. For more, *see* Ministry of Internal Aff. & Comm., *White Paper on Local Public Finance Japan, 2012*, www.soumu.go.jp/iken/zaisei/24data/chihouzaisei_2012_en.pdf.

93 On that shift, *see* Ministry of Internal Aff. & Comm., *White Paper on Local Public Finance Japan, 2006*, www.soumu.go.jp/iken/zaisei/18data/2006e_c_visual.pdf.

not unsustainable debt levels, but rather the inability to find lenders and assume debt.[94] If the law structures a solid, trustworthy lending environment, international investors are much likelier to step into the breach and offer credit, thereby aiding localities in their time of fiscal need.

B Legal reforms to better the sale of municipal assets

While, if structured and aided effectively by state laws, the private market could provide a check on, and efficient regulation of, local borrowing, it cannot be expected to achieve the same result with respect to the sale of local assets. Quite the opposite: in this field the market should be expected to do its utmost to render deals as unsuccessful as possible for cities. In a one-off deal, buyers do not share the interests of sellers: the buyer of a municipal asset would like to attain the lowest price possible, while the selling city should strive to obtain the highest consideration. In this competition, rather often, it has been the private buyers who have prevailed. In Canada, Montréal's dealings with the private corporation managing its bike share plan (Bixi) have been exceptionally fraught, as the city kept infusing its funds while the private entity entered bankruptcy. Chicago's sale of its parking meters revenue was a notoriously bad deal: the city was underpaid by more than a billion dollars. Other sales of municipal assets in the U.S., such as waterworks, have followed similarly lamentable patterns.[95] In Germany, the courts have been asked to rule in a dispute between the city of Leipzig and UBS. The case relates to a complex sale-and-leaseback agreement that the city signed for its local waterworks; making good on the city's commitments to the bank in the deal may bankrupt the city.

The reason for local governments' failings in their negotiations with private buyers is often simple. The buyers are experienced, and repeat, market players. Local governments are not. Private buyers have sophisticated professional infrastructures—both within their organizations and outside of them—that they rely on and that allow them to strive for the best deals possible. Local governments do not. After all, they are governments, not businesses. If local governments are to negotiate with buyers on equal terms, this professional gap must be closed. Local governments must undertake serious internal procedures before committing themselves to a sale of assets or any other complicated market deal. The value of the asset must be determined before the sale by an objective assessor; an invitation to multiple bidders should be made; bidders' offers must be compared along multiple dimensions and by disparate stakeholders; deliberations must precede any decision; more than one decision point should be assured;

94 *See* Martinez-Vasquez, *supra* note 6, at 26.

95 *See* Max Schanzenbach & Nadav Shoked, *Reclaiming Fiduciary Law for the City*, 70 Stan. L. Rev. 565 (2018).

professional, and preferably, outside, counsel on legal and economic elements of the transaction must be obtained.

The IMF thus recommends a set of best practices for cities engaging market actors.[96] To one degree or another, such recommendations were adopted through legislation in Australia and in some European countries.[97] In another article, one of us has suggested that in the absence of legislation, courts in common law countries could impose such procedural duties on local governments through corporate law doctrines.[98]

Raising funds through the sale of assets is assumed to be—and is—an easy, and thus attractive, way to raise funds in tight budgetary times. Securing a good deal is not so easy, however, and must not be assumed to be. For the facially simple task of selling assets on the market local governments must develop their own sophisticated market infrastructure. Due to costs, inertia, laziness, and perhaps officials' self-interest, such infrastructure is unlikely to materialize organically. Local governments must be forced—through legislation or court order—to institute it.

C. Legal reforms to better municipal investments

For the next tool traditionally popular among private market actors and recently adopted by local governments—financial investments—the recommendation respecting the need to develop sophisticated internal infrastructure applies with even greater force—and urgency. Spectacular failures in local governments' investment of funds are easy to pinpoint. In the U.S., Detroit was pushed into bankruptcy in 2012 by the failure of its bet on swaps.[99] Almost two decades earlier, Orange County, California, one of the most affluent locales in the nation, had entered what was then the largest municipal bankruptcy in history because of the disastrous investment strategy employed by its treasurer, ignoring almost uniform contrary advice, and eventually costing the county $1.8 billion.[100] These ruinous occurrences, very much like the investing practices giving them birth, are no longer purely American. In France, Saint-Étienne's deputy-mayor decided to invest in swaps to very bad effect.[101] In Italy, Milan's 2005 investment in interest-rate derivatives (means of converting the city's fixed-interest rate payments on its bonds to a lower, floating rate, supposedly with a limit on the losses

96 *See Public–Private Partnerships*, Fiscal Aff. Dep't, (Int'l Monetary Fund, 2004), at 15–16.
97 *See* Istrate & Puentes, *supra* note 70.
98 Schanzenbach & Shoked, *supra* note 96. Administrative law may, in certain instances, be used for this purpose as well, though it too requires adjustments to the unique settings of local governments. Nestor M. Davidson, *Localist Administrative Law*, 126 Yale L.J. 564 (2017).
99 *See* In re City of Detroit, 504 B.R. 97, 115–16 (Bankr. E.D. Mich. 2013).
100 *See* Mark Baldassare, Government Fails: The Orange County Bankruptcy 1–6 (1998).
101 *See* Alan Katz, *The City that Got Swapped*, Bloomberg Newsweek (Apr. 22, 2010), www.bloomberg.com/news/articles/2010-04-22/the-city-that-got-swapped.

that a bad bet on the future level of interest rate could generate) soured within a few years, leading to acrimonious litigation.[102]

As the litigation in the Italian court exposed, in almost all such cases the problem's root is city officials' misunderstanding of highly sophisticated investment vehicles. Since these officials are not bankers or investment professionals, they cannot be expected to perform much better. A more robust support staff and better decision-making processes, as suggested for selling municipal assets in the preceding section, offer themselves as a solution here as well. Still, we doubt that they will be sufficient. Sophisticated investing is a much more complicated, and speculative, endeavor, than the relatively straightforward assignment of selling an asset. Believing that cities can develop the necessary mechanisms to handle such a task might be too aspirational. A large staff of financial advisors will have to be retained—and those advisors, if they are to truly represent the top of the profession, will not be cheap. Most, almost all, cities could not afford such a commitment.

The more realistic solution, therefore, is for legal systems to establish centralized authorities—on the national or state/provincial levels—to advise, if not fully handle, local investments. This central authority could also, conceivably, take the form of a collective endeavor funded and established by the disparate local governments themselves, pulling their resources together to construct a joint bureaucracy each individual government could not afford to maintain on its own.[103] The central government will probably still have to incentivize—if not actively force—the formation of this joint authority handling local investment decisions, yet reliance on inter-local agreements would represent a more subtle form of centralization.

Regardless of the manner in which it is established, such an authority could economize on expenses, employ economies of scale, and draw on retained experience, to improve the performance of cities as investors. Many states already maintain such systems for disparate aspects of local finances, such as local borrowing, and the model can be replicated.[104] In 2010, Italy did so, when it moved to force local governments to get an opinion on any proposed derivative deal from the Ministry of Economy and Finances. Local governments are required to prove to the Ministry's satisfaction that a transaction would leave them better off than simply repaying their current debt. Though such centralization decreases the potential for local experimentation, in this specific context, and given the extraordinary financial costs and risks involved, this loss should be tolerated—if a system insists on allowing localities to turn to the investment market (systems can of course simply block localities access to that market, and an example for a recent prohibition is found in China, where government policy implemented in May 2017 restricts local governments from using loans to set up investment funds).

102 *See Cities in the Casino*, ECONOMIST (Mar. 18, 2010), www.economist.com/node/15731538.

103 We are grateful to Nestor Davidson for making this suggestion to us.

104 In the U.S., North Carolina is the best example.

D. Legal reform to better impact fees

Since the last tool reviewed in Part II—impact fees—is the most traditionally governmental in nature, it requires the least dramatic adjustment to existing legal practices. Acquaintance with, and adaptation to, private market practices is not as indispensable here as it is when local governments employ the preceding three tools that are much more private market-focused in nature. Still, because impact fees involve the modification of public requirements in exchange for private investment and services, they heighten the risks associated with the intermingling of public and private in local government action.[105] Worldwide, land use decisions, particularly those incorporating zoning permits and variances, are a major producer of corruption cases. Furthermore, even in the absence of any type of corruption, such decisions tend to create inequities: major developers, as repeat players, will be able to negotiate with the government and get the deals and variances they desire much more easily than smaller developers or individuals.[106]

One means for overcoming these dangers is to minimize the role played by the factor responsible for their emergence: the individualized form of negotiations ahead of the setting of an impact fees charge. An opening for favoring some developers over others is created when the government's decision-making process is not clearly structured but rather relies on discrete determinations with respect to each and every project. Therefore, the requirement, nature, and amount of impact fees should—to the extent possible—be predetermined in clear local regulations. Logical and coherent formulas must be made available. Interested developers should be able to consult the local law book or database and determine the amount of funds they will have to dedicate to a particular project if they are to receive the governmental concession they seek. Naturally, some flexibility must be preserved. Not all projects and legal permissions are amenable to precise and uniform rules determined in the abstract ex-ante. But guidelines, at the very least, can and must be accessible to the relevant public.

As international organizations often preach, the arbitrariness that is inherent to any ad-hoc decision-making process and that inevitably favors those in the know must be removed from the impact fees' legal realm. Clear local ordinances could do much to promote this goal. These ordinances will enable impact fees—a financial tool local governments often must rely on in these fiscally turbulent

105 Poor design of the policy can engender further risks (for example, if the fees are not paid up front the city might end up taking the obligation on itself—as sometimes happened with respect to sports facilities; or if the city requires the developer to provide services or infrastructure these might prove to be not those desired by the public). *See*, for example, Almos T. Tassonyi, *Financing Infrastructure in Canada's City-Regions, in* Urban Governance and Finance: A Question of Who Does What 171 (Paul Hobson & France St. Hilare eds., 1997); *and see* Bird & Slack, *supra* note 11, at 152.

106 For a formal discussion of the problem in the specific legal context of American federal law see David A. Dana, *Land Use Regulation in an Age of Heightened Scrutiny*, 75 N.C. L. Rev. 1243, 1297 (1997).

days—to serve their beneficial public financing role. Still, it is important to always acknowledge a perhaps inconvenient reality: impact fees, even if wisely administered, will not be the panacea for local governments' fiscal predicament. Through impact fees, developers fund infrastructure and services the city desires. Impact fees thus presuppose developers. Developers, in turn, can be found in cities that are doing well enough to entice development. Impact fees can help, for example, a New York or a São Paulo, but not other, more rural or suburban, communities in the U.S. or Brazil.

Conclusion

The twenty-first century is materializing as a good century for cities. It is arguably the century of the city: in the developing world cities are growing at unheard of rates and in the developed world cities are regaining their cultural and economic bearing. But not all the changes brought about by the last two decades have been positive for cities worldwide. A dramatic shift in ideological, political, and economic realities upset the existing funding regimes cities had relied on for decades. The Great Recession of 2008 was the first global economic upheaval to take place against this new background, and its effects on local finances were hence unprecedented. In legal systems that leave little room for autonomous means of local revenue raising, vital grants from higher level governments were drastically cut. In systems that afford some fiscal autonomy, local flexibility in designing taxation schemes that could effectively react to the downturn was limited by new laws or political and economic trends. Consequently, in their plight, almost everywhere, local governments have turned to new tools for generating revenues. These tools, inevitably, are much more private market oriented than ever before. Local governments' borrowing has ballooned, local governments now sell to private buyers assets they have held for decades if not centuries, many local governments invest their holdings in financial markets, and often local governments try to shift infrastructure costs on property owners and private developers through the charging of impact fees. While these tools can, and do, aid governments in plugging budgetary holes generated by new fiscal realities, they pose risks, risks that only shrewd legal reforms can attenuate. In thinking of such reforms, and in ensuring that their novel financing practices are rational, legal systems and local governments should draw on the experience of other governments and systems; they should take advantage of the availability of global perspectives on urban law.

9 Keeping municipal law making democratic

A critical appraisal of the legal position of third party rights from the state of Victoria, Australia

Rebecca Leshinsky

Introduction

> … we have a duty to the community … we're planning for the whole of Melbourne, so we're planning for the developers and the people who live here and the people who work here, people who come here every day. So we're planning for everybody and we've got to balance everybody's needs and when something's been to council and there's a decision on it, we've got to represent that view and we feel that's a community view, meaning all those parts, including developers. That's why we do it.
>
> (City of Melbourne: Land use planning officer)

With the spread of democracy, and its decline,[1] it is important for community involvement to play an active role in local government decision making. Citizen involvement offers another check and balance on municipal transparency and assists in avoiding conflicts of interest. Globally, urbanization continues in its growth phase and cities are challenged by population growth; infrastructure renewal; affordable and available housing; climate change and adaptation, among many other issues – all of which impact local law making. These challenges are situated in a period of economic austerity where governments are rationalizing public spending.

(Re)education, rather than strict enforcement is the starting place at the local government level in the state of Victoria, Australia. In turn, or, by virtue of, there is mature juridical support for citizen involvement in municipal decision making, despite a lack of constitutional protection. The current political economy favours the maintenance of the status quo and, as Wilson and Swyngedouw have observed,[2]

1 In this chapter, when we speak of "democracy," we are following the Freedom in the World Methodology used by Arch Puddington and Tyler Roylance, *Anxious Dictators Wavering Democrats*, 27 J. DEMOCRACY 86 (2016). *See also Methodology: Freedom in the World 2016*, FREEDOM HOUSE (2016), https://freedomhouse.org/report/freedom-world-2016/methodology; Marc F. Plattner, *Is Democracy in Decline?* 26 J. OF DEMOCRACY 5 (2015).

2 THE POST-POLITICAL AND ITS DISCONTENTS: SPACES OF DEPOLITICISATION, SPECTRES OF RADICAL POLITICS (Japhy Wilson & Erik Swyngedouw eds., 2014).

> [agnostic] political disagreement has been replaced by an ultra-politics of ethnicised and violent disavowal on the one hand, and the exclusion and containment of those who pursue a different political-economic model on the other. These extremes are placed outside the post-democratic inclusion of different opinions on anything imaginable in stakeholder arrangements of impotent participation and "good governance," which ensure that the framework of debate and decision-making does not question or disrupt the existing state of the neoliberal political-economic configuration. This process is generally referred to as one of post-politicisation, institutionally configured through modes of post-democratic governance.[3]

With cities facing austerity measures that dig deep into citizen pockets, such as the public bailout of irresponsible financial institutions, rising tuition fees, and a price hike in public transport, it is important for opportunities for public participation to be recorded so as not to allow for a further withering of community involvement in public decision making. The model discussed in this paper, as a type of community and legal memory stems from the state of Victoria, Australia, and is by no means utopian. Rather, it is a starting point that shares from a jurisdiction not often cited, and carries insight into an open and (relatively) inclusive system, which also faces a strong neo-liberalist agenda that hinders dissenting community positions. Local government governance touches lives on a daily basis and, to be for the people, the people must be allowed to have their say in this process.

Whilst democracy is not an absolute state, allowing people to exercise democratic rights seems so natural to Australians, particularly after the *Australia Act 1986* (Cth),[4] which significantly severed legal ties with the United Kingdom, allowing for a real sense of independence as a sovereign nation.[5] Notwithstanding legal excise from Britain, Australia is still very much connected with Britain and this is based on the nature of the Queen remaining the Constitutional monarch (Head) of the Commonwealth of Australia.

Australia does not have a U.S. style Bill of Rights. Rather, it has a written constitution[6] that provides some sense of rights but in many ways is an operational directive on how to run the Commonwealth of Australia.

In this chapter, we first outline the political and economic position of Australia, with an emphasis on Melbourne, the capital city of the state of Victoria. Then, some of the legal opportunities afforded to the community to participate in local law making are discussed. Throughout the chapter, we share findings from a

3 *Id.* at 5.

4 *Australia Act 1986* (Cth) (Austl.); *See also* Australia Act 1986, c. 2 (U.K.).

5 The effect of the Australia Act is the termination of power of the Parliament of United Kingdom to legislate for the Commonwealth of Australia and the Australian states and territories.

6 Commonwealth of Australia Act, 1900, 63 & 64 Vict. c. 12, 9 (U.K.).

recent study where stakeholder views on local law making in Melbourne were gathered.[7] We conclude with the message that expressions of citizen involvement in local law making must be shared glocally so that municipalities can learn reciprocal lessons for more transparent law-making processes.

I. A case study – Melbourne, Australia

A. Background

Australia is a federation, emerging in 1901 from an amalgamation of former British colonies to become the Commonwealth of Australia.[8] The country has always enjoyed a laissez-faire economic system, albeit within quite a regulated regime. Whilst the country has never provided the type of welfare experienced as, say, in the Scandinavian nations, there has been comprehensive health cover, but over time, governments at all levels have reduced public spending on health, housing, welfare, and infrastructure, leaving much to be regulated by market forces. Australia has adopted a strong neo-liberalist approach and this is evidenced in the growth of public–private partnerships now being experienced in the upgrading of its ageing infrastructure.[9] Melbourne has grown into one of the most "liveable" cities in the world.[10] It experienced a successful gold rush in the 1860s and 1870s, with money from this period assisting to build a well-planned city with world class infrastructure. This infrastructure is now in urgent need of upgrading, as the city of Melbourne continues to attract about 100,000 additional people per year.[11] The city has changed quite dramatically, particularly over the past 25 years, shifting from medium rise built environment to a more dense city housing many hundreds of high rise developments.[12] At the same time, as the city has become more complex, there has been a need for greater local regulation.

7 This study formed part of a larger project for U.N.-Habitat. We thank U.N.-Habitat for their support and research grant. A special thanks is extended to Robert Lewis-Lettington and Melissa Permezel from U.N.-Habitat Nairobi.

8 *See* Stuart MacIntyre, The Oxford History of Australia 4 (1986).

9 *See* Andrew Beer et al., *Neoliberalism, Economic Restructuring and Policy Change: Precarious Housing and Precarious Employment in Australia*, 53 Urb. Stud. 8, 1542 (2016).

10 *See* The Data Team, *The World's Most "Liveable" Cities*, Economist (Aug. 18, 2015), www.economist.com/blogs/graphicdetail/2015/08/daily-chart-5.

11 *See Melbourne Our Fastest-growing Capital*, Austl. Bureau Stat. (Mar. 30, 2016), www.abs.gov.au/ausstats/abs@.nsf/lookup/3218.0Media%20Release12014-15.

12 *See* Leanne Hodyl, *To Investigate Planning Policies That Deliver Positive Social Outcomes in Hyper-dense, High-rise Residential Environments*, Winston Churchill Mem'l Trust Austl. (2015), www.churchilltrust.com.au/media/fellows/Hodyl_L_2014_Social_outcomes_in_hyper-dense_high-rise_residential_environments_1.pdf.

B. Local law making: the role of the local government act

In Australia there are three tiers of government: Federal, State, and Local. The *Local Government Act 1989* (LG Act) is the state statute in Victoria that governs the operations of 79 local councils in the state. Melbourne is the capital city of Victoria and is in many respects just another local council in the state of Victoria. As it is also the capital city of the state of Victoria, additional regulation governs the city. For the purposes of this chapter, we will outline the process of community involvement in local law making from the perspective of the municipality of the City of Melbourne.

Melbourne is one of the local councils in Victoria, and carries some further special categorization due to it being the state capital. The City of Melbourne, like other Australian local councils, consists of elected Council members and day-to-day operational officers. A Chief Executive Officer (CEO) heads this operational council team, all of whom are expected to act at all times with due diligence and in a transparent and fair manner, free of any conflicts of interest. These requirements are mandated in the LG Act. The City of Melbourne, only since the 1980s, has become more residential in character. Traditionally it was a central business hub, but has changed now to accommodate a mixed-use position.[13]

> There's a schedule to the [Local Government] Act, so the procedure for making local laws, the availability of local laws, commencement of local laws and ... local laws have a life of 10 years and revocation by the governing councils all within the body of the Local Government Act.
>
> (NGO2: Officer)

There is a dedicated transparent legal methodology for making local laws and this involves some community consultation. For instance, s. 208 of the LG Act notes that councils must develop a program of regular consultation with its community in relation to the services it provides[14] and further, it must report regularly to its community on its achievements.[15] The LG Act and the various regulations made under that statute set out the extent and nature of local government law-making authority and the operation of local government. Local government is not recognized by the Australian Federal constitution. Lacking a place for local government in the Commonwealth Constitution further weakens the power balance of local councils as compared to State and Federal governments.

Councils, as local governments, consist of independently elected councillors, as well as operational staff being local government officers. The LG Act carries very

13 *See Postcode 3000 – A City Transformed?*, City of Melbourne: What's On Blog (Aug. 21, 2013), http://blog.thatsmelbourne.com.au/postcode-3000-a-city-transformed/.

14 *Local Government (Best Value Principles) Act 1999*, (Vict.) s 208(e) (Austl.).

15 *Id.* at s 208 (f).

strict civil and criminal penalties for any deliberate misconduct by councillors or council staff, including facilitating with conflicts of interest.[16]

Local governments are responsible for land use zoning and the determination of land use and development applications, local roads, waste management, and services for local communities. Local governments are funded by the collection of local property rates but also rely on levies and grants from State and Federal Governments who hold a great deal of power over councils. Local law-making can be seen to be filling in a "missing gap" because local government is said to be "in closer" touch with the community for local issues on a daily basis. For such issues, local councils become the first point of contact for citizens who have a civic concern or grievance. In this way, there is a level of accountability at the "grassroots" local government level.[17]

The preparation of local laws is governed by the enabling Act and provisions in Schedule 8 of the LG Act, whereby, local law-making procedures must be followed to be valid. Guidance is provided by the Victorian State Government document "Guidelines for Local Laws Manual."[18] However, following the manual is only a "suggestion" and is not mandated by legislation that may limit the scope of its effectiveness. At the creation stage, the sectorial experience required comes from local Council staff drafting and reviewing draft law, and presenting the proposed local law to Council for adoption. The legislative requirements relate to community engagement, and adoption of the local law by Council. A proposed local law must be passed by a majority of elected councillors present at a Council meeting. The implementation stage follows adoption of a local law by a local Council. It requires the publication of a notice in the Victorian State Government Gazette stating details of the new local law and a copy of the local law must be sent to the Minister for Local Government. A copy of the local law must also be kept available at local Council offices for inspection. The enforcement of the local law requires experienced local Council officers.

The LG Act sets out strict conduct principles for all local Councils and requires all staff in the course of their employment to act impartially, act with integrity including avoiding conflicts of interest, accept accountability for results, and provide responsive service. There is also a requirement for the CEO of each local Council to develop and implement a Code of Conduct. Additionally, there are strict requirements placed on the election process and appointment of local councillors, and the selection of the CEO and senior officers. This includes the specification that the employment of Council staff is based on merit and the

16 *See, e.g., id.* at ss 28A, 78B, 79, 80B.

17 *See* Andy Inch, *Ordinary Citizens and the Political Cultures of Planning: In Search of the Subject of a New Democratic Ethos*, 14 Plan. Theory 404 (2014).

18 Vict. Dep't Plan. Cmty. Dev., Guidelines for Local Laws Resource Book 3 (2010), www.localgovernment.vic.gov.au/__data/assets/pdf_file/0021/48720/Local_Laws_Resource_Book.pdf.

obligation for the Council to review the performance of the Chief Executive Officer and for the Chief Executive Officer to review the performance of every senior officer at least once each year.

As part of the procedure for making a local law, a council must give notice in the Government Gazette and a public notice stating:

(a) the purpose and general purport of the proposed local law; and
(b) that a copy of the proposed local law and any explanatory document can be obtained from the Council office; and
(c) that any person affected by the proposed local law may make a submission relating to the proposed local law.[19]

This provision allows for participation by an affected party, which in effect, narrows third party involvement to those only "affected" by the proposed local law.

> In terms of the decision making process, I think it's as robust as you could possibly get. All of those who are submitters have an interest of some sort in the local law. That's not a conflict of interest. It's good that they have an interest and that they are making a submission in respect to it. So yes, that's about it.
>
> (NGO 1, Officer)

Other than the review of proposed local laws by local council staff and the Council at the time of adoption, there are no other mechanisms for review before adoption. The LG Act provides the Executive branch of the Victorian State Government the power to revoke a local law if it exceeds the powers conferred to it under its enabling Act or is inappropriate for any other reason. Therefore, the Victorian State Government has the final say in whether a local law and thus the preparatory work, drafting and local council adoption, has been appropriate. Additionally, the validity of a local law can be challenged under the *Supreme Court Act 1986* (Vic). Ultimately, all of this detracts from the actual hands-on control local government has over its own law-making processes.

Should there be any legal inconsistency between the laws of the Australian Government and any State legislation, s. 109 of the Commonwealth Constitution provides that the Federal law shall prevail to the extent of the inconsistency. The Australian Federal Government is thus not directly involved in the regulation or administration of local government. However, it provides significant support to local government through provision of funding, including financial assistance, grants, and running the National Award for Local Government. There is a Federal Minister for Local Government whose role is largely to oversee the allocation of State funding to councils. The Federal government therefore plays

19 *Local Government Act 1989* (Cth) s 119(2)(a).

an important role in local councils because it provides some of their essential funding. This is seen in particular via large infrastructure projects that are often financed by the Federal and State government working together and/or, and more commonly of late, in a Public Private Partnership (PPP) relationship. Local councils affected by these projects will have a say but are not as persuasive as the State and Federal decision makers.

Amendments to the LG Act over the past couple of years have tightened up expectations on council officers and councillors to ensure that the operational side of local government is kept free from unlawful behaviour. The local government inspectorate is run from the State government with strong investigative and enforcement powers. Whilst there is always the chance for untoward behaviour to slip through the system, and there have been matters that have been reported over time, overall, by virtue of the way the law is set up and operates in Victoria, it can be said that the system of law is effective and efficient.

The LG Act allows for each local government to make "local laws" to assist it in carrying out its functions and powers in its district. The City of Melbourne has three such local laws dealing with a wide range of community, environmental, and governance issues. The Activities Local Law 2009 and the Environment Local Law 2009 provide City of Melbourne with the ability to prescribe various matters including exemptions and forms. The Conduct of Meetings Local Law 2010 provides guidelines for the conduct of Council and committee meetings.

> Governance and legal departments in the City are intentionally kept separate to ensure best practice and transparent law making . . . the Local Government Act has teeth to ensure law making in the City of Melbourne is fair and transparent. There is very little case law to suggest differently. All local laws once adopted are publicly available and need to be on councils' websites.
>
> (NGO 2: Officer)

Local laws sunset in the state of Victoria after 10 years and such legal procedure forces the system to disallow enduring laws. It is an added check and balance on the system. If local law making does not accord with the Local Government Act procedure, there is an opportunity to appeal to the Victorian Supreme Court on the grounds of natural justice and procedural fairness. There is very little case law to suggest differently.

A new initiative for public participation was trialed in 2014 in the form of a people's panel. Whilst citizen juries have never been a part of local law making in Melbourne, a novel exercise was carried out in 2014.[20] A people's panel was randomly assembled to advise the council on a 10-year financial plan for the city. The panel met five times between August and November 2014 and 11

20 *See* Rosanna Ryan, *Melbourne Citizens' Jury Success Offers Fresh Hope for Democratic Renewal*, Austl. Broadcasting Corp. (Jul. 3, 2015), www.abc.net.au/radionational/programs/sundayextra/citizens'-jury-success-offers-fresh-hope-for-democratic-renewal/6589630.

recommendations were put forward, covering a range of areas from rates, the environment, sustainability and climate change, managing assets, community services, and capital works.[21] Whilst it was an excellent initiative for the City of Melbourne in terms of community engagement, some sceptics might argue why this is not a more common exercise and whether this endeavour is more show than substance.

II. Perceptions on local law making

A. *A view from Melbourne*[22]

Peppered throughout this chapter are quotations from respondents who participated in our recent study, which examined stakeholder perceptions on local law making in the City of Melbourne. Nine semi-structured, face-to-face interviews were also conducted to explore local law making for land use planning and waste management in the City of Melbourne. Findings from these interviews were used to establish stakeholder impressions and perceptions on local law making. Included in these discussions were views and experiences on transparency and honesty in the local law-making process.

The interviews were conducted with representatives from the City of Melbourne and non-government organizations (NGOs from the local government sector), and a representative from the Victorian State Government. Unfortunately, during the scheduled interview period, councillors from the City of Melbourne were unavailable to be interviewed due to conflicting commitments. No member from any community engagement group or resident or business people from the City of Melbourne were interviewed. This is a shortcoming in the findings and opens the door for further research work to be undertaken in this area. We acknowledge that the sample size is small and that this study is more exploratory in nature. Findings from the semi-structured interviews contribute therefore to a pilot project that broadly addressed the following themes and topic areas:

- Perceptions on local law making
- Understanding of local law making
- Where local law making fits in the Australian system of law
- Process of local law making
- How local laws are passed and by what institutions

21 *See 10 Year Financial Plan Asset Management Strategy 2015–25*, City of Melbourne: Participate Melbourne (Oct. 20, 2015), http://participate.melbourne.vic.gov.au/10yearplan.

22 I would like to thank U.N.-Habitat Nairobi for funding the research project discussed in this article. Special thanks also to Dr. Judy Rex, ACU and to Dr. Melissa Permezel from U.N.-Habitat for all of their support with the research project.

- Perceptions about fairness and transparency in local law making
- Awareness of conflicts of interest in local law making
- Opportunities for community engagement
- Different roles of decision makers in the local law-making process
- Decision making in local law making
- Operational frameworks in local law making.

Respondents explained that ideas for new local laws could be presented to the local Council for consideration by anyone who was interested in having the law introduced or interested in changing an existing law. This could include residents and business people including commuters and those who own and/or manage local businesses within the City of Melbourne. The requirements for community engagement under the LG Act emphasizes that there should be proper consultation and community involvement in the local law-making process. Respondents interviewed were well aware of these provisions.

> In preparing a local law, the council will generally go beyond its statutory consultation requirements and consult with the community generally and particular stakeholders who are identified who may be impacted to a greater extent.
>
> (City of Melbourne: Officer)

> There are certain requirements under the statute about consulting and how they should be exhibited but we always do extra to make sure that whoever we think is going to be affected is notified.
>
> (NGO2: Officer)

The process that they follow is: they are required to advertise in the Victorian Government Gazette, local newspapers, and on the web. The Council also does a direct mail out to all the stakeholders and property owners who may be affected.

> We don't hide ads on page 64 of a newspaper.
>
> (City of Melbourne: Governance officer)

Not all respondents were so supportive of the community engagement process. When a law is proposed, some respondents commented, it appears that submissions regarding the local law are in fact rather limited in number. The exception is when a particular stakeholder group may pick up on an issue. This has occurred with more contentious developments such as a proposal to erect a high-rise building.

> You must put it [local law] in the Government Gazette. You must put it on your website. We don't play ... minimums.
>
> (City of Melbourne: Officer)

> In terms of what local laws can deal with, they are not at liberty to deal with any matter that is the subject of state legislation, but they are able to address gaps in state legislation and provide finer grain requirements for occupiers and a range of activities within municipalities.
>
> (City of Melbourne: Legal Officer)

There was a feeling from respondents that Federal and State governments could try to work closer with local governments because, being closer to the community, local government is in a better position to make laws that are relevant to their local communities.

Reinforcing that local government is close to the community, some respondents were proud to claim that sometimes, when new laws were passed by local governments, they were adopted by other municipalities at a later date. It was also suggested that more should be done to make local laws more uniform and relevant to a broader range of councils across the state.

> We are the area that actually people contact – in local government, people actually contact their local government and talk to people. State government is far away.
>
> (City of Melbourne: Land use planning officer)

> ... it is important to make sure that residential associations or other community groups are aware that this is their opportunity to say, no, we don't want any change or we want change of this type, to ensure that you do get representative input and not simply input from those who have a particular vested interest.
>
> (City of Melbourne: Officer)

This comment was in contrast to another opinion where a respondent felt that:

> A local law is to deal with things which are relevant to your municipal district which may not be in common with the rest of the community. That's the intent of it.
>
> (City of Melbourne: Officer)

Law making at the local level touches people's lives at first instance. It is not uncommon, when citizens are unsure how to proceed with a daily endeavour, to contact their local council at first instance.[23] Yet, in Australia, local government is a poorly funded institution heavily reliant on Federal and State government for financial support.

23 *See* Gerald E. Frug, *The City as a Legal Concept*, 93 HARV. L. REV. 1056 (1980); *see also* GERALD E. FRUG, CITY MAKING: BUILDING COMMUNITIES WITHOUT BUILDING WALLS (1999).

> We are the area that actually people contact – in local government, people actually contact their local government and talk to people. State government is far away.
>
> (City of Melbourne: Land use planning officer)

> I think what we also see is that globally, local government or municipal government depending on how it's called in different contexts, plays a really critical role in city development. Even the local bylaws or ordinances that they develop can have an impact on people's everyday lives.
>
> (NGO2: Officer)

B. Movement towards sharing glocal engagement experiences

A number of findings emerged from the City of Melbourne study. These have been reported in greater detail elsewhere.[24] One significant finding was that it is education rather than hard-core enforcement that provides for better compliance with local law requirements. We suggest that a more inclusive step that is necessary even before re(education) is for the community and the state itself to provide robust opportunities for citizens to be involved in local law making. The state of Victoria supports a strong system of enforcement and accountability and this has been architecturally built in to the local law-making process, particularly through the LG Act. We argue that whilst the Rule of Law and strong democratic processes are supported by the state of Victoria, and by the various municipalities in the state, there is still much greater scope for community involvement. The literature in this area suggests that ownership of local policy and law breeds confidence in the system.[25]

Conclusion

Chan[26] speaks of city diplomacy and "glocal" governance and holds the belief that world affairs can be managed by cities, as diplomacy and democracy originated in the Greek city-states. In itself, this may be still a utopian ideal, and one that was never even achieved when Greece was a global power, but certainly geo-connectivity has been made very real in the twenty-first century. From this perspective, we agree that there are certainly reciprocal lessons for cities, both

24 *See* Rebecca Leshinsky, *Touching on Transparency in City Local Law Making: Experiences from the City of Melbourne, Australia*, 8 Int'l J. L. Built Env't 194 (2016).

25 *See* John F. Forester, The Deliberative Practitioner: Encouraging Participatory Planning Processes (1999); *see also* Patsy Healey, Collaborative Planning: Shaping Places in Fragmented Societies (2nd ed. 2006).

26 *See* Dan Koon-hong Chan, *City Diplomacy and "Glocal" Governance: Revitalizing Cosmopolitan Democracy*, 29 Eur. J. Soc. Sci. Res. 134 (2016), http://dx.doi.org/10.1080/13511610.2016.1157684.

nationally and internationally, to learn from each other on how to better involve citizens so that views and needs can be met in a more inclusive and just manner.[27]

The next logical steps for the study reported on in this chapter are for a more thorough examination of where public participation has been robust and most effective in local law making and what this has meant in terms of equitable and inclusive outcomes, as well as community satisfaction with particular local laws that touch on their lives. Compliance and enforcement are important in this context. There is also opportunity via public participation to lobby law makers as many voices must play an active role in inclusive local law making.

27 *See* Susan S. Fainstein, The Just City (2010).

10 Saving sriracha, fighting city power

An LA school view of urban law in a hot sauce conflict

Ernesto Hernández-López

Introduction

In November of 2013, national newspapers reported that sriracha, an extremely popular hot sauce with a cult-like global following, could have its production shut down by Irwindale, a city in Greater Los Angeles.[1] This city of less than 1,500 residents sued its maker Huy Fong Foods, Inc. (Huy Fong) in court, soon after their relocation there. Irwindale argued that their chile pepper grinding created a public nuisance with smells affecting resident health.[2] A judge issued a preliminary order for the company to stop producing obnoxious odors.[3] Trial was set to start twelve months later. These legal proceedings appear to focus on a local conflict.

Meanwhile, foodies, chefs, hipsters, and Asian food lovers obsessed over legal nuisance proceedings, which moved to Irwindale's city council in February of 2014.[4] In April, the council formally declared Huy Fong to be a public nuisance.[5] With attention far from Los Angeles, the dispute fed larger debates, casting California as anti-business, and Republican politicians and rival states begging the $20 million plus a year company to leave Irwindale. The fact that

1 *See* Frank Shyong, *Sriracha Sauce Factory Odor Causing Headaches, Burning Eyes, City Says*, L. A. Times (Oct. 28, 2013), http://articles.latimes.com/2013/oct/28/local/la-me-ln-irwindale-sues-sriracha-20131028.

2 *See* Mark Memmott, *Sriracha Factory Under Fire for Fumes; City Sues*, NPR: The Two Way (Oct. 29, 2013, 9:23 AM), www.npr.org/blogs/thetwo-way/2013/10/29/241587163/sriracha-factory-under-fire-for-fumes-city-sues.

3 *See* Frank Shyong, *Sriracha Plant Must Cease Operations that Cause Odors, Judge Rules*, L.A. Times (Nov. 26, 2013), http://articles.latimes.com/2013/nov/26/local/la-me-judge-rules-no-sriracha-20131126; *See also* Patrick T. Fallon, *Judge Orders Sriracha Hot Sauce Plant Partly Closed Over Odors*, CNBC (Nov. 27, 2013), www.cnbc.com/2013/11/27/judge-orders-sriracha-hot-sauce-plant-partly-closed-over-odors.html.

4 Caleb Hannan, *Sriracha Hot Sauce Catches Fire, Yet "There's Only One Rooster,"* Bloomberg Bus. WK. (Feb. 21, 2013), www.businessweek.com/articles/2013-02-21/sriracha-hot-sauce-catches-fire-with-only-one-rooster.

5 *See Agenda for the Regular Meeting of the City Council (Resolution No. 2014-14-2674)*, City of Irwindale (Apr. 23, 2014), www.ci.irwindale.ca.us/AgendaCenter/ViewFile/Agenda/04232014-176 (Hereinafter *Resolution No. 2014-14-2674*).

this was an artisanal sauce made by a charismatic elder Vietnamese refugee only spiced up the attention.[6] By June, the city dropped the lawsuit and failed to act on its declaration.[7] This avoided plant occupation and the feared shutdown. It is presumed that the company and Irwindale informally resolved the conflict, even though these details were not fully disclosed.[8]

This chapter looks at the role local government law played in the so-called "sriracha-apocalypse."[9] The dispute developed locally, but its causes, its resolution, and whom it affected were regional, national, and global. Most observers, usually from outside the city, viewed Irwindale as irrational, abusive, duplicative, possibly corrupt, or an example of NIMBYism (meaning "not in my backyard").[10] Irwindale eagerly supported Huy Fong's move to Irwindale with redevelopment financing for years, and then sued them. It knew Huy Fong made chile based sauces and nothing else. The company operated for decades in nearby Rosemead with no complaints or smells before its relocation. During the conflict, state air quality regulators found no violations or odors.[11] As such, Irwindale's positions were severely doubted. This controversy was over odors and likely

6 For basic information about Huy Fong's history and sriracha, see Huy Fong's webpage. HUY FONG FOODS INC., www.huyfong.com (last visited Mar. 23, 2018). *See also Huy Fong's Sriracha Hot Sauce*, BON APPÉTIT (Mar. 6, 2013), www.bonappetit.com/trends/article/huy-fong-s-sriracha-hot-sauce; Roberto A. Ferdman, *The Highly Unusual Company Behind Sriracha, the World's Coolest Hot Sauce*, QUARTZ (Oct. 21, 2013), http://qz.com/132738/the-highly-unusual-company-behind-siracha-the-worlds-coolest-hot-sauce; Frank Shyong, *Sriracha Hot Sauce Purveyor Turns Up the Heat*, L.A. TIMES (Apr. 12, 2013), http://articles.latimes.com/2013/apr/12/business/la-fi-himi-tran-20130414.

7 *See* Frank Shyong, *Sriracha Lawsuit Dropped; Irwindale Tables Public Nuisance Resolution*, L. A. TIMES (May 29, 2014), www.latimes.com/local/lanow/la-me-ln-sriracha-lawsuit-dropped-20140529-story.html.

8 Donald J. Waldie, *Sriracha and Irwindale: The War May Not Be Over as Questions Remain*, KCET (June 6, 2014), www.kcet.org/updaily/socal_focus/commentary/where-we-are/sriracha-and-irwindale-questions-still-loom-the-war-may-not-be-over.html.

9 Matthew Bramlett, *Srirachapocalypse, Now: California Stops Shipments of Hot Sauce [UPDATE]*, LAIST (Dec. 11, 2013), http://laist.com/2013/12/11/sriracha_shipping_halted_until_mid-.php.

10 *See* Steve López, *Irwindale's a Town Where Something Always Smells Funny*, L.A. TIMES (Apr. 26, 2014), http://articles.latimes.com/2014/apr/26/local/la-me-0427-lopez-sauce-20140425; *See also* The Times Editorial Board, *For California's Sake, Irwindale Needs to Save Its Sriracha Plant*, L.A. TIMES (Apr. 24, 2014), www.latimes.com/opinion/editorials/la-ed-sriracha-factory-too-spicy-for-irwindale-20140425-story.html; Ernesto Hernández-López, *Fight Over Sriracha Factory Smell Heating Up*, SAN DIEGO UNION-TRIB. (May 1, 2014), www.utsandiego.com/news/2014/may/01/sriracha-smell-Irwindale/; Ernesto Hernández-López, *Save Sriracha!: Save a Beloved Hot Sauce from Smelly Politics*, CHI. TRIB. (Mar. 21, 2014), http://articles.chicagotribune.com/2014-03-21/opinion/ct-perspec-sriracha-0321-20140321_1_huy-fong-foods-irwindale-raider-crater; *Editorial: Chilling Treatment of Hot Sauce Maker*, ORANGE COUNTY. REG. (Dec. 24, 2013), www.ocregister.com/articles/sriracha-594641-california-sauce.html.

11 *See* Sharon McNary, *Update: Your Sriracha's Safe. Judge Denies Attempt to Close Hot Sauce Plant*, SCPR (Oct. 31, 2013), www.scpr.org/news/2013/10/31/40126/sriracha-hot-sauce-high-tech-odor-cops-follow-thei/.

affected only one street block of homes. But its impact was felt far away, given sriracha mass appeal.

These impacts motivate placing the dispute in a larger theoretical picture, eyeing where it took place and the forces that created Irwindale, informed its legal powers, and shaped relations between the region, city residents, and city leaders.[12] Local controversies like this occur all over the world and policymakers and judges are left trying to resolve them. For something as popular and commonplace as sriracha, local power received widespread attention, but surely most examples of urban law and the conflict it creates and resolves escape public scrutiny. Looking at the sriracha-apocalypse with an urban theory lens helps identify how to make sense of disputes when residents and a city seem at a standstill with businesses and neighboring communities. This local public nuisance conflict provides an example of how cities rely on urban law to respond to global forces and economic restructuring.

This chapter employs analytical frameworks from the Los Angeles School of Urbanism (LA School). Since the 1980s, the LA School has represented a group of writers and urban-focused scholars examining Los Angeles as a model for global urban conditions, exemplified by decentralized public authority, powerful imagery in popular culture, changing industries, and insecurity trends.[13] It includes authors, geographers, and urban planners such as Mike Davis, Edward Soja, Michael Dear, Michael Storper, and others. A recent generation of LA School scholars has begun to focus on the politics of urban transformations, adding to prior geography and socio-economic approaches.[14] This essay follows these suggestions, examining how local legal ordering contributed to a nuisance conflict, narrowly sourced but widely noticed, in a small city in Greater Los Angeles.

Section I describes the LA School of Urbanism. Section II provides a quick place-specific history of Irwindale and Huy Fong. Section III describes how Irwindale initiated public nuisance proceedings against Huy Fong, claiming offensive smells. The legal powers exercised by Irwindale, and belonging to most cities, appeared abusive to outside observers. Section IV identifies the legal doctrines cooking up the sauce fight. Given its small population and the economic influence of mining companies, Irwindale has often been weak to

12 This chapter provides an abbreviated description of the dispute. More detailed analysis of the conflict, along critical race and nuisance terms and food studies terms, is available at Ernesto Hernández-López, *Sriracha Shutdown: Hot Sauce Lessons on Local Privilege and Race*, 46 SETON HALL L. REV. 189 (2015), papers.ssrn.com/sol3/papers.cfm?abstract_id=2676140; *See also* Ernesto Hernández-López, *Sriracha: Lessons from the Legal Troubles of a Popular Hot Sauce*, 15 GASTRONOMICA: J. CRITICAL FOOD STUD. 27 (2015).

13 For two good primers on the LA School, see Michael Dear, *Los Angeles and the Chicago School: Invitation to Debate*, 1 CITY & COMMUNITY 1 (2002); *See also* Walter J. Nicholls, *Los Angeles School: Difference, Politics, City*, 35 INT'L J. URB. & REGIONAL RES. 189 (2011).

14 For these observations see Nicholls *supra* note 13; *See also* Michael Dear & Nicholas Dahmann, *Urban Politics and the Los Angeles School of Urbanism*, 44 URB. AFF. REV. 266 (2008).

outside actors and forces. For internal matters however, such as nuisance actions or the powers of a city attorney and a city council, Irwindale's city powers are quite influential, able to meet the objectives of local leaders. The city's history illustrates this dichotomy. City authority is powerful for actions inside and but it is also very vulnerable to the outside. Local law created this, setting up city borders (excluding outsiders), residency voting requirements (empowering members), and council standards (creating a body of leader-insiders).

Section V places this conflict into a theoretical discussion, useful for comparative analysis. LA School perspectives show how cities such as Irwindale, municipalities outside metropolitan centers and undergoing economic restructuring, experience varied forms of polarization. From this, spatial justice disputes develop with residents, private actors, and public institutions fighting over influence at a particular location. Irwindale efforts to shut down sriracha production exemplify this. Soja describes these disputes as part of a larger regional urbanization. The Irwindale–Huy Fong dispute reflects four discourses of regional urbanization: economic restructuring; globalization of capital, labor, and culture; a spatial stretch of urban form; and polarization. In the sriracha-apocalypse, law played a vital role in these discourses determining: public nuisance grounds, the city attorney's authority, standards for urban redevelopment, overlapping public authority, and who served as and voted for Irwindale's leaders.

I. The LA School of Urbanism

In *My Los Angeles: from Urban Restructuring to Regional Urbanization*,[15] Edward Soja explained that "regional urbanization" will fill entire metropolitan areas, and from this, "spatial-justice" disputes arise.[16] Regional urbanization is a process by which metropolitan forms evolve, creating poly-centric and networked regions and urbanized suburbia.[17] This builds on LA School assumptions, regarding decentralized urban cores, economic restructuring, global influences, and critical landscapes. Generally, Soja and other LA School theorists see cities as poly-centric and subject to significant economic changes.[18] Accordingly, they view urban geographies not as neatly divided into governmental, manufacturing, and residential sectors, as maybe Chicago School urban sociologists describe. Most important in methodological terms, the LA School emphasizes the spatial aspects of socio-economic change, as opposed to focusing on the chronology of transformations and consequent clashes. The LA School argues that cities are subject to reindustrialization, instead of just an end to manufacturing or heavy

15 Edward Soja, My Los Angeles: From Urban Restructuring to Regional Urbanization 21–22 (2014).

16 *Id.* at 23. *See also* Edward Soja, Seeking Spatial Justice (2010).

17 *See*, Soja, My Los Angeles, *supra* note 15, at 22.

18 For criticism of the LA School see D.W. Miller in *The New Urban Studies*, Chron. Higher Educ., Aug. 18, 2000.

industry. Similarly argued, cities have their futures shaped by global flows of capital, migration, and culture.

Soja and others contend that these urban landscapes reflect geographies that are not neutral or natural. LA School social scientists see actual locations as important actors in socio-economic change. Locations and physical settings are intentionally utilized to benefit public and private interests. Businesses and governments may control access to physical attributes such as rivers, coasts, or elevated terrain and to infrastructure such as ports, highways, and railways. City residents and local governments often can only react to these dynamics versus proactively creating policies favoring local constituents. For LA school perspectives, local economic crises do not cause industrial restructuring. Instead, the constant restructuring by private actors generates these crises. This is most obvious locally. Spatial-justice disputes result from this inter-play between global and local forces and popular mobilization articulated in spatial terms. This essay takes the methodological view that there were two important places in the sriracha conflict. One was Huy Fong's new plant in a converted mining pit in Irwindale. Second was Irwindale as a small city in Greater Los Angeles cloaked with city powers after incorporation in 1957.[19]

LA School writers identify these trends – decentralized cores, economic restructuring, global influences, and critical landscapes – as the backdrop for disputes between people, business interests, and public institutions over how a particular place is utilized. Examples of these spatial-justice conflicts include protests by public transport users, communities against large stores such as Wal-Mart, and right to the city movements.[20] LA School perspectives analyze this context, explaining why controversies occur. They argue that private interests can capture or actually control how city, regional, or state governments make decisions. In these settings, citizens, residents, and voters are less influential than electoral politics suggest. Building on this, this chapter sees urban law as exercising a critical role. Urban law delineates how city and regional governments determine their jurisdiction, and how private interests protect their economic investments in court and in public institutions at local, county, or state levels. Law can be a powerful tool to exclude resident participation, evade public accountability, and protect commercial and financial interests.

This essay tracks law's complex role in one such spatial-justice dispute, i.e., the sriracha-apocalypse transpiring in a classic Greater Los Angeles setting. Law helped cause, feed, and resolve this local place-based conflict. The controversy was over presumed smells from food production and the consequent choices of a local government. A quick reading of news beyond-the-headlines shows that the conflict encompassed insider–outsider, Latino–Asian, established migrant–new

19 This history is described in Michael Broggie, The History of Irwindale: Jardín de Roca (2009); Ernesto Hernández-López, *Sriracha Shutdown: Hot Sauce Lessons on Local Privilege and Race*, 46 Seton Hall L. Rev. 189 (2015).

20 Soja, My Los Angeles, *supra* note 15, at 226–45.

migrant, private–public, city–state, and local–global dynamics.[21] Huy Fong was new to Irwindale, relocating in 2012. Its owners, the Tran family, are of Vietnamese descent. They make a sauce initially crafted for Asian food, specifically Vietnamese pho soup.[22] For over a century, the Irwindale area has been almost entirely populated by Mexican and Mexican-American communities. Since the 1990s, cities east of Irwindale have become home to some of the nation's largest Chinese, Vietnamese, Filipino, Korean, and Indonesian communities.[23] The city of Irwindale, state of California, and the regional South Coast Air Quality Management District (SCAQMD) all exerted overlapping public authority over Huy Fong's operations. Sriracha demand and the financing for Huy Fong represented global economic forces, penetrating this suburb.

Soja's ideas on regional urbanization are used to argue three points about local government law's role in the sriracha-apocalypse. First, local government law made Irwindale both weak and powerful to outside forces. Second, for internal local issues, such as public nuisance determinations and the powers of the city attorney and city council, Irwindale is actually quite powerful. Third in this setting, Irwindale's leaders, whether elected or appointed, had the precise but limited authority to react to distinct forces of regional urbanization. A public nuisance lawsuit, city council hearings, the consequent threat of shutdown, and the public relations impact all exemplify this local strength, sourced in a city's legal powers.

II. Irwindale and sriracha

Irwindale's role in the sriracha-apocalypse shows how a city's physical and legal characteristics shape the political and economic choices it makes. This influence has been historic. With fewer than 1,500 residents, Irwindale is located 21 miles east from downtown Los Angeles, in the suburban San Gabriel Valley (SGV).[24] It was incorporated in 1957, in order for mining companies to capitalize on extraction operations there. Since early last century, the area has been exploited for gravel and other aggregates to make concrete. Here the San Gabriel River meets the base of mountains of the same name, creating a rich and easily accessed supply of gravel. These resources were in high demand after the Federal Highway

21 Hernández-López, *Sriracha Shutdown, supra* note 19; *See also* Anita Mannur & Martin Manalansan, *Dude, What's That Smell? The Sriracha Shutdown and Immigrant Excess*, From the Square: NYU Press Blog (Jan. 16, 2014), www.fromthesquare.org/?p=5903.

22 John T. Edge, *A Chili Sauce to Crow About*, N.Y. Times (May 20, 2009), www.nytimes.com/2009/05/20/dining/20united.html?pagewanted=all&_r=0.

23 *See* Wendy Cheng, The Changs Next Door to the Díazes: Remapping Race in Suburban California (2013); *See also* James S. Lai, Asian American Political Action: Suburban Transformation (2011); Leland Saito, Race and Politics: Asian Americans, Latinos, and Whites in a Los Angeles Suburb (1998).

24 Irwindale is comprised of 9.5 square miles with a population of 1466. *Demographics*, City of Irwindale, www.ci.irwindale.ca.us/Index.aspx?NID=262 (last visited Feb. 6, 2015).

Act in 1956 required concrete for suburban developments and a vast freeway network between city centers, bedroom communities, and metro areas nationwide. When incorporated, the city had seventeen mining pits, covering over 70 percent of its 9.5 square mile area.[25] In 2015, only six pits continued to be mined.[26]

Gary Miller describes how mining companies moved to incorporate Irwindale in order to avoid the Los Angeles County or another city having quarries within their borders.[27] These companies feared increases in sales tax imposed on mining. This would happen if the quarries were subject to another city's legal authority. They also worried about potential city residents influencing a local government with jurisdiction over their operations. To avoid these two problems, Irwindale was incorporated to have city borders over as many mining pits as possible with the smallest number of people living inside city borders.[28] This experience with municipal incorporation would influence later California efforts including the Lakewood Plan, when cities were specifically formed to exclude residents and to benefit private enterprise.[29] The cities of Lakewood and Downey exemplify this history. Throughout California, small cities were incorporated politically with legal powers of a local government, but also able to minimize city expenses by contracting public services with the county. Miller examines the diverse trends to exclude evidence in the incorporation of cities like Bradbury, Irwindale, Commerce, and Cerritos.[30] Private economic interests and a desire to exclude minority or immigrant habitants motivated municipal incorporation. LA School authors see these numerous incorporations, sixty between 1940 and 1970, as making cities weak and segregated culturally.[31]

Importantly for Irwindale, the area barely had 1,400 residents in 1957. Almost all of them were Mexican or Mexican-American.[32] The latest census in 2010 reports that Irwindale's population is less than 1,500 and over 90 percent Hispanic or Latino.[33] Recently, as mining operations face an inevitable end, with extraction predicted to be depleted by 2050, Irwindale searches for new

25 Broggie, *supra* note 19, at 27; *See also* Bob Pool, *Surroundings/Irwindale*, L.A. Times, Mar. 13, 2003, at 2, *available at* 2003 WLNR 15177070.

26 Courtney Tompkins, *Irwindale Stands by Decision to Reopen Olive Pit Mining Quarry*, Pasadena Star-News (Jan. 29, 2015), www.pasadenastarnews.com/government-and-politics/20150129/irwindale-stands-by-decision-to-reopen-olive-pit-mining-quarry.

27 Gary J. Miller, Cities by Contract: The Politics of Municipal Incorporation 57 (1981).

28 *Id.* at 57.

29 *Id.* at 20.

30 *Id.* at 35.

31 Nicholls, *supra* note 13, at 197.

32 Miller, *supra* note 27, at 56.

33 Based on data from the 2010 U.S. Census, 90.6 percent of Irwindale's population is Hispanic or Latino. Hispanic or Latino population in Irwindale City, California in 2010 from U.S. Census Bureau, American FactFinder, http://factfinder2.census.gov/faces/nav/jsf/pages/community_facts.xhtml (search "Irwindale City, California," then select "Race and Hispanic of Latino Origin").

industries. The city's main economic task has been finding ways to repurpose unused quarries to provide a city tax base.[34] Without new businesses, the city's small population may not have a tax base to support municipal services. The city is seeking to convert its mining pits, many of which are superfund sites, into places for lighter industry. Irwindale now houses a pet-food factory, major brewery, auto speedway and a small amount of business parks and commercial shopping. All of these point to Irwindale's reindustrialization. When Huy Fong came to Irwindale, the city was undergoing a slow economic transformation, while the SGV was increasingly globalized, as a home to Asian and Latino migrants, their investments, and diverse cultures. In this critical geography, Huy Fong constructed its new plant.

For food production and business reasons, Huy Fong has had to heavily depend on Irwindale's location. In 2013, Huy Fong moved into new $40 million dollar facilities, spanning over 655,000 square feet.[35] Irwindale and Huy Fong worked together to buy the land and build the largest commercial real estate project in Los Angeles County in 2012. Huy Fong invested heavily in sriracha and Irwindale. It capitalized on Irwindale's location and public support to construct state-of-the-art facilities. Irwindale's redevelopment agency secured the land and used Huy Fong as a shining example for business opportunities in this city.

Named after a coastal town in Thailand, sriracha has been made by David Tran, Huy Fong's owner, since he came to California over thirty years ago.[36] Tran started in Los Angeles's Chinatown, but soon moved to a plant in Rosemead in the SGV. The name Huy Fong refers to the boat Tran took as a refugee fleeing communist Vietnam. The company continues to grow. Recently reported figures put company sales between $35 and $65 million per year.[37] Sriracha is loved by legions of fans, who wear T-shirts, costumes, baby onesies, and basically any paraphernalia with Huy Fong's fire-engine red, green cap, and rooster image. Sriracha has become a pop culture icon, spreading its spicy kick far beyond its initial use for pho.

Sriracha production is almost an entirely local operation. Its recipe calls for high-quality jalapeño chile peppers to be ground, and then garlic, sugar, salt, vinegar, and preservatives added.[38] Chiles become unusable if not ground within a few hours of harvest. This fragility makes it difficult for large sauce producers to use freshly picked peppers. Most hot sauce makers use dried chiles or chile

34 Pool, *supra* note 25.

35 Roger Vincent, *Spicing Up An Irwindale Lot*, L.A. Times, Oct. 9, 2010, at B1, *available at* 2010 WLNR 20190148.

36 *See* sources cited *supra* note 6.

37 *Id.*

38 Willy Blackmore, *When Sriracha is Made, a Different Kind of Fire Season Comes to L.A.*, Take Part (Oct. 29, 2013), http://dev.takepart.com/article/2013/10/29/sriracha-public-nuisance/index.html.

powder.[39] Importantly, sriracha chiles are locally sourced, to guarantee quality and freshness. Huy Fong works solely with Underwood Ranches, in Ventura and Kern counties, less than a two-hour drive from Irwindale.[40] Chiles are harvested and ground from late August to November. During this time of year, people in Irwindale complained about smells. This annual process grinds 100 million pounds of chiles.[41] With this paste, Huy Fong makes sriracha and its other two products, the *sambal oelek* and chili garlic condiments. The company is highly dependent on local peppers, local processing, and Irwindale's business conditions.

III. Local nuisance over smelly hot sauce gets noticed

The global eye and foodie demand for sriracha became readily apparent when Irwindale employed municipal legal powers and took Huy Fong to court. In 2013, the new plant was at risk of being shut down, after the city government sued Huy Fong in Los Angeles Superior Court. The tensions between Huy Fong and Irwindale began to stew in September of 2013 when residents complained about odors caused by grinding chiles at the new plant.[42] Court papers filed by Huy Fong, along with reports from newspapers, trace the initial complaint to the son of a city council member.[43] He complained the year before and quickly raised the gripes in 2013, directly with Huy Fong and later with the city.[44] Tran explained that Huy Fong installed new filters each year because the council member's son complained.[45] The company had not transferred all of its

39 *Sriracha: From the Farm to Your Table*, FARM TO TABLE (Oct. 14, 2014).

40 Craig Underwood, *Huy Fong Sriracha: How Vision, Trust and Loyalty Combine to Make One of the World's Best-Loved Sauces*, EDIBLE OJAI & VENTURE CO. (May 1, 2013), http://edibleojai.com/online-magazine/huy-fong-sriracha/.

41 Blackmore, *supra* note 38.

42 Complaint for Public Nuisance and Injunctive Relief at 3, People *ex rel.* City of Irwindale v. Huy Fong Foods, Inc., No. BC525856 (L.A. Super. Ct. Oct. 28, 2013) [hereinafter *Complaint*]. A timeline of events is available at *Sriracha Hot Sauce Controversy Timeline of Events*, PASADENA STAR-NEWS (Mar. 12, 2014, 8:04 PM), www.pasadenastarnews.com/environment-and-nature/20140312/sriracha-hot-sauce-controversy-timeline-of-events.

43 The first complaint is attributed to Manuel H. Ortiz from September 16, 2013. *See* Plaintiffs' Ex Parte Application for Temporary Restraining Order and Order to Show Cause Re Preliminary Injunction at Exhibit 2, People *ex rel.* City of Irwindale v. Huy Fong Foods, Inc., No. BC525856 (L.A. Super. Ct. Oct. 31, 2013) [hereinafter *Plaintiffs' Ex Parte*]. *See also* Sarah Favot, *Sriracha Hot Sauce Complaints Began with Irwindale Councilman's Son*, SAN GABRIEL VALLEY TRIB. (Oct. 31, 2013), www.sgvtribune.com/business/20131031/sriracha-hot-sauce-complaints-began-with-irwindale-councilmans-son.

44 City Council records show that resident complaints about Huy Fong odors had begun as early as November 2012. *See* CITY OF IRWINDALE, AGENDA FOR THE REGULAR MEETING OF THE CITY COUNCIL NO. 1A1, 28 (Dec. 12, 2012), *available at* www.ci.irwindale.ca.us/AgendaCenter/ViewFile/Agenda/12122012-10.

45 Declaration of David Tran in Opposition to Application for Temporary Restraining Order at 2, People *ex rel.* City of Irwindale v. Huy Fong Foods, Inc., No. BC525856 (Oct. 31, 2013)

operations from Rosemead to Irwindale. The move began the prior year, gradually shifting to the larger plant. The legal saga sparked on October 28, when Irwindale argued that odors and fumes created a public nuisance.

Irwindale used its powers to seek a finding of a public nuisance, to enjoin sauce production, and to force corrective measures. In its complaint, Irwindale argued that Huy Fong plant operations constituted "a public nuisance due to the emanation of odors and irritants" that caused "physical harm and discomfort for the people of the city of Irwindale."[46] The odors were described as "offensive,"[47] and "injurious to the health, enjoyment and the life and use of property of residents."[48] It said that these odors were irritating eyes and throats; causing coughs, difficulty breathing, headaches, bloody noses, and heartburn; and forcing residents to limit outdoor activities.[49]

Seeking to end a harm suffered by a community, public nuisance doctrine is intrinsically an expression of the legal intentions of a city.[50] Local governments employ the law of public nuisance to protect a community. Typically, a city points to harms created by heavy industry, mining, factory smoke, slaughterhouses, and other businesses. Irwindale's Municipal Code defines a public nuisance as something "adverse or detrimental to the public peace, health, safety or general welfare."[51] California's Civil Code requires that public nuisances affect "an entire community or neighborhood, or considerable number of persons."[52] Public nuisances are less common than in the past century, since statutory land-use and environmental regulations address many of these problems.

Irwindale's actions caught immediate public attention beyond Southern California. It all seemed odd. Irwindale not only approved Huy Fong's ongoing relocation, but in 2009 it enticed the company with redevelopment funds to buy an empty mining pit for the plant.[53] Irwindale employed its municipal authority

[Hereinafter *Declaration of David Tran*]. Ironically, the council member had been reportedly happy with Huy Fong's move to Irwindale. *See*, J.D. Velasco, *New Headquarters for "Rooster Sauce" Company Nearing Completion in Irwindale*, San Gabriel Valley Trib. (July 5, 2011, 12:01 AM), www.sgvtribune.com/general-news/20110705/new-headquarters-for-rooster-sauce-company-nearing-completion-in-irwindale.

46 *Complaint, supra* note 42, at 2–4.

47 *Id.* at 5; *see also Plaintiffs' Ex Parte, supra* note 43, at 2.

48 *Plaintiffs' Ex Parte, supra* note 43, at 3.

49 *Id.* at 2; Motion for Preliminary Injunction at 4, People *ex rel.* Irwindale v. Huy Fong Foods, No. BC525856 (L.A. Super. Ct. 2013).

50 Osborne M. Reynolds, Jr., Handbook of Local Government Law § 115 (2d ed. 2001) (describing the public nuisance tort action as a means of land use regulation as it leads to abatement or injunction); *id.* at § 115 n.1 (summarizing examples of how courts normally accept determinations of a public nuisance made by municipal legislative bodies, unless they are "clearly arbitrary or unreasonable"); *id.* at § 115 n.3 (describing how public nuisance statutes provide governments "broad powers to shutdown" public nuisances).

51 Irwindale Mun. Code § 8.08.010 (2013), www.ci.irwindale.ca.us/index.aspx?NID=273.

52 Cal. Civ. Code § 3480 (2014), http://leginfo.legislature.ca.gov/faces/codes_displayText.xhtml?lawCode=CIV&division=4.&title=1.&part=3.&chapter=&article.

53 Vincent, *supra* note 35.

to argue that Huy Fong created a public nuisance. They said Huy Fong did not cooperate with requests to implement additional filter systems. Huy Fong claimed that the city would not stop making requests, after it responded to prior demands by installing air filters.[54] Huy Fong further argued against the stop, before any trial, because it was chile grinding season and shutdown would force the company to risk losing its annual chile harvest.[55]

These tensions fueled a series of legal maneuvers, relying on local government law. Irwindale's first legal step was to go the Superior Court repeatedly seeking a court order to stop all Huy Fong operations. On October 31, 2013, the city sought a temporary restraining order,[56] which the court characterized as "rather edgy."[57] This was denied. Four days after that, Irwindale reappeared and requested a preliminary injunction.[58] All the while the press began observing and worrying about sriracha's shutdown.

On November 26, the court issued its order and ruling.[59] A preliminary injunction was issued on December 16.[60] The city viewed this as a victory over Huy Fong, even though the judge had serious doubts over the nuisance harms Irwindale raised.[61] In the order, the court directed Huy Fong to "immediately make changes in its site operation reducing odors" but it did not enjoin plant operation or the use of the property as Irwindale requested.[62] The court explained that there was "a lack of credible evidence linking the complained about health problems as being caused by the odors or emissions."[63] It did not enjoin any of its operations.[64] The city succeeded in having a court take note of odors. A court told Huy Fong to stop but it effectively doubted all of the negative impacts the city raised. The dispute was set to move to trial with a date scheduled for November of the next year.

Irwindale shifted its legal attack to its city council. This body had the power to formally declare a public nuisance, which could lead to abatement and a

54 *Declaration of David Tran, supra* note 45, at 2.

55 *Id.* at 3.

56 *Plaintiffs' Ex Parte, supra* note 43.

57 Frank Shyong, *Sriracha Fight: Irwindale Officials Not Backing Down After Ruling*, L.A. Times (Oct. 31, 2013), www.latimes.com/local/lanow/la-me-ln-irwindale-officials-sriracha-20131031-story.html.

58 Frank Shyong, *Sriracha Plant Must Cease Operations That Cause Odors, Judge Rules*, L.A. Times (Nov. 26, 2013), http://articles.latimes.com/2013/nov/26/local/la-me-judge-rules-no-sriracha-20131126.

59 Order Re: Preliminary Injunction, People *ex rel.* Irwindale v. Huy Fong Foods, No. BC525856 (L.A. Super. Ct. 2013) [Hereinafter *Order Re: Preliminary Injunction*].

60 Preliminary Injunction, People *ex rel.* Irwindale v. Huy Fong Foods, No. BC525856 (L.A. Super. Ct. 2013).

61 The city attorney presented the ruling as favorable to Irwindale's position. *See* Rory Carroll, *Sriracha: Judge Orders Partial Shutdown of California Factory*, Guardian (Nov. 27, 2013), www.theguardian.com/world/2013/nov/27/sriracha-partial-shutdown-california-factory

62 *Order Re: Preliminary Injunction, supra* note 59, at 2.

63 *Id.* at 1–2.

64 *Id.* at 2.

shutdown of the factory by Irwindale.[65] A council declaration would vitally support any Irwindale position in its ongoing court proceedings with Huy Fong. On February 26, 2014 Irwindale's city council held public nuisance proceedings, when air quality experts, residents, plant workers, SGV politicians, business organizations, and Huy Fong spoke about the alleged problems.[66] This included the owners of Huy Fong and Underwood Ranches. While a few Irwindale residents raised grievances about Huy Fong, neighbors in Rosemead and a children's nursery across the street never complained. Nearby residents explained that there was no smell or that it was minimal and expected for sauce making.

Huy Fong, the city, and the state environmental agency, SCAQMD, presented different opinions from air quality experts. The consultants hired by Irwindale explained what potentially caused the odors at specific times and weather conditions. They highlighted potential scenarios, but the exact causes and potential remedies were far from clear. The company argued that since the causes and any remedies were unknown, a public nuisance determination was premature.

Regardless, in April the council formally determined that there was a public nuisance, with a resolution. This happened despite the SCAQMD finding no harmful effects from any fumes or odors.[67] To cool consumer panic, Huy Fong quickly announced it had plenty of sriracha in storage to avoid shortages.[68] Newspaper editorials criticized Irwindale for acting so quickly and not waiting for more evidence from the SCAQMD.[69]

Meanwhile hot sauce polemics fired up, like a spicy kick, from a neighborhood grievance to a global problem. This progressed for months, and the political attention widened as more voices chimed in, heating up larger debates. It quickly went from local, to regional, to state, to national level problems. The *Los Angeles Times* editorial board (2014) pleaded with Irwindale to stop harassing Huy Fong,

65 Irwindale, Cal., Code of Ordinances, § 8.08.020 (2015), *available at* www.ci.irwindale.ca.us/index.aspx?NID=273 (stating if the City Council finds a public nuisance, abatement can be achieved by "rehabilitation, demolition, or repair"); *id.* at § 8.08.110 (requiring costs of abatement by city to become a lien against the property).

66 Sarah Favot, *Sriracha Hot Sauce Factory Smell Decision Delayed by Irwindale City Council*, San Gabriel Valley Trib. (Feb. 26, 2014) www.sgvtribune.com/business/20140226/sriracha-hot-sauce-factory-smell-decision-delayed-by-irwindale-city-council. I took notes for the February 26 public hearings. An abbreviated version of the public comments, taken by the City, is available in the City Council's Agenda, when it approves activity from prior sessions. For the February 26 public hearing, *see Agenda for the Regular Meeting of the City Council, City of Irwindale*, (Apr. 9, 2014) at 19–27, www.ci.irwindale.ca.us/AgendaCenter/ViewFile/Agenda/04092014-173.

67 Steve Gorman, *California Town Moves Against Sriracha Hot Sauce Plan*, Reuters (Apr. 10, 2014), www.reuters.com/article/2014/04/10/usa-sriracha-california-idUSL2N0N226V20140410.

68 Frank Shyong, *Sriracha Shortage Unlikely; Company Has 18-month Supply*, L.A. Times, (Apr. 10, 2014), http://articles.latimes.com/2014/apr/10/local/la-me-ln-sriracha-shortage-unlikely-company-has-18month-supply-20140410.

69 *See* Orange County. Reg. *supra* note 10; *see also* Hernández-López, *Save Sriracha!*, *supra* note 10.

or California would suffer.[70] After the public nuisance declaration, Huy Fong announced its possible relocation.[71] Politicians from all over the country tried to lure Huy Fong to their cities and states.[72] This spiced up inter-state rivalries, especially debates about California being anti-business with stifling regulations and hostile local rules. Republican politicians saw the issue as a way to court Latino and Asian voters.[73] All of this attention, brewing in a small locality, only added pressure on Irwindale to stop these proceedings. Newspapers all over the United States, Europe, Asia, and beyond followed the developments of a city suing sriracha's maker.

By any account, only a miniscule number of residents complained, between eleven and thirty. On October 31, in papers filed in court, Irwindale referred to eleven resident complaints.[74] The city council's April 23 resolution declaring a public nuisance stated that "approximately thirty residents" have "raised concern about strong odors and other irritating symptoms" and described the odors as "aggressive" and "spicy."[75] Based on complaints filed with the SCAQMD, the *Pasadena Star News* reported that only sixty-one grievances were made, that four of those were traceable to Huy Fong, and that the overwhelming number of grievances came from four households.[76] Even for a city of less than 1,500 residents, these numbers are minute.

Irwindale's lawsuit and public hearings provided local newspapers an excuse to bring up the city's troubled history with corruption and negative attention. With such a small number of complaints, and given that air-quality violations were unlikely, the city's honesty was doubted. Observers questioned whether there really was any smell or whether the city process was fair. This skepticism was

70 Editorial, *For California's Sake, Irwindale Needs to Save Its Sriracha Plant*, L.A. Times (Apr. 24, 2014), www.latimes.com/opinion/editorials/la-ed-sriracha-factory-too-spicy-for-irwindale-20140425-story.html.

71 Emma G. Gallegos, *Sriracha Creator Talks About Moving, Invites Texas Politician for Tour*, LAist (Apr. 16, 2014), http://laist.com/2014/04/16/sriracha_creator_says_hes_thinking.php; Frank Shyong, *Sriracha Considers Moving Factory Amid Smell Complaints*, L.A. Times (Apr. 16, 2014), www.latimes.com/local/lanow/la-me-sriracha-may-move-ln-20140416-story.html#axzz2z5oqgoYW.

72 Ian Lovett, *Sriracha Factory Irritates Some California Noses, But Entices Politicians*, N.Y. Times (May 13, 2014), www.nytimes.com/2014/05/14/us/sriracha-factory-irritates-some-california-noses-but-entices-politicians.html.

73 Stephanie McNeal, *Hot-Button Issue: Calif. Republicans Rally Behind Sriracha in Fight Against City*, Fox News (Apr. 22, 2014), www.foxnews.com/politics/2014/04/22/hot-button-issue-calif-republicans-rally-behind-sriracha-in-fight-against-city/.

74 *Plaintiffs' Ex Parte Application*, *supra* note 43, at 6–9.

75 *Resolution No. 2014-14-2674*, *supra* note 5, at 29–34.

76 *See* Sarah Favot, *Majority of Complaints About Sriracha Factory Came from 4 Households*, Pasadena Star-News (Feb. 25, 2014), www.pasadenastarnews.com/business/20140225/majority-of-complaints-about-sriracha-factory-came-from-4-households; *See also* Sarah Favot, *Sriracha Smell Traced Back to Irwindale Factory 4 Times in 61 Complaints*, Pasadena Star-News (Mar. 12, 2014), www.pasadenastarnews.com/environment-and-nature/20140312/sriracha-smell-traced-back-to-irwindale-factory-4-times-in-61-complaints.

fueled by ongoing corruption scandals of city officials. Irwindale's mayor and a City Council member appeared in court within days of City Council hearings on Huy Fong.[77] Former city officials pled guilty to charges involving expensive trips to New York City on this working-class city's public budget. Meanwhile, the city was at risk of losing insurance for its public officials due to misconduct by police and other city staff.[78]

Sriracha's legal troubles, plus what appeared like corrupt city governance, re-ignited the mismanagement and corruption memory Irwindale had in Los Angeles area history. Many people still think of the city as the "Raider Crater," from the failed attempt to lure the NFL team to a new stadium in an old mining pit in 1987.[79] Newspapers brought up the "spiked enchilada" story from 1972, when a council member was fed drug-laced enchiladas in order to take compromising pictures of him.[80] In sum, Irwindale used its local legal powers, as an incorporated city, to act against a new business. The place and politics, a small suburb known for mining and insular residents, shaped how this law was applied.

IV. Urban law in Irwindale: from single-use to specific exclusion

In 1957, Irwindale was incorporated to take advantage of the city as a legal entity.[81] The immediate result was that mining companies had their physical access guaranteed to aggregates, needed for a mid-century construction boom. Private economic interests secured a location to extract and process rocks. These resources would not be inside another city's jurisdiction. With Irwindale incorporated for the interests of an industry, it is an example of a "single-use industrial city." Victor Valle and Rodolfo Torres describe Irwindale, and such cities as the City of Industry, City of Commerce, Santa Fe Springs, Azusa, and Vernon.[82] They present single-use industrial cities as having the basic municipal purpose to

77 *See* Nicki Arnold, *City Council Election in Irwindale Comes Down to Three Votes*, CAL. CITY NEWS (Nov. 7, 2013), https://www.californiacitynews.org/2014/06/city-council-election-irwindale-comes-down-three-votes.html; *see also* Sarah Favot, *Former Irwindale Official Sentenced to 3 Years Probation in Corruption Case*, PASADENA STAR-NEWS (Apr. 7, 2014), http://www.pasadenastarnews.com/general-news/20140407/former-irwindale-official-sentenced-to-3-years-probation-in-corruption-case; *and see* Adam Poulisse, *Arraignment Delayed for 4 Irwindale Officials Suspected of Embezzlement, Conflict of Interest*, SAN GABRIEL VALLEY TRIB. (Feb. 27, 2014), http://www.sgvtribune.com/general-news/20140227/arraignment-delayed-for-4-irwindale-officials-suspected-of-embezzlement-conflict-of-interest.

78 Sarah Favot, *Irwindale at risk of losing insurance due to allegations of corruption*, PASADENA STAR-NEWS (Sept. 8, 2013), http://www.pasadenastarnews.com/government-and-politics/20130908/irwindale-at-risk-of-losing-insurance-due-to-allegations-of-corruption.

79 Pool, *supra* note 25.

80 *See* López, *supra* note 10; Richard Winton, *The "Spiked Enchilada Caper" and Other Irwindale Scandals*, L.A. TIMES BLOG (Oct. 27, 2010), http://latimesblogs.latimes.com/lanow/2010/10/the-spiked-enchilada-caper-was-irwindales-last-political-scandal.html.

81 *See* Hernández-López, *Sriracha Shutdown, supra* note 12, at 226–27.

82 VICTOR VALLE & RODOLFO TORRES, LATINO METROPOLIS 26–27 (2000).

operate like a private enterprise but with municipal powers to determine local taxes, expropriate private property, and determine city boundaries.[83] California has many such cities, where an industry or company has physical access to a factory, mine, manufacturing plant, refinery, or another asset, with an almost non-existent number of residents. When a city has a small residential population, with the power to vote or influence local governance, this benefits the industry. Public leaders can cater to economic actors with less concern or voice from residents. Likewise, when a city's physical borders encapsulate little more than the industry's economic activities, city policies can be fashioned to be supportive of private interests. This kind of city is common in California.

With such a small size evident in Irwindale's geographic reach and its residential numbers, private interests gained a capacity for greater influence over city politics. In Irwindale residents live extremely close to the mining operations, and not separated from industry. This has resulted in 700 businesses and 40,000 workers in a city with less than 1500 residents.[84] Because of this small population, Irwindale city residents can greatly influence how the city treats local businesses. A small group of citizens has the ability to make its impressions become issues of city concern.

This section describes how law's role in the sriracha-apocalypse develops from Irwindale as a single-use industry city. The city was formed to limit resident numbers and to exclude outside participants. Over fifty years later, this framed how Irwindale could treat an outsider business such as Huy Fong. This section identifies a series of legal powers influential in the hot sauce conflict.

In the sriracha-apocalypse, four areas of law significantly influenced this city-and-company conflict. These doctrines include public nuisance, addressing alleged harms of chile grinding; the powers of the city attorney, most important being to initiate and sustain lawsuits on behalf of the city; city council proceedings and governance, used to approve the city's legal actions, conduct hearings, and issue formal declarations; and redevelopment authority, permitting the city to attain tax revenues and encourage specific investments inside city borders. Seen in an analytical light, public nuisance is *what* the city argued substantively against the company, while city council and city attorney powers are *how* they acted against it. But the geographic location of this conflict, the *where*, is addressed by redevelopment. The law of redevelopment brought this business inside city borders. In sum, the first three doctrines – public nuisance and city attorney and city council powers – protected local decisions, while redevelopment provided the city with far less influence. This chapter's next section examines the theoretical significance of this duality between local-influence and local-weakness.

83 *Id.*

84 *See* Keely Webster, *City That Sued Chili Sauce Plant Had Portrayed It as Redevelopment Success*, Bond Buyer (Dec. 19, 2013), www.bondbuyer.com/issues/122_243/city-that-sued-chili-sauce-plant-had-portrayed-it-as-redevelopment-success-1058394-1.html.

Public nuisance law provided the city a way to legally cite and perhaps even economically penalize Huy Fong for the alleged harms. Public nuisance is *what* Irwindale raised as a legal claim regarding its operations. As opposed to private nuisance, in which individuals or private entities raise claims, public nuisance is as a public doctrine with the city representing its residents. Public nuisance is a common law tort, which permits a city a way to regulate land use but without any specific regulations.[85] For the sriracha-apocalypse, the city raised nuisance claims in court and made similar findings after council hearings. In response, Huy Fong looked to air quality measures under the public authority of the SCAQMD to address the issue. This enforcement belongs to a regional public entity governing parts of three counties and is sourced in the state of California's authority.

Provided in its city charter, Irwindale had the ability to bring a lawsuit and seek remedy for public nuisance harms.[86] This provided a way to bring these matters to Huy Fong's attention, try and seek a response, and force them to take on the costs of attending to the matter with expenses of legal representation. Irwindale had much deference in this matter, employing its authority with city staff and city attorney.

Had the dispute gone to trial, this local deference for Irwindale would have most likely been tempered. In deciding public nuisance cases, courts use a test to balance harms to a community posed by the nuisance with the benefit of the activity that is argued to be causing a problem (in this case pepper grinding).[87] Importantly, California courts interpret public nuisance law as protecting and redressing community interests and not just the harms suffered by individuals.[88] The Supreme Court of California, in *Gallo v. Acuña*, explained that "not every interference with a collective social interest" is a public nuisance and that "to qualify, and thus be enjoinable, the interference must be both *substantial* and *unreasonable*."[89]

With sriracha, a court would most likely not side with Irwindale given the small number of complaints. The largest number of grievances raised by the city was "approximately thirty."[90] This is not substantial. Moreover, Irwindale knew what

85 Public nuisance is tort action used as a means of land use regulation that leads to abatement or injunction by a government. Cities and states have developed nuisance statutes providing for this action. These statutes provide governments "broad powers to shutdown" public nuisances. Courts normally accept determinations of a public nuisance made by municipal legislative bodies, unless they are "clearly arbitrary or unreasonable." *See* Reynolds, *supra* note 50, at § 115.

86 Irwindale Ordinances, *supra* note 65.

87 *See Gallo*, 929 P.2d at 605 (citing Restatement (Second) of Torts §§ 826–31 (1979)); *see also San Diego Gas & Elec. Co.*, 920 P.2d at 697; *and see* Regulation of Public Nuisances, 3 Local Government Law § 14:3 (John Martinez, March 2015).

88 *Gallo*, 929 P.2d at 603; 1 Cal. Civ. Prac. Torts § 17:3 (June 2013) (summarizing the doctrine's emphasis on community interests and rights of a community at large).

89 *Gallo*, 929 P.2d at 604 (emphasis added).

90 *Resolution No. 2014-14-2674, supra* note 5.

Huy Fong made in its plant and approved of the relocation in so many other forums. As such the effects of chile grinding could not be unreasonable or unexpected.

A court did not have the opportunity to apply this reasoning, since there was no trial. But before any final decision, the city did capitalize on its legal powers in public nuisance doctrine, as it attempted to motivate Huy Fong to change its operations. This took place before any trial. Exercised by city staff and in council hearings, this legal power was collateral to any courtroom proceedings. Local government law provides for all of these abilities, deriving from the powers of a city attorney.

Sourced in urban law, city attorney powers illustrate *how* a city acted against a business. In California, the duty of the city attorney is to advise officials in all legal matters pertaining to city affairs and to frame ordinances and resolutions for the legislative body. The city attorney has no authority until the legislative body authorizes it.[91] Generally, these powers are inferred from the power to manage city affairs and are inferred "unless expressly forbidden."[92] Specifically, the Irwindale city charter provides for the city attorney to: be legal advisor for the city; appear and defend the city in "all matters in civil litigation involving the city;" and prosecute violations of city ordinances.[93]

Moreover, the city council has a great deal of authority over the city attorney. He or she is "directly responsible to the City Council for the performance of his [or her] duties."[94] Irwindale's city charter states that the city attorney shall "prepare all ordinances, resolutions, contracts, opinions and other legal documents" and shall "perform such other duties" as the city council requires.[95] The office of the city attorney creates a legal capacity to act on alleged public nuisance harms. As with sriracha, this can be influential even without a trial or lawsuit. The city attorney can act based on what the city council approves.

Similarly, city council powers reflect another *how* in this dispute. For this, the makeup of the city council, its legislative authority, and direction over the city attorney stand out. To serve on the city council someone must be a resident of Irwindale.[96] The council functions as a legislative body[97] and can establish by ordinances how the city exercises its powers.[98] The council passes ordinances and these can direct the city manager for this council-manager form of government.[99] In executive sessions, closed to the public, the city council meets with the city attorney

91 27B Cal. Jur. 3d, *District and Municipal Attorneys* § 10 (2015).

92 Reynolds, *supra* note 50, at § 50.

93 Irwindale, Cal., Charter art. 7, § § § 705(a)(b)(c) (2015), *available at* www.ci.irwindale.ca.us/index.aspx?NID=273.

94 *Id.*, at § 704.

95 *Id.* at § 705(c).

96 *See supra* note 91, at art. 5 § 502(b).

97 *See id.* at art. 6 § 600.

98 *See id.* at art. 402.

99 *See id.* at art. 700 & 703.

to consider litigation matters.[100] As a city, Irwindale has many legal powers usually associated with local powers, such as land use regulations and tax authority. With Irwindale, the city council determines many issues, as is common with many cities, as a way to effectuate the political wishes of local residents. But with Irwindale, residents are small in number. Moreover, the city's history has kept these numbers at around 1,500, with the council limited to only residents of the city.

In addition to these city council powers, it may become easily subject to residential sentiments. In Irwindale, city residents exert a great deal of influence over the city council, not only because the local electorate is small, but because the city charter provides a means to influence the council. Section 504 points to the electorate's right of referendum for any legislative act by the council and right to recall any elective officer.[101]

The law of redevelopment authority helped determined *where* the conflict developed, i.e., in Irwindale, since its redevelopment agency brought Huy Fong from nearby Rosemead. Redevelopment is the financing measure by which a city can declare a location blighted and in need of investment in which a particular project, usually something commercial or manufacturing, moves into the location.[102] The city uses its power of eminent domain to gain control of the project's location. Redevelopment's objective is to bring in economically beneficial actors to an area in need of investment. For this, the city secures the conditions for an investor to profit and it is presumed that this helps the local economy. To incentivize this, a city forms a redevelopment agency which is able to gain revenues from property taxes attributed to land values in the redeveloped areas. With redevelopment, the agency receives revenue from taxes that would usually be collected by the county and state to go to other public services in the city, such as schools. The tax revenue levels before the project's implementation are locked-in for the city and county, but the redevelopment agency acquires the increases in property tax revenue after the project. Huy Fong's relocation to Irwindale was presented as a success story for redevelopment.[103]

There is an important geographic element to redevelopment, also called tax-increment financing, since projects are designated to take place only at a specific location, like a city neighborhood, former factory, or an unused mining pit as in Huy Fong's case. Redevelopment has been used to convert economically disenfranchised areas into a host of projects such as tourist, shopping, entertainment, and mix-used economic zones.

In legal terms, redevelopment poses a few complications, when delineating the influence from local and outside actors. It represents a mix of local and state

100 *See id.* at art. 603(d)(2).

101 *See id.* at art. 405 a & c.

102 This is a simple description of redevelopment, its history, legislative changes, and recent lawsuits, for more detailed accounts see Seth Merewitz and Ethan J. Walsh, *Redevelopment after RDAS*, Los Angeles L. (2013); *see also* William R. Maurer, *California Redevelopment Ass'n v. Matosantos: Fiscal Meltdown Leads to Victory for Property Owners, School Districts, and Taxpayers*, Orange County L. (2012).

103 Webster, *supra* note 84.

authority. The state created these powers. It actually collects the taxes and approves of the agency creation. But local actors have significant roles. A city forms the agency and receives the funds, presumed to be the result of the project's success, diverted from tax revenue going to other local public services. At times, redevelopment has been used by cities to avoid new housing from being built, thereby protecting existing local political interests. Irwindale is such an example. In California redevelopment was criticized as allowing agency creation without a popular vote, indebtedness without voter approval, and using public eminent domain powers to acquire private property.[104]

Similarly, there is a mix of private and public parties involved for these projects. Real estate developers or a business actually acquires title to the land, proposes the project, and profits from it. They are not public. Redevelopment agencies are formed as private entities by a city. They perform different functions than a city, yet have city council members serving on their board. In California, redevelopment began in 1952 and by 2011 over 80 percent of all cities had such an agency. Irwindale was one of the smallest cities with a redevelopment agency.[105]

A further complexity developed in 2012, when the state effectively stopped new redevelopment projects from being approved, by eliminating the agencies and beginning a drawn-out wind down process. California had absorbed too much economic loss from local redevelopment agencies, whose projects failed or did not get implemented. For years, great expenses were taken on to buy land, build private partnerships to move in, and acquire approval for these projects. After the financial crisis of 2008, it became economically difficult to secure private financing and demand for many projects. Since 2012, around the time that Huy Fong moved into Irwindale, redevelopment efforts have been in flux in California. Most new projects, since then, have stopped. Meanwhile, the state is working with the hundreds of agencies to settle what debt exists, who can pay it, and what projects can proceed.

Despite these complexities outside the city, for Irwindale and Huy Fong the redevelopment project created tensions between the company and the city. The company was an outsider and private while the city was an insider and public. Full details of the project have not been attained. Many news reports point to how after its move, Huy Fong did not like how the city treated the company. Likewise, the city likely lost out on funds when the company paid off its loans. This happened as Irwindale, like many cities, could no longer look to redevelopment financing after 2012. Some reports state that the city provided Huy Fong a ten-year interest-only loan for $15 million and a balloon payment at the end to cover the land, while the company would pay the city $2.5 million a year for ten years in lieu of sales tax.[106]

104 Maurer, *supra* note 102.

105 Sue Ehrlich, *Tax Increment Financing in California: The End of an Era?*, 40 No.4. REAL ESTATE REV. J. ART 8 (2011).

106 *See* Webster, *supra* note 84. Other reports say the company's annual payment to the city was $1.5 million per year; Randyl Drummer, *Hot Sauce Maker Adds Zip to 23-Acre Site in L.A. County*, COSTAR NEWS (Oct. 12, 2010), www.costar.com/News/Article/Hot-Sauce-Maker-Adds-Zip-to-23-Acre-Site-in-LA-County/123588.

City records suggest that Huy Fong's initial loan with the city would provide the city with payments of over $600,000 a year for the loan.[107] Most likely, the city planned to earn $250,000 a year from Huy Fong as in-lieu payments for ten years.[108] With redevelopment, Huy Fong invested heavily in sriracha and Irwindale.

Similarly, the city also profited from Huy Fong's move from Rosemead. Its redevelopment agency secured funding to purchase the property.[109] In 2007, the city bought the property that had belonged to CalMat mining and had been empty for over a decade.[110] The agency described the property as "previously vacant and underutilized, constituting a physical and economic burden on the City."[111] Huy Fong's entry was presented as serving "to eliminate existing physical and economic blight" and "address stagnant property values and issues of vacant properties."[112] It also would provide additional annual revenues to the city from Huy Fong in the form of loan payments, in-lieu of the company paying sale tax payments.[113] This loan represented a significant economic relationship between the city and the company.

Before the public nuisance conflict, Huy Fong had paid off the loan principal provided by Irwindale to relocate and build the new plant.[114] It is also believed that the city lost years of loan payments and interest on the principal.[115] This was likely a significant amount of money, which the city counted on, especially given

107 Full redevelopment and loan agreements were not attained but various Irwindale reports provide details about these payments. *See 2010–2014 Five-Year Redevelopment Implementation Plan*, City of Irwindale, Cmty. Redevelopment Agency 44, www.ci.irwindale.ca.us/DocumentCenter/View/77 (last visited Sept. 18, 2015) [hereinafter *Irwindale Redevelopment Plan*] (listing net-income projections from the Huy Fong installment payments to the city's redevelopment agency of $677,070 for years 2010 and 2011 and $674,268 in years 2013 and 2014); *see also Comprehensive Annual Fin. Report for the Fiscal Year Ended June 30, 2010*, City of Irwindale, Cal. 56 (2010), www.ci.irwindale.ca.us/Archive/ViewFile/Item/49 (describing the city's redevelopment agency sale of the property to Huy Fong for $15,046,000, with Huy Fong's down payment of $677,070, and a loan from the agency to Huy Fong for $14,363,930 for "a term of ten years bearing annual interest at a rate of 4.5%"); *City Council Budget Workshop FY 2012/13*, City of Irwindale 25 (May 23, 2012), www.ci.irwindale.ca.us/Archive/ViewFile/Item/54 (listing anticipated revenues of $250,000 from Huy Fong's in-lieu payment for each fiscal year for 2011/12 and 2012/13).

108 Martin Lomeli, *City Manager's Budget Message*, City of Irwindale Annual Budget 2011/12 2, 7 (June 22, 2011), www.ci.irwindale.ca.us/ArchiveCenter/ViewFile/Item/61.

109 Stephen LeDoux, *Commentary: All Stimulus is Local*, Daily J. Commerce, Oct. 27, 2010, *available at* 2010 WLNR 27776306; Vincent, *supra* note 34.

110 Tania Chatila, *Sriracha Sauce Maker Gets Too Big for Rosemead*, San Gabriel Valley Trib., Oct. 29, 2009, *available at* 2009 WLNR 21518572.

111 *Irwindale Redevelopment Plan, supra* note 107, at 36.

112 *Id.*

113 Drummer, *supra* note 106. *See also California Cultivates Food Projects*, Site Selection, https://siteselection.com/issues/2010/nov/ (last visited Nov. 24, 2017).

114 Joe Mathews, *What Makes Sriracha Stink: Not the Sauce. It's Cities Like Irwindale*, Zócalo Pub. Square (Dec. 5, 2013), www.zocalopublicsquare.org/2013/12/05/what-makes-sriracha-stink/inquiries/connecting-california/.

115 *Id.*

economic difficulties after 2008 and the dissolution of California's local redevelopment agencies in 2012.[116] Because of this, city leaders resented Huy Fong. In this context, the city used its legal powers against the company. With public nuisance doctrine and city council and city attorney powers, urban law permitted this city to act in a specific spatial-dispute, while larger forces shaped Irwindale's economic challenges.

V. Law's duality in regional urbanization: local-influence and local-weakness

Culminating decades of work, Soja published *My Los Angeles* in 2014, the year before he passed away. In the book, he explained how since the 1980s the LA School made two significant contributions to urban study. First is that for cities there is a constant economic restructuring, often incorrectly labeled as de-industrialization or misunderstood as individual economic crises. Second is that these changes heavily impact economic development, cultural and technology creation, and social movements in cities. Looking at this, he predicted that major world cities would undergo regional urbanization. This can be summarized as the metropolitan form changing to peripheral urbanization with polycentric and networked city regions.[117] For this, the metropolitan notion of an urban center surrounded by residential suburbs ceases to make analytical sense. These changes would be similar to Greater Los Angeles's century transformation. He predicted a species change from traditional metropolitan forms to entire regions, dominated by urban extension. Fueling these changes is economic restructuring, with lighter industries replacing manufacturing within cities, and heavy industry relocating to rural sectors, further away from urban centers, or overseas, all to evade city politics, liability, or economic costs.

Huy Fong's move to Irwindale points to just such an economic shift, with food processing replacing mining. Soja explains that "spatial justice" disputes erupt from such transformations, when residents, governments, and businesses fight over how a specific place is used. These disputes are reactions to unjust geographies caused by economic restructuring.[118] Irwindale's public nuisance claims about pepper grinding exemplify such a conflict. In these controversies, political and legal forms are contested. City governments, regional agencies, and state and federal entities exercise varied authority, which is often unclearly delineated. For Irwindale, over fifty years of mining functioned with a small resident and electorate population influencing city government. This imbalance provided a minor number of residents with great influence over city politics. It suited the economic and political needs of mining companies in 1957, and residents since then. Concentrated political power aggravated tensions between Huy Fong and

116 *Id.*

117 Soja, My Los Angeles, *supra* note 15, at 22.

118 *Id.* at 23, 226–45.

the city. This enflamed the dispute, however it was classified. With details never fully disclosed, the conflict can be painted as community-based with residents, by the plant complaining about smells; personal and emotional between Huy Fong and city personnel, vindictive after the company moved in; a series of misunderstandings between individuals; or the product of ambivalent and conflicting regulatory regimes such as public nuisance claims and air quality measures. For any of these readings though, the place-base politics of Irwindale only increased the tensions. In a more diverse or larger city, these tensions would be resolved without the city resorting to lawsuits and council hearings.

Soja explains how regional urbanization is fueled by six discourses: industrial restructuring, cosmopolis, expolis, polarization, social control, and simulated landscapes.[119] Influencing the sriracha-apocalypse, Irwindale experienced the first four, as the small city reacted to larger forces felt in Greater Los Angeles. The first discourse points to economic restructuring. Cosmopolis refers to how global and migration forces change a city. Exopolis is the stretching between urban forms and their use by persons and businesses. Polarization regards how urban populations are increasingly divided in social, economic, and political terms. Not influential for the Irwindale–sriracha conflict are the fifth and sixth discourses. The fifth discourse refers to insecurity felt and city policing responses. The last discourse is how cities recreate nature, fantasylands, or downtowns for entertainment such as in Disneyland or Las Vegas. This section examines law's role in four discourses during the Huy Fong–Irwindale controversy. They illustrate how local legal authority is actually effective and strong for internal matters but weak in influencing outside matters. For this reason, Irwindale could rely on powers in public nuisance doctrine and city attorney and city council powers, but less so in matters regarding air quality, migration, and sauce demand.

The first discourse, describing the industrial metropolis, develops as urban governments search for new industries to provide jobs and taxes. As high-technology, cultural, or information-intensive industries grow in a city, new sectors of the urban geography are devoted to this. Cities seek to replace heavy industries that require labor, resource, and capital-intensive investments, such as with the automobile sector, energy production, and durables manufacturing. Soja explains that often this is incorrectly viewed as de-industrialization. He argues that in reality it is reindustrialization, seeking post-Fordist industries. For this change, lighter, less capital-intensive and less labor-intensive sectors are sought. These industries can adapt to demand and supply fluctuations. Heavier industries require permanent and limiting investments in terms of location, infrastructure, and workers. All of these restrict the options a city government has to support or check businesses. Soja describes the Los Angeles example of how after the auto sector and aerospace manufacturing died then new industrialization developed in high technology, financial services, and creative culture industries.

119 *Id.* at 21–22, 141–43.

The relocation of Huy Fong to a mining pit in a city known basically for gravel extraction exemplifies this. For the past few decades, Irwindale has tried to convert these quarries for other economic uses. Success stories include business parks, shopping strips, a dog food factory, and a MillersCoor brewery. Importantly, the city needs this to support its tax base, which falls as the number of residents stays the same but income from mining decreases.[120] The city has rigidly guarded itself against building new housing and inviting new residents, who could participate in governance and elections. In 2010, it was reported that Irwindale spent $87 million to build 42 new homes, rehabilitate 62 older units, and rehabilitate a mining pit for the building of a hot sauce plant.[121] For most of its history, Irwindale had a small number of residents and a smaller number of mining companies committed to being there, while tens of thousands of workers entered and left the mining operations and the city each day. The law most obviously at work in this discourse is redevelopment efforts. Here, the city could focus and select private investments for Irwindale, but financing was provided by the state and by private lenders.

Cosmopolis, the second discourse, identifies how cities are subject to the globalization of capital, labor, and culture. Soja describes how international migration and investments characterize Los Angeles, especially as previously white suburbs become increasingly diverse with migrant populations and places such as the SGV rejuvenated with overseas Asian investment. The most important aspect of this is that global forces impact local settings and their institutions. Here, capital refers to the financial mobility of overseas investments, the spending of migrants and tourists, and local production to meet foreign demand. In terms of labor, worker populations increasingly are foreign-born or second-generation migrants. Los Angeles exemplifies this with workers who are from Mexico, Central America, Asia, Eastern Europe, Western Europe, Africa, and the Middle East. The cultural impacts of this are a diversification of language, religions, food, entertainment, and social relations. Cultural industries such as film, music, art, and tourism invite and seek this diversity.

For sriracha, this globalization appears in various ways. The sauce has a global demand. In fact, Tran has argued that the reason Huy Fong had to expand was to keep up with consumers in Asia. Next, Irwindale has been nearly entirely Hispanic or Latino, since before its founding. This small nearly homogenous city has experienced global cultural influences with Huy Fong's move there along with the development of Asian shopping and residential areas throughout the SGV. Most Irwindale residents trace their history to migration from Mexico early in the twentieth century. The SGV, especially immediately east of Irwindale, has seen large increases in migrants since the 1990s. In terms of local law's influence,

120 Pool, *supra* note 25.

121 Jessica Garrison, Kim Christensen & Doug Smith, *Cities Often Give Short Shrift to Affordable Housing*, L.A. Times (Oct. 3, 2010), http://articles.latimes.com/2010/oct/03/local/me-redevelop-housing-20101003.

this is perhaps where local government law is weakest. Soja identifies capital, labor, and culture as the components of this global influence. The most apparent law shaping this involves financial regulation, telecommunications, and immigration laws. Cities have limited influence over these, most likely finding it hard to displace federal and state doctrines. A city of Irwindale's size has even less influence.

Exopolis, the third discourse, is most evident in how Irwindale's actions had regional and global impacts. Soja describes this discourse as the "socio-spatial restructuring" created by a "disjuncture" between the place of employment, housing, and transit to and from.[122] His focus is on a city and where persons live and work, with the public sector stretched by demands of workers living further away from jobs. For Irwindale, the aspect of workers, housing, and transit is less relevant, given its small size. But there is an important disjuncture in the city's public capacity to provide services and the demands placed on it by those outside the city.

Irwindale's exopolis transpired even though it's a tiny city with a small population who chose to regulate one company at its sole location. Irwindale was incorporated in theory to politically benefit the persons living within its borders. The hot sauce fights show that city choices have ramifications far beyond Irwindale's jurisdiction. Huy Fong's demand is global and its loyal consumers are almost entirely located outside Irwindale. These consumers may have positions regarding local legal authority applied to Huy Fong, but in strictly political terms Irwindale's city council could overlook these positions. These concerns came from outside Irwindale. For public nuisance controversies the problems were inside the city. Irwindale chose to act locally. Public nuisance determinations, to bring the lawsuit or have a council declaration, could ignore consumer positions, which were from outsiders.

But if the same harms were examined by air quality measures, Irwindale's local influence was severely lessened. Air quality regulations illustrate the limits of Irwindale's geographic reach. The SCAQMD was viewed as the regulatory agency with the most appropriate authority here. Whether it did or did not find any infractions, Irwindale residents who complained had a more receptive audience in city leaders. Public nuisance and the powers of the city attorney and city council provided an alternative venue to voice and act on gripes of obnoxious smells. These examples show how Irwindale's urban form was stretched regarding alleged odors.

The city was also incapable of meeting its local economic demand. With mining operations decreasing Irwindale's tax base has been shrinking. The city was incorporated with few residents, whose income would not be all that necessary for a city tax base. Instead, mining operations would be taxed and these funds used by the city government for the benefits of residents. Huy Fong and other businesses have moved in, with the city seeking their economic

122 Soja, My Los Angeles, *supra* note 15, at 149–50.

contributions. New arrivals could be taxed. Huy Fong did not disrupt the small resident numbers the city has had for over fifty years. The saucemaker potentially added funds to the city but kept the concentrated political power the same, by not bringing in any new residents.

The last applicable discourse, polarization, appears in how Irwindale is in many ways insulated from so many things around it. With a 90 percent resident population of Latino or Hispanic, it is less diverse than its neighbors to the west. Its population represents longer-term residency when compared to more recent migrant arrivals surrounding the city. It is a working-class city with a median income that is on the lower spectrum of Greater Los Angeles. Its small but stable numbers create a political environment with few participants and repeat players.[123] The city's political history shows the same family names serving as council members and mayors.[124] Many news stories comment on how so much of this politics is between family members or persons with long-established ties to the city. To add to that, elections for public position are often won or lost by just a handful of votes.[125]

Perhaps, the most polarizing aspect of city governance is the corruption and policing problems that plague the city. During the sriracha-apocalypse, the mayor, former council members, and former staff appeared in court responding to allegations of taking public funds. Most of these complaints focused on lavish trips to New York supposedly to meet with financial institutions. Likewise, Irwindale was at risk of losing municipal insurance, after many allegations and lawsuits involving corruption and misconduct by council members, city staff, and police.[126] Predicted ways to avoid this was for city leaders, staff, and policy, to undergo training on public institution management.

Conclusion

An LA School examination of law's role in this dispute suggests a few points. City complaints about chile smells from a local business indicate a spatial-justice

123 Lee Romney, *Irwindale's Family Values: The City's Close-Knit Residents Have Carved Out a Bit of Paradise Amid the Rock Quarries – and They're Keeping It to Themselves*, L.A. TIMES (Jan. 20, 1994), http://articles.latimes.com/1994-01-20/news/ga-13432_1_irwindale-residents.

124 Robert Moran, *Family Ties Link City's Voters to Campaigners – Except Mayor*, L.A. TIMES (Apr. 5, 1992), http://articles.latimes.com/1992-04-05/news/ga-641_1_city-manager.

125 Nicki Arnold, *City Council Election in Irwindale Comes Down to Three Votes*, CAL. CITY NEWS (Nov. 7, 2013), www.californiacitynews.org/2014/06/city-council-election-irwindale-comes-down-three-votes.html.

126 *See* Sarah Favot, *Irwindale at Risk of Losing Insurance Due to Allegations of Corruption*, PASADENA STAR-NEWS (Sept. 8, 2013), www.pasadenastarnews.com/government-and-politics/20130908/irwindale-at-risk-of-losing-insurance-due-to-allegations-of-corruption; *see also* Sarah Favot, *Irwindale Police Chief Talks Department Reforms, Fewer Internal Investigations*, SAN GABRIEL VALLEY TRIB. (Sept. 22, 2014), www.sgvtribune.com/government-and-politics/20140922/irwindale-police-chief-talks-department-reforms-fewer-internal-investigations.

dispute. Law was vital to the substance of these gripes. Public nuisance doctrine framed city arguments in court and in city hall. City council and city attorney powers provided the means to act on nuisance complaints. This severely threatened Huy Fong, not just because it possibly could shut down sriracha production, but more importantly because the company heavily depended on its location in Irwindale. Huy Fong relied on being close to pepper farms and accordingly built a new plant, corporate headquarters, and storage facilities there. Eventually, the city's local powers could only go so far as the nuisance findings and a lawsuit gave way to an informal resolution between the city and the business, with pressure from the California governor's office.[127]

These themes reflect how larger forces such as the effects of redevelopment projects, global culture and capital, and economic restructuring caused and resolved the dispute. Gripes about chile smells from a new business reflect many of the discourses that Soja explains transform suburbs and edge cities as part of regional urbanization. Specifically, sauce making, and other businesses, moved into where mining occurred. The widely popular hot sauce represented global trends, with foreign and national demand markets and fast-moving financing fueling trend spicy tastes. Irwindale's public influence was limited geographically, it could use local and internal powers to influence, some say intimidate, Huy Fong. All the while, the city and its place in Southern California seemed polarized, internally by a few votes among the same electorate, and regionally, with its reputation for public misconduct and corruption.

Soja's six discourses of regional urbanization help place the hot sauce fight in a larger context. The city was reacting to outside influences and in reality, was quite weak to economic, financial, and political pressure far beyond its borders. The city was incorporated to meet industrial objectives of mid-century America, i.e., to control access to gravel and to limit political participation of city residents and of other cities in the region. Southern California's political history is littered with the stories of small cities formed to benefit big business. Decades later, their afterlife is felt in corruption scandals by city staff or elected leaders, city bankruptcy, or environmental crises. Huy Fong's struggles with Irwindale in 2012–14 brought light to this, only because sriracha is so popular. If Huy Fong was in another industry, Irwindale would have probably escaped consumer, political, and newspaper attention. Soja and the LA School help explain why social justice conflicts happen and where to look in terms of geography, economics, and history to explain them. Ideally, this chapter has suggested ways to identify law's ambivalent but effective role in these local conflicts when regional and global economic actors step into local histories.

In conclusion, an LA School view of the sriracha-apocalypse points to urban law's ambivalent duality, when addressing conflicts between cities and outside

127 Reid Wilson, *How Jerry Brown Saved Sriracha for California*, Wash. Post (May 31, 2014), www.washingtonpost.com/blogs/govbeat/wp/2014/05/31/how-jerry-brown-saved-sriracha-for-california/.

businesses. Internally, city influence is quite strong and effective at meeting local objectives. Irwindale could voice and act on opinions that chile odors and fumes were a public nuisance, requiring city attorney and city council attention. Up until the lawsuit was dropped in May of 2014, Irwindale had a very specific and precise way to deal with Huy Fong. But, the city was actually quite weak when responding to regional and statewide concerns. Redevelopment law, air quality regulations, and political pressure curtailed their influence beyond Irwindale's jurisdiction.

11 Cities as stakeholders

Corporate social responsibility in an urban environment

Ronit Donyets Kedar

Introduction

The city and the corporation are two of the most influential phenomena of the twenty-first century. Current literature on both the city and the corporation has recognized the significance of these two institutions for our societies, and has dealt extensively with each separately. However, little has been written on the intersection between the city and the corporation. The literature on corporations, and specifically on corporate social responsibility, has generally ignored the urban space as a unique locus of corporate activity and influence. Similarly, urbanism literature has for the most part overlooked the ethical, legal and social implications of corporate activity, as such, within cities. This chapter aims to offer a preliminary discussion of these largely neglected issues.

The chapter briefly describes the rise of both the city and the corporation, focusing on the centrality of both institutions for life in the twenty-first century. It then offers two different perspectives to analyze the relations between the city and the corporation. Finally, the chapter analyzes the normative duties and responsibilities that the interaction between corporations and cities may give rise to.

The first perspective on the interrelation between the city and the corporation focuses on *the operations of the corporation within the city*. The question this perspective focuses on is whether the fact that a corporation is settled in a particular urban community, and fosters complex ties with it, gives rise to special responsibilities by the corporation, towards the city. Through the forthcoming analysis I conclude that it does.

The second perspective of the interaction between the city and the corporation focuses on *the city*, questioning the role of cities as regulators vis-à-vis corporations that operate (distinctively) within their jurisdiction. The focus of this part is the special responsibilities that cities may have in mitigating the impact of such corporate activity. It therefore investigates the extent to which issues such as unique urban character, local identity and urban democracy should influence municipal deliberations. An example for this type of regulation is the large-corporation "free-zones" that some cities in the US have tried to implement, battling sameness and attempting to protect the diverse nature of the city.[1]

I. Cities and corporations

The city and the corporation are two of the most significant phenomena of the twenty-first century. Since 2009, more than half of the world's population resides in cities. In 2014, the portion of the world's population that lives in urban areas reached 54 percent, and is estimated to reach 66 percent by 2050.[2] While the rates of urbanization differ from one part of the world to the next (in average-lower income countries, the rates are highest),[3] accelerated urbanization is nonetheless a global phenomenon: each year, 65 million people across the globe are migrating to cities, and by 2030, the number of urban residents worldwide is estimated to reach 4.7 billion people.[4] The number and size of the world's mega-cities is constantly rising. However, most city-residents worldwide still live in medium-size cities of less than half a million inhabitants.[5]

The urbanization process bears far-reaching social, economic and environmental influences. First, cities are centers of diverse economic activity: almost half of the gross world product is produced by 600 major cities.[6] Similarly, two thirds of the world's energy consumption occurs therein. As transportation hubs and centers of governance, education and health, cities are significant growth engines in their respective countries, as well as globally.[7] Indeed, urban areas are often linked to a rise in the general level of well-being, leading to improved health, better accessibility to culture, and to political institutions and influence, and more.[8] Undergoing the same processes, Israel is a good example: the urban

1 A few dozen cities in the US have used zoning regulation to ban chain corporations from parts of the city, aiming to protect their unique, local character ("formula regulation"). For an overview of this phenomenon, *see* Mark Bobrowski, *The Regulation of Formula Businesses and the Dormant Commerce Clause Doctrine*, 44 Urb. Law. 227 (2012).

2 *See* the UN's DESA (Department of Economic and Social Affairs) report, *World's Population Increasingly Urban with More Than Half Living in Urban Areas* (July 10, 2014), www.un.org/en/development/desa/news/population/world-urbanization-prospects-2014.html. Interestingly, in 1950, the portion of the population that resided in urban areas was at around 30 percent. Since then, the world's urban population has grown rapidly, from 746 million in 1950 to 3.9 billion in 2014. This growth is even more striking in North America (84 percent of the population lives in urban areas) and Latin America (80 percent).

3 *The Working City: A Strategic Plan for Sustainable Urbanism*, Israeli Ministry Envt'l Protection (2015) (in Hebrew).

4 UN-DESA, *supra* note 2.

5 Mega-cities are defined in the literature as cities with over ten million residents. Today, one in eight persons on earth lives in one of twenty-eight mega cities worldwide. *See The Working City*, *supra* note 3.

6 *See id.* at 7.

7 Avirama Golan & Ronit Donyets-Kedar, *Introduction*, in Business of Cities, Cities of Business: Corporatizing Urban Spaces 10 (2017).

8 *Id.*

population rate in Israel is among the highest in the world, whereas circa 90 percent of the country's population resides in cities.[9] In 2013, almost half of the entire Israeli population lived in its fourteen major cities alone.[10]

Importantly, the global urbanization processes occur in tandem with other significant social and political global developments, primarily that of the weakening of the nation state as the primary provider of social goods, and the significant drop in its dominance as the source of social and political justice. This decline in the power of the state has brought about a shift in the status of municipalities, which have consequently become more independent, and increasingly thought of as free-standing economic units. Thus, cities and townships across the globe are exceedingly expected not to rely on government funds and local taxes, but are encouraged to obtain independent sources of income.[11] Toronto, for instance, has handed the development of its eastern waterfront in the downtown area over to Google's sister company, Sidewalk Labs, partly due to its promised investment of millions of dollars in the project.[12]

These processes have transformed the local public arena into a market where municipalities are pitted against each other in an attempt to draw more businesses their way. According to Harvey, this "urban managerialism is embedded in a framework of zero sum inter-urban competition for resources, jobs and capital."[13] As a result, a new imbalance of powers between cities and corporations is struck, with significant implications for the nature of the urban space.

Like cities, corporations are becoming increasingly significant institutions. In the past decades, some aspects of corporate power have become ubiquitous and overwhelming. Economically, for example, the income of some large multinationals exceeds the budgets of most sovereign states.[14] Similarly, the net worth of

9 Yishai Blank, *The Location of the Local: Local Government Law, Decentralization and Territorial Inequality in Israel*, 34 HEBREW U. L. REV. 197 (2004) (in Hebrew).

10 *Id.*

11 *See, e.g.*, David Harvey, *From Managerialism to Entrepreneurialism: The Transformation in Urban Governance in Late Capitalism*, 71 GEOGRAFISKA ANNALER: SERIES B, HUM. GEOGRAPHY 3 (1989). (Discussing how entrepreneurialism in urban governance has become a dominant urban strategy in the last decades, and showing how mechanisms of inter-urban competition that it involves produce macroeconomic consequences).

12 Molly Sauter, *Google's Guinee-Pig City: Will Toronto Turn its Residents into Alphabet's Experiment? The Answer has Implications for Cities Everywhere*, ATLANTIC (Feb. 13, 2018), www.theatlantic.com/technology/archive/2018/02/googles-guinea-pig-city/552932/?utm_source=pocket&utm_medium=email&utm_campaign=pockethits.

> The urban-development corporation that owns the majority of the Quayside site [...] needs a new partner with deep pockets to continue its mission [of development]. That makes Sidewalk's $50 million commitment (about 63 million Canadian dollars) all the more attractive.

13 Harvey, *supra* note 11, at 5.

14 Brian Roach, *Corporate Power in a Global Economy*, GLOBAL DEV. & ENV'T INST., TUFTS UNIVERSITY, www.ase.tufts.edu/Gdae/education_materials/modules/Corporate_Power_in_a_Global_Economy.pdf (last visited Mar. 23, 2018).

assets owned by these corporations exceeds the gross national product (GNP) of most of the world's countries.[15] Naturally, this economic power translates into significant social and political power, one important channel of which is lobbying.[16] As discussed in the next part of the chapter, large corporations can leverage this power to negotiate favorable terms in contracts vis-à-vis cities, which become increasingly reliant on their business.

Importantly, however, corporate strength is not manifested through economic or political power alone, but is also expressed in other, sometimes covert ways. To name just a few, big corporations have a huge influence not only on jobs, but also on the position of women in the workplace and society;[17] not only on the prices of produce, but on what we eat, or even consider as food;[18] not only on what we buy, but on what we consider to be a commodity.[19] On a local level, this could have an even greater impact: corporations that operate in cities may have transformative power on cities' distinct character, on the degree and range of their diversity, their safety, accessibility and aesthetics.

Focusing on the impact modern corporations have on the public sphere, it has become increasingly accepted by scholars and the industry alike, that large corporations should not be considered merely as economic institutions the purpose of which is to maximize shareholder gains, but rather as social institutions as well. As such, corporations are thought to bear a (limited) responsibility for the social implications of their conduct.[20] Thus, in recent years the Corporate Social Responsibility (CSR) discourse has gained ground.[21] Whether derived

15 *See* John Christopher Anderson, *Respecting Human Rights: Multinational Corporations Strike Out*, 2 U. Pa. J. Lab. & Emp. L. 463 (2000).

16 Lawrence Lessig, Republic Lost: How Money Corrupts Congress and a Plan to Stop it (2011); Steven R. Ratner, *Corporations and Human Rights: A Theory of Legal Responsibility*, 111 Yale L. J. 443 (2001).

17 The number of white, young, male tech new recruits in Seattle's Amazon, for instance, is said to have influenced the city's make-up, and consequently its cultural scene. *See You've Got Male: Amazon's Growth Impacting Seattle Dating Scene*, Jeff Reifman Blog (May 12, 2014), https://jeffreifman.com/2014/05/12/youve-got-male-amazons-growth-impacting-seattle-dating-scene/.

18 Ronit Donyets-Kedar, *The Social Responsibility of Food Corporations*, Food Law: Law, Soc'y, & Culture (2017) (in Hebrew).

19 Think of bottled water, for instance.

20 The debate on the nature of the corporation (between the conservative approach that considers the corporation an economic institution the purpose of which is to maximize shareholder benefit, and the social approach that holds the corporation a social as well as a financial institution, bearing social responsibility toward all of its stakeholders) has accompanied the corporate literature for decades. For a historical review *see* David Millon, *Frontiers of Legal Thought: Theories of the Corporation*, 39 Duke L.J. 201, 216–225 (1990).

21 A growing number of corporations, especially transnational ones, invest considerable capital and attention in socially beneficial projects. Virtually all of the Fortune 500 companies have a CSR policy that commands compliance with human rights and environmental standards, and leading businesses have become increasingly involved in various multi-stakeholder initiatives. CSR managers, a commonplace position in today's business world, introduce new modes of monitoring and certification for compliance with CSR standards. Simon Zadek therefore

from notions of social legitimacy, ethical concerns, or economic rationale, the underlying assumption of CSR relies on the understanding that corporations have *some* commitment to their stakeholders – those who are influenced by corporate practices.[22] Interestingly, however, and while the literature on stakeholder theory is voluminous, it has generally ignored the urban space as a unique locus of corporate activity and influence. While the "community" or the "environment" are recognized and discussed,[23] the city as a distinct stakeholder is almost entirely absent from the CSR discourse. The task of the next part of the chapter is to fill this void by offering two perspectives – that of the corporation and that of the city – discussing the city as a distinct stakeholder vis-à-vis the corporations that operate distinctively within it.

II. Cities as stakeholders

Does the urban setting as a unique locus of social activity give rise to distinct normative relationships between cities and corporations? And, if so, what does this special relationship consist of? Does the impact corporations have on cities warrant special duties on behalf of the corporation to the city? Does the city bear a distinct responsibility to society when inviting corporations to conduct their business within its jurisdiction? What comes next offers some preliminary thoughts on these issues.

A. The corporation in the city

The first perspective on the interrelation between the city and the corporation focuses on the operations of the corporation within the city. The question this

defined the CSR discourse as "the 21st century's most important and contentious public policy issue." *See* SIMON ZADEK, THE CIVIL CORPORATION: THE NEW ECONOMY OF CORPORATE CITIZENSHIP 29 (2007).

22 *See, e.g.*, the definition offered by the Commission of the European Communities, which defines CSR as follows:

> A concept, whereby companies integrate social and environmental concerns in their business operations and in their interaction with their stakeholders on a voluntary basis. Being socially responsible means not only fulfilling legal expectations, but also going beyond legal compliance and investing "more" into human capital, the environment and the relations to stakeholder. The experience [has been] that going beyond legal compliance can contribute to a company's competitiveness.

The Green Chapter on Promoting a European Framework for CSR, http://ec.europa.eu/employment_social/soc-dial/csr/greenchapter_en.pdf (last visited Mar. 23, 2018). On stakeholders as a contested concept, *see* Samantha Miles, *Stakeholder Theory Classification: A Theoretical and Empirical Evaluation of Definitions*, 142 J. BUS. ETHICS 437 (2017).

23 *See generally* R. EDWARD FREEMAN, ET AL., STAKEHOLDER THEORY: THE STATE OF THE ART (2010), especially ch. 2.

focuses on is whether the fact that a corporation is settled within a particular municipality and fosters complex ties with it, gives rise to special responsibilities by the corporation toward the city. Such special relations could be fostered in a number of ways: first, the company could be interested in unique natural resources that are located in a specific urban area. Such, for example, is the case with regard to the thermal spring waters of the French town of Vichy and the cosmetics company L'Oréal; or the case of the US "rust-belt" cities and the factories and companies that operated there – milling steel and coal. Corporations may also choose to settle in a particular city due to its geographic location and the benefits that may accrue. Israel, for instance, offers significant tax breaks for large corporations that set up their plants in the periphery of the country. Intel, for one, gained significant tax reductions for locating two of its main production plants in the southern part of Israel, in the city of Kiryat Gat.[24]

Some corporations target not a particular city, but rather the urban fabric *as such*. Sharing economy corporations are a good example. As noted by Professors Davidson and Infranca, as well as other scholars,[25] the sharing economy is an urban phenomenon. The urban benefits of density, proximity, diversity and specialization allow companies such as Airbnb, Uber, TaskRabbit, WeWork and others to bring together peer-to-peer providers and consumers, as well as business-to-consumers initiatives, leveraging the urban conditions to their advantage.[26] The benefits of agglomeration of the urban environment allow not only creation of favorable settings for collaborative exchange, but also, the urban environment is thought to speed the adoption of sharing economy platforms, as cities are more open to innovation, and new ideas tend to spread more rapidly in cities.[27]

Some corporations, then, operate distinctively in cities (either in specific cities targeted by the corporation for a variety of reasons, or cities as such), and thus give rise to the question what is the nature of the special ties that are formed between these corporations and cities, and what are the duties and responsibilities they warrant.

It is important to note that the special link between city and corporation that I discuss here does not refer to corporations that happen to operate in a

24 *See, e.g.*, Ora Coren, *Which Corporation Gets the Biggest Tax Break in Israel? Teva*, HAARETZ (July 23, 2013), www.haaretz.com/israel-news/business/.premium-who-gets-the-biggest-tax-breaks-teva-1.5298412.

25 Nestor Davidson & John Infranca, *The Sharing Economy as an Urban Phenomenon*, 34 YALE L. & POL'Y REV. (2016) (hereinafter Davidson & Innfranca). *See also* Michèle Finck & Sofia Ranchordàs, *Sharing and the City*, 49 VAN. J. TRANS'L L. 1299 (2016) (arguing that "sharing initiatives are naturally facilitated by the city's geography, population, infrastructures, and economic activities") (hereinafter Finck & Ranchordàs).

26 On the advantages of the urban environment (such as reduction of transportation costs, the benefits of labor-market pooling; quality, accelerated matching; and knowledge spillovers) to sharing economy companies, *see* Davidson & Infranca, *supra* note 25, at 225–235.

27 Davidson & Infranca, *id.* at 226. *See also* JANE JACOBS, THE ECONOMY OF CITIES (1970).

city, while also conducting their business nation-wide. In such cases (think of Citibank and Kansas City, Coca-Cola and Minneapolis, or Microsoft and Denver, for example), there do not seem to be any special relations between the city and the corporation in the sense that renders the city a distinct stakeholder. This is not to say, of course, that these firms do not bear any responsibility to the communities of these cities, or to their physical or human environment. However, in these cases, such responsibilities would be grounded in a more general duty of CSR, rather than in the particular relations to the city, which is what I am interested in here.

While some interrelations between corporations and cities have been extremely successful,[28] others have been mixed, as the corporation's activity in the city brought economic welfare to some, at the cost of significantly transforming, sometimes harming, the urban character of the city. Seattle, for instance, underwent a significant transformation of its former character with the arrival of Amazon, which, today, is the largest employer in the city (with over 40,000 employees), and the owner of almost a fifth of the city's office space.[29] Drawing other giant corporations in its footsteps, the thick corporate presence in the city is also said to have pushed housing prices up, as well as the cost of living, and to have effected traffic congestion.[30] A city ethos once rich with diversity of music and art is said to have made its way to a corporate cultural one.[31]

Other interactions between cities and corporations have had devastating ramifications for the city. Some companies have exploited the resources of cities and towns, stripping them of their most valuable assets.[32] Others have abandoned flourishing urban communities to relocate to cheaper production sites, usually overseas.[33] Such, for instance, is the case of Youngstown, Ohio, and the steel

28 Wolfsburg, one of the richest cities in Germany, was established as a Volkswagen factory town, and remains heavily reliant on this factory even today. *See Germany's Motown is Country's Richest City*, LOCAL (July 29, 2013), www.thelocal.de/20130729/51105.

29 *See* Kirk Johnson, *5 Lessons Seattle can Teach Other Cities about Amazon*, N.Y. TIMES (Nov. 16, 2017), www.nytimes.com/2017/11/16/us/amazon-seattle-headquarters.html.

30 Ken Kalthoff, *Amazon's Growth Leads to Congestion, Higher Cost of Living in Seattle*, NBC NEWS (Sep. 27, 2017), www.nbcdfw.com/news/business/Amazons-Growth-Leads-to-Congestion-Higher-Cost-of-Living-in-Seattle-448371233.html.

31 *Id.* See also the testimony of a Seattle born blogger, stating that "Seattle is dead and Amazon killed it." *How Amazon Swallowed Seattle*, GAWKER (Aug. 18, 2015), http://gawker.com/how-amazon-swallowed-seattle-1724795265.

32 Such, for example, is the case of the city of Arad in the southern part of Israel, and the mining corporation "Israel Chemicals Ltd." The city, located on the border of the Judean desert mountains, was renowned for its clean air and other environmental benefits. The corporation's phosphate mining in a nearby location (Sde Barir) has been argued to have robbed the city of its most valuable assets. *See* Batya Roded, *City and Phosphate Mine in the Arad Valley – Actors in a Struggle*, in BUSINESS OF CITIES, CITIES OF BUSINESS: CORPORATIZING URBAN SPACE 53 (Avirama Golan & Ronit Donyets Kedar eds., 2017) (in Hebrew).

33 The cases of company-towns, or of towns and cities the economy of which relies heavily on a particular company, that ended up abandoned by the corporation that was at the center of their

factory that closed down in the 1980s, leaving an entire city without its primary economic anchor.[34]

The effects of the sharing economy companies on the city are typically similar. While the activity of sharing companies within cities can contribute to a thriving urban life (sharing economy initiatives encourage new types of interactions that may never have occurred in its absence),[35] and alleviate some of the challenges of urban space (carpooling initiatives, for instance, may reduce traffic congestion), its operations may also exacerbate existing challenges, or even produce new frictions. The presence of Airbnb in some cities, for example, has led to a steep rise in the cost of rent, as well as to a significant transformation of the nature of some neighborhoods.[36] Cities such as Barcelona, Berlin and others have considerably restricted Airbnb, due to its detrimental influence on the city's character, among other things.[37] Similarly, ridesharing platforms (such as Uber and Via) have exacerbated traffic congestion in some cities.[38] In addition, stronger corporations (both sharing economy companies that are able to define and adjust

economic and cultural life, are abundant. Such, for example, is the case of Ann Arbor, MI, and the pharmaceutical company Pfizer, which was Ann Arbor's largest private employer and the recipient of significant tax abatements. Pfizer decided to shut down its activities in the city in 2008, leaving the community stunned. *See* Nathan Bomey, *5th Anniversary of Pfizer Gut Punch: Ann Arbor Leaders Recall "Rallying Cry,"* ANN ARBOR NEWS (Jan. 22, 2012); Tom Gantert, *The Business Lesson of Pfizer and Ann Arbor*, MICH. CAPITOL CONFIDENTIAL (Apr. 9, 2012), www.michigancapitolconfidential.com/16745.

Other prominent examples in the US are Flint, MI and GM motors. Prominent examples in Israel are Pri Galil, a canning company that was the economic axis of the town of Ha'tzor-Hag'lilit. The plant closed down in 2013; and Delta Ltd., one of Israel's largest clothing manufacturers, that significantly downsized its activities in the city of Karmiel, moved its entire production overseas.

34 See analysis below.

35 *See, e.g.*, JANE JACOBS, THE DEATH AND LIFE OF GREAT AMERICAN CITIES 147 (1961) ("A city's collection of opportunities of all kinds, and the fluidity with which these opportunities and choices can be used, is an asset").

36 ROY SAMAAN, AIRBNB, RISING RENT, AND THE HOUSING CRISIS IN LOS ANGELES (2015), (showing how Airbnb's density overlaps with higher rents and lower rental vacancy, and noting that Airbnb creates incentives to take units off the rental market. Samaan argues that Airbnb incentivizes

> the large-scale conversion of residential units into tourist accommodations [and] forces neighborhoods and cities to bear the costs of its business model. Residents must adapt to a tighter housing market. Increased tourist traffic alters neighborhood character while introducing new safety risks.
>
> SAMAAN, at 4)

www.ftc.gov/system/files/documents/public_comments/2015/05/01166-96023.pdf.

37 *See* Finck & Ranchordàs, *supra* note 25, at 38.

38 Winnie Hu, *Your Uber Car Creates Congestion. Should You Pay a Fee?*, N.Y. TIMES (Dec. 26, 2017) (noting that "an explosion of ride-hailing app services has transformed the way that people get around the city and is choking the streets"), www.nytimes.com/2017/12/26/nyregion/uber-car-congestion-pricing-nyc.html.

their activity to circumvent local regulation, and the more "old-fashioned" companies that are strong enough to enjoy a favorable negotiating position vis-à-vis some local authorities), tend to engage in "regulatory arbitrage" between different municipalities, working their way around local regulation.[39] Amazon's recent bid for a city to host its second largest Head Quarters in North America is a good example.[40] In its Request for Proposals, Amazon flat out stated that it has a preference for cities that can offer regulative flexibility, as well as tax incentives, and that are "creative" with regard to land cost and uses.[41] Amazon bluntly declares that "as this is a competitive project, Amazon welcomes the opportunity to engage with [bidding cities] in the creation of an incentive package, real estate opportunities, and cost structure to encourage the company's location of the project in your state/province."[42] Interestingly, Amazon's search for a new location for its second HQ has stirred up a remorseful response from some of Seattle's city officials, stating that if Amazon chose to look elsewhere for its new offices, it must mean that Seattle wasn't "competitive enough."[43]

The negative effects of corporations on their urban locations may be significant, then. These negative local externalities need to be mitigated. It is the claim of this chapter that the central role some corporations play in the city's economic, cultural and social life, and the growing power of some corporations to affect the urban landscape *as such* give rise to corporate responsibility to the city as a distinct stakeholder. This recognizes that the responsibilities of corporations

39 *See* Davidson & Infranca, *supra* note 25, at 241.

40 Press Release, Amazon Opens Search for Amazon HQ2 – A Second Headquarters City in North America, http://phx.corporate-ir.net/phoenix.zhtml?c=176060&p=irol-newsArticle&ID=2299039; and *Amazon HQ2 RFP*, https://images-na.ssl-images-amazon.com/images/G/01/Anything/test/images/usa/RFP_3._V516043504_.pdf (last visited Mar. 23, 2018).

41 "Communities that think big and creatively when considering locations and real estate options." *See Amazon RFP*, at 2. See the following as well:

> Please provide a summary of total *incentives offered* for the Project by the state/province and local community. In this summary, please provide a brief description of the incentive item, the timing of incentive payment/realization, and a calculation of the incentive amount. [...] With respect to *tax credits*, please indicate whether credits are refundable, transferable, or may be carried forward for a specific period of time. If the incentive includes *free or reduced land costs, include the mechanism and approvals that will be required*. Please also include all timelines associated with the approvals of each incentive. *We acknowledge a Project of this magnitude may require special incentive legislation in order for the state/province to achieve a competitive incentive proposal. As such, please indicate if any incentives or programs will require legislation or other approval methods.* Ideally, your submittal includes a total value of incentives, including the specified benefit time period.
>
> (emphasis added – R.K)

42 *Id.* at 8.

43 See further discussion below.

should flow from their influence on the public sphere (in this case – the urban environment) and on the ability of the public to shape it.[44] When corporate activity hinders this ability, it is the corporation's responsibility to rectify the damage. Importantly, the urban attributes that facilitate the thriving of a corporation in the city are also those that are often threatened by corporate conduct, once it is established in the urban environment.

For example, Airbnb flourishes exactly because it is able to offer customers a genuine urban experience.[45] However, its aggressive policies, of taking over large sectors of neighborhoods and cities and transforming them into short-term rental apartments (beneficial in the short term for the company), threaten the unique nature of these neighborhoods and cities, and undermine the special urban culture. This bears detrimental effects for the city as such, and gives rise to the corporation's duty to avoid the harming behavior. Interestingly, these policies are also damaging for the company itself, as they are undermining its most valuable asset – the city itself – in the long run.

It is for these reasons that corporations that operate within a city should be thought to be responsible to the city itself.[46] This means that companies are to integrate urban social and environmental concerns in their business operations within the city. This may mean that Airbnb, for instance, will have to consider the impact of its operations on the special character of cities or neighborhoods, and limit the number of its apartments in certain geographical areas, rather than to aggressively encourage apartment holders to convert their property into neighborhood hotels.[47] Such a policy, when harming the unique fabric of the city, may be considered an infringement of its responsibilities. Similarly, the decision to demolish two steel plants in Youngstown, Ohio in the 1980s may not have met the suggested standard of the responsibility regime offered here.[48] In this case, the board of directors of United States Steel Company decided to close down its two plants in the city, a decision with considerable ramifications,

44 For a comprehensive discussion of the responsibility of corporation as flowing from their influence on the ability of the public to constantly and effectively shape the public sphere, see, Ronit Donyets Kedar, *Rethinking Responsibility in Private Law*, in PRIVATIZATION, VULNERABILITY AND SOCIAL RESPONSIBILITY (Martha Fineman et al. eds., 2016).

45 According to Airbnb's own research, 91 percent of travelers want "to live like a local." *See The Economic Impacts of Home Sharing in Cities Around the World*, www.airbnb.com/economic-impact.

46 Whether this responsibility is legal and should be enforced in case the corporations fails to comply, or whether it is a softer, voluntary, type of responsibility, goes beyond the scope of this chapter. While I believe that in some cases the corporations should be under a *legal duty* to respect the interests of the city, the purpose of this chapter is merely to draw attention to the special relations between the corporation and the city, as relations that give rise to normative responsibilities more generally.

47 SAMAAN, *supra* note 36.

48 Joseph W. Singer, *The Reliance Interest in Property*, 40 STAN. L. REV. 611, 611–614 (1988) (citing N.Y. TIMES, Apr. 29, 1982, at A20, cols. 3–5 (picture caption)).

not only for the workers, but for the entire Youngstown township.[49] The court, in its discussion, stated that

> [f]or all of the years United States Steel has been operating in Youngstown, it has been a dominant factor in the lives of its thousands of employees and their families, and in the life of the city itself. The contemplated abrupt departure of United States Steel from Youngstown [...] will doubtless mean a devastating blow [...] to the City of Youngstown itself.[50]

While the court was sympathetic to the workers, their families and to the entire town, it nevertheless held that the corporation is the owner of the plants, and as the owner, it was entitled to handle its property as it wished.[51] The court therefore decided that the corporation had no legal obligation to find a less devastating alternative. However, under the proposition here, that considers the city as a distinct stakeholder, the corporation would have been thought to be under an obligation to take into account the ramifications for the city of closing down its business in it.[52] The implications of the suggested principle may therefore be that a corporation that operates within a certain city may, in cases of significant dependency of the city, lose its "leave-at-will" exit rights.

B. The city and the corporation

The second perspective through which to think of the interaction between the city and the corporation focuses on *the city*, questioning the role of cities as regulators of corporations that operate distinctively within their jurisdiction. The focus of this part is the special responsibilities that cities may have in mitigating the impact of such corporate activity for the city as such (rather than for certain groups within it). It therefore investigates the extent to which issues such as unique urban character, local identity, and urban democracy should have in municipal deliberations. While the duty of municipalities (as well as that of other governmental bodies) to act as a trustee for the public interest is clear, the question here is more specific: whether or not the municipality has a special duty

49 *Id.*

50 United Steel Workers of Am. v. U.S. Steel Corp., 631 F.2d 1264 (6th Cir. 1980) (quoted in Singer, *id.* at 616).

51 United Steel Workers of Am., Local No. 1330 v. U.S. Steel Corp., 492 F. Supp. 1 (N.D. Ohio 1980), *aff'd in part, vacated in part sub nom.* Local 1330, United Steel Workers, 631 F.2d 1264 (6th Cir. 1980) (quoted by Singer, *id.* at 617).

52 Joseph Singer criticized the court's decision by arguing that the relationship between the constituencies of the corporation could have been legally recognized as a property right. The court, he claims, should have interpreted the law as recognizing a property right for the workers, possibly by finding a right of first refusal of either the workers' union or the town.

Singer, *supra* note 49, at 617. *See also* Joseph Singer, *The Reliance Interest in Property Revisited*, 7 UNBOUND: HARV. J. LEGAL LEFT 79 (2011).

of care to the urban fabric as such, safeguarding its unique nature as an open and diverse social arena.[53]

It is the contention here that since these ingredients – diversity, openness, local democracy, free-interaction, mixed-uses, innovation, contradictions, idiosyncrasy and more are what makes a city, a responsibility by the municipality to safeguard these unique features in its dealings with corporations is essentially the flip side of the corporate responsibility towards the city. In this sense, the very urban conditions that generate much of the value for corporate activity in cities and that render the city a distinct stakeholder, are those that forge a similar responsibility for the municipality itself. In both cases, it is the value of the city as such to human life that is at stake.

One central urban characteristic, often under threat by corporate activity, is diversity. One of the claims against Airbnb is that by overtaking entire neighborhoods, converting them to short-term rent apartments, rather than allowing vibrant communities of actual residents to flourish, they are undercutting the diversity of truly residential areas. A similar claim has been made against Amazon in Seattle, whose arrival to the city has transformed its nature, and harmed its diversity. Jane Jacobs suggests that the mixture of uses a city offers, made possible by its diversity, is the essential phenomenon to understand cities.[54] Jacobs stresses that a

> mixture of uses [. . .] needs an enormous diversity of ingredients. So the first question – and I think by far the most important question – about planning cities is this: How can cities generate enough mixture among uses – enough diversity – throughout enough of their territories, to sustain their own civilization.[55]

However, instead of "sustaining their own civilization," cities have started to conduct themselves in alignment with the corporate way of thinking: as part of the hegemony of the neo-liberal discourse, municipalities are now expected to perform as economic organizations the operations of which are measured primarily by a financial bottom line. As such, cities are made responsible for attracting investors and finding their own sources of income. Municipal privatization is part of the same idea.

53 In his "*Building and Dwelling: Ethics for the City*," Richard Sennett reiterates the linguistic difference between the French *ville* and its *cité*, whereby the former refers to the city itself, and the latter means "the character of life [. . .] the feelings people harbor to neighborhoods, and strangers, and attachment to places." It is this latter meaning of "city" that I refer to in discussing the municipality's duty to the city – *cité* – as such: not merely the built environment, but the ways in which people actually live in it. *See* Richard Sennett, Building and Dwelling: Ethics for the City (2018).

54 Jane Jacobs, *supra* note 35, at 144 ("To understand cities, we have to deal outright with combination of uses, not separate uses, as the essential phenomena.").

55 *Id.* Jacobs goes on to stress the importance of diversity, and its ingredients, as she says:

> The diversity, of whatever kind, that is generated by cities rests on the fact that in cities so many people are so close together, and among them contain so many different tastes, skills, needs, supplies, and bees in their bonnets.

This type of logic has driven the Israeli government to devise a plan to merge the coastal city of Bat Yam, the fourteenth largest city in the country in terms of population, with its neighboring city of Tel Aviv, since the former was not "profitable," and was unlikely to cover its budgetary deficit without state support.[56]

This line of thinking has led to the infiltration of corporate agenda and business jargon into the municipal discourse, which became saturated with the managerial thinking that measures performance according to parameters of cost and benefit or that attributes supreme importance to the value of efficiency, at the expense of an open, pluralistic, urban discourse.[57] An entire business vernacular has permeated urban governance, aligning the dominant values of the public sphere with those of the market. An example is the UK's Urban Development Corporations (UDCs), created by the Local Government, Planning and Land Act 1980, which were non-departmental government bodies, set up to address cities' economic hardships of the de-industrialization of the Thatcher era. Thought of as an "amalgam of free enterprise and de-regulated decision making,"[58] the UDCs, whose appointed (not elected) board members were typically private sector business figures, were handed the responsibility for urban regeneration, responsibilities that were stripped off local municipalities.[59] Similarly, many Israeli cities operate through economic companies that allow the municipality to apply a market-oriented *modus operandi*, otherwise less available for the city as a public body. See, for instance, the Tel Aviv-Yafo Economic Development Authority Ltd.'s website, stating that the company was established with the aim of "realizing the raw business-economic potential of the municipality's tangible and intangible assets, [...] for the purpose of creating new and significant income sources [...] for the benefit of Tel Aviv residents and the City's active business community."[60] The regulatory arbitrage that companies tend to engage in feeds off this type of thinking and pits municipalities against each other, encouraging a regulatory race to the bottom. The goals of local regulation – zoning,

56 Zafrir Rinat, *Tel Aviv May Merge with Bat Yam*, HAARETZ (July 7, 2014), www.haaretz.com/. premium-tel-aviv-may-merge-with-bat-yam-1.5254875.

57 See, for instance, the reaction of the president of the Seattle Metropolitan Chamber of Commerce to Amazon's RFP for its HQ2 outside of Seattle, suggesting that the city did not compete well enough, and that Amazon's decision was thus the responsibility of Seattle's local politics, that were not business friendly enough. *See* Daniel Beekman & Joseph O'Sullivan, *Amazon's Announcement of HQ Outside of Seattle send Ripples Through State's Political Circles*, SEATTLE TIMES (Sep. 7, 2017), www.seattletimes.com/business/amazon/amazons-announcement-of-hq-outside-of-seattle-sends-ripples-through-states-political-circles/. For a different approach to achieve a similar goal (of holding municipalities responsible to the city's stakeholders), see Max Schanzenbach & Nadav Shoked, *Reclaiming Fiduciary Law for the City*, 70 STAN. L. REV. (forthcoming, 2018), (Arguing that city officials, when acting in a business capacity, should be held to standards of care and loyalty that apply to corporations under corporate law).

58 ROB IMRIE & HUW THOMAS, BRITISH URBAN POLICY: AN EVALUATION OF THE URBAN DEVELOPMENT CORPORATIONS 17 (1999).

59 *Id.*

60 *See* Tel Aviv-Yafo Economic Development Authority Ltd.'s website, www.ta-eda.co.il/the-tel-aviv-yafo-economic-development-authority/.

health and safety, diversity and others – are thus circumvented. While stronger municipalities may sometimes fend-off some of the corporate pressure to soften regulation, smaller and weaker municipalities lack such negotiating power.[61] This imbalance contributes in turn to municipal inequalities, and accelerates the process of regulatory leniency toward some of the powerful corporations.

These negative effects of the intersection between corporations and cities that are sometimes the outcome of municipal policies themselves threaten the nature of cities as an arena of an open, diversified, public interaction. Municipalities should play an active role in implementing policies that will maintain the special nature of the city, safeguarding the special fabric of the urban environment. An example for such policies is the local regulation by some American cities to form "chain corporation free-zones," as a way of battling sameness and attempting to protect the diverse nature of the city.[62]

Conclusion

This chapter discussed the unique challenge posed by the interrelations between corporations and cities. By analyzing the special relations between cities and corporations from two perspectives – that of the corporation and that of the municipality – it claims that the city should be recognized as a distinct stakeholder vis-à-vis corporations that operate within it, and that, correspondingly, the city must use its regulatory powers to protect its distinct urban nature. This implies that corporations have a responsibility towards the city as such, and should conduct their business within it accordingly. In the same manner, the municipality itself is responsible for safeguarding the special fabric of the urban environment. The hope that underlies the chapter's argument is that this dual concept of responsibility will mitigate the negative influences corporate conduct may have on cities as such, and secure a better protection for the city as a unique, meaningful human arena, for its residents as well as to society at large. Indeed, cities are not only materialistic centers of capital – a commodity[63] – but are also singular human creations, with their own peculiarities and idiosyncrasies, and, as such, are a platform for inimitable human interaction, voice and imagination. Their distinctive value must not be neglected, either by the corporations that operate within them, or by the municipality itself.

61 Uber's refusal to conduct background checks for drivers in smaller cities, but its compliance with the same demand in larger ones is a good example of the regulatory arbitrage described in this section. *See* Davidson & Infranca, *supra* note 25, who note that NYC and Houston are the only two cities in the US where Uber operates under a legal requirement to conduct criminal background checks for its drivers, while leaving cities such as Austin, and threatening to leave others in case the city will insist on such a requirement. Davidson & Infranca, *supra* note 25, at 251–252 and the corresponding footnotes.

62 *See, e.g.*, the campaign of New York's East Village Community Coalition, stating that "Like many in other municipalities, the EVCC has determined that the presence of chain businesses can be detrimental to community character and local economies." *See* East Village Community Coalition, *Report: Preserving Local, Independent Retail* (June 12, 2015), http://evccnyc.org/2015/06/12/preserving-local-independent-retail/.

63 *Cf.* Alan Blum, The Imaginative Structure of the City, 188–189 (2003).

Index

Note: page numbers in *italic* type refer to Figures those in **bold** type refer to Tables.

www.ingramcontent.com/pod-product-compliance
Ingram Content Group UK Ltd.
Pitfield, Milton Keynes, MK11 3LW, UK
UKHW011003180926
475701UK00004B/530